Dream Family

— A MEMOIR —

JERRY KEEFE

Pie House Publishing

Pie House Publishing
7045 SW Ventura Drive
Tigard, OR 97223

Ordering Information
For details, contact jkeefes@q.com

ISBN: 979-8-9856822-3-6

Printed in the United States of America

First Edition

To Bill, Ann, Connie, and Katy

PROLOGUE

WE SIT DOWN at the dining room table in our house on Monroe Street, Granpa to my left at the head of the table, which is more by chance than by design, Bill on my right, Mom at the opposite end facing Granpa. Dad, Gramma, and Ann are sitting across from me. It is Thanksgiving, or Easter, or a Sunday dinner.

There is turkey, or roast beef, or baked ham, potatoes and gravy. We are a meat and potatoes family. The corn and carrots are from Gramma and Granpa's garden across the street. Gramma's dinner rolls have filled the neighborhood with sweet smells. Glistening and oozing berries, a cherry pie awaits in the kitchen.

Granpa passes me the butter and angles it in such a way that I stick my thumb in it.

"You're losing it bud," he says, waving his index finger at me, the one that's gone at the knuckle.

"Not half as much as you," I reply, eyeing his finger. He curls his lip over his false teeth in a grin.

"Shut up and pass the butter," Bill says, eager to get into the meal. I try the same trick on him but he's on to me. He's too cool. Anyway, if it had worked he would have pounded me after dinner in the backyard or in the bedroom or in the garage. Each year Bill's New Year's resolution includes pounding me on every square foot of our property by year's end. I truly believe this.

Dad tells Bill not to say "shut up" at dinner. The butter goes around the table with each family member taking a slice. Mom warns Ann about elbows on the table. Gramma, the wise one, says little, but when she does everyone listens:

"Jerry, your friend's father Mr. Hall came over yesterday and wanted to buy some of my coins. He's quite the talker, just like on T.V."

"The the old man downs a six pack before doing those commercials," I say. "John told me. It's really embarrassing."

"It should be," Bill says. "Makes a butt of himself."

"That's enough Bill," Dad says.

There's more banter and warnings and passing of butter. Later we eat slices of the cherry pie, clear off the dishes, wash up. Then it's time for bridge. The atmosphere changes—anticipation, tension, a foreboding of bad things to come. The players—Mom, Dad, Gramma, and Granpa, and sometimes Paul, who drops in from Santiago, or Lima, or Paris, or Mexico City, or Lisbon—understand this is no parlor game. Reputations are won and lost. During play I imitate Howard Cossell and narrate the game making up names for the players: Gramma is Ferocious Forrest, Paul is Pope Paul, Granpa is Feudin' Rasputin.

Paul is Dad's younger cousin who works in international accounting for Arthur Andersen. From the places he's lived he brings us carved redwood fertility dolls with bulging stomachs, maracas painted in bright red and green flowers, thick dark liqueurs with foreign words printed on the labels. He gets me thinking about what I want to do with my life.

　　　　DREAM FAMILY ◆ A MEMOIR

Although I haven't a clue how the game is played, I pick up enough bridge lingo to add some color.

"Two no trump," Dad bids.

"It's a two no trump bid," I whisper into an imaginary microphone I'm holding. I'm squeezed between Mom and Granpa. "A daring bid at this stage of the game."

"Four Hearts," Gramma counters.

"You heard it folks, four Hearts. Four Hearts," I repeat, pausing for effect. "You gotta love this game. A veritable bloodletting. Who'll be left after this clash of Titans. It's anybody's guess. Stayed tuned!"

Sooner or later they tell me to hush up, so I leave to have my nightly bowl of Wheaties and toast before heading upstairs for homework or reading or bed. From upstairs I sometimes hear heated arguments over the game, even when my door is closed. The arguments are more than about bridge.

✳ ✳ ✳

"I don't think he's going to make it," Dad says.

It is March 1971 and Dad and I are standing next to the hospital bed where Granpa is lying. Several tubes with fluids racing in and out are attached to his body. His skin is pale and paper thin, pulled tight over his face, his unfocused eyes open and close in cavernous sockets. He's breathing deeply, rasping, fighting for his life. He does not recognize me or acknowledge that I'm there. A blood vessel has burst in his brain.

"Go on your trip," Dad says.

Reluctantly I leave with friends the next day for California—it's Spring break my senior year of college and the trip's been planned for a while. In a few days I'm with my brother in Lompoc where he lives with his wife Nancy. Early one morning we get the phone call from Dad.

"He's gone. Pop's gone." I sense Dad can barely keep from crying.

"I knew it," I mumble to myself, choking up, "I knew it."

We drive straight through to Eugene. All kinds of family are there when we arrive at Monroe Street. A night or two later I slip out the front door and begin walking. Finally I'm alone. I walk up 20th Street and

Friendly Street past Adams Elementary and Jefferson Junior High. I walk down 24th past Uncle Ed's house and Washington Park. I angle over to Lincoln Street where Wilson used to be and the corner grocery where after school we drank coke mixed with Dr. Pepper. Between sobs I talk to myself like a crazy man. Later, when I arrive home, Dad asks "where you been?"

"Just walkin."

OUR HOUSE ON Monroe Street had peach, walnut, apple, tulip, cherry, and maple trees. As well as their beauty and fruit, they were a source of great fun when Bill and I would hang Cousin Jay by his feet from one of their branches and pepper him with tennis balls. But they were a source of great labor too when each Fall I collected walnuts by the hundreds in their thick green skins, which left black stains on my fingers that took weeks to wash out. There was danger in them when I was underneath the Blais's gigantic tulip tree when it cracked like a powerful firecracker and crashed to the ground during the Columbus Day storm. Each Fall I raked leaves from these various trees too, leaves that certainly numbered in the tens of thousands over the years and varied in their reds, yellows, and golds, and in their geometrical shapes. In bags and wheelbarrows

I'd haul them across the street to Gramma and Granpa's for composting in their garden.

I was born in a house not far from the Monroe Street house, it's still there, a small bungalow on College Hill, with a single car garage neatly tucked under the dining room. On the left of the main entry is the small living room where once stood a Brazilian coffee table inlaid with exotic South American butterfly wings Dad got in the Navy, which I still have. In the back of the house are two bedrooms where we slept. I remember the tiny dining room barely big enough for us to sit around. In the small front yard is a holly bush where Bill threw Cousin Jim Hunt's car keys. Parallel to the driveway a high retaining wall keeps the tiny front yard from tumbling down the hill to Washington Park. Fronting the house 20th Street slashes an angle from the crest of College Hill down to Lincoln Street, east to west, and I remember cars resembling ladybugs quietly inching up and down, motors purring, silent drivers bundled in heavy coats behind large round steering wheels. Towering laurel bushes enclose the backyard where Mom hung clothes in the summer on a line and we kids played on the two-seater swing set.

* * *

With Gramma and Granpa's advice and help, Mom bought the house in 1945 for $5,000. Auntie Jean and Uncle Buryl were renting it at the time, but couldn't afford it when it came up for sale. The war was winding down, Dad was soon to be released from the Coast Guard, and it was common knowledge that houses were going to be at a premium once the soldiers started coming home. Later, when he first caught sight of the house after his discharge, Dad said to Mom, "You paid that much for this?"

After the war Mom had us three children while living in that house: Bill in 1946, me in 1948, and Ann in 1951. Mom, an energetic and practical woman, was not only eager to have children and raise a family, but also eager to be a part of a complete family that she never had in South Dakota. She filled those early days taking care of us kids and Dad, making sure we were fed, clothed, taken to the doctor, and, for us kids, kept from killing each other. In spite of being from the same parents and raised under the same roof, we children were hardly similar.

From the beginning Gramma and Granpa Keefe—Dad's parents—were simply called "Gramma and Granpa" by us, and they always seemed to be close by. Even when we left Eugene for a period after Dad's graduation from college in 1952, and lived in Olympia and Salem, they were never long out of sight. They lived on Monroe Street directly west of 20th street by six blocks.

Like our house on 20th street, Gramma and Granpa's house was small and tidy; painted white, it had a lone bedroom on the main floor and an attic where Granpa played his violin and wrote his memoir. On the same lot behind the house was an even smaller house where Gramma's mother Ollie Belle Scott McDaniel lived until the main house was built; she passed away in 1950 just after I was born. They owned the vacant lot next door as well, where each spring they cultivated tulips, roses, and daffodils, followed later in the season with annual dahlias, zinnias, and marigolds, which Gramma and Granpa planted next to the street for show. Gramma's dahlias—reds, yellows, variegated—won prizes at the Lane County Fair. Further back were green beans, corn, squash, pumpkin, and lettuce. Each year Granpa consulted the Farmer's Almanac for the best time to plant, usually during the first full moon in the Spring. There were plum and apple trees on both lots too, and a towering Douglas Fir next to the detached garage. Sunday drivers motoring down Monroe Street would slow down for a better view of the flowers in full bloom.

Granpa was a meter reader for the Eugene Water and Electric Board (EWEB), the local utility. A vigorous and strange man, he'd come through our neighborhood once a month checking our water and electric meter, using his metal stick with a hook on the end to lift the cover off the buried meter in the tree lawn. By then he was in his mid-fifties; he wore rimless and oft-times dirty glasses, smoked a pipe which left burn holes in his pockets, and religiously wore his false teeth on community orchestra night. He was missing half his right index finger from an ancient cannery accident and was partially blind in his right eye, which was crossed. He bathed only when pressured by Gramma. Many in the family considered him a curmudgeon and steered clear of him. His memoir was about life in the 1890's and early 1900's.

Gramma was a large woman with a large presence. She was a McDaniel from Missouri. She wore rimless glasses and flowery dresses, black brogue shoes; she had thick dark hair and intelligent eyes and long exacting fingers. Her button and doll collections were world class and people would visit her to buy and sell them. Next to Mom she held the female sway in the family. Her values and beliefs came from 19th century common sense and folklore: "a penny earned is a penny saved," "beauty is as beauty does." These maxims reside in me as if from a long lost world.

Gramma and Granpa were the tip of the iceberg regarding the larger family beyond the five of us. Both Mom and Dad had numerous cousins, aunts, uncles, nieces, and nephews, Mom, her maiden name White, from Mitchell, South Dakota, Dad a Keefe from Hurd, North Dakota. By the time I was born Mom's father had passed on, but her mother— Gramma White—would visit us from Bismarck, North Dakota every year for a week. She was the polar opposite of Gramma Keefe: short, intense, religious, opinionated. She and Bill squabbled over how many cereal boxes should be opened at one time. We kids didn't like her very much, not like we did Gramma Keefe, but like Gramma Keefe, she was nimble with her fingers—she loved playing solitaire and checkers—and the intricate and beautifully designed maroon afghan she knitted for me in the 1950's I still keep and treasure. She made one for each of us kids.

The only family Mom had in Eugene in those days was my Auntie Jean, Mom's older sister, who physically resembled Mom to the point that people often mistook one for the other. Mom followed Auntie Jean to Eugene shortly after Mom graduated from high school in 1940. Auntie Jean had married Buryl Shoff, and their children—cousins' Patty, Denny, and Peggy—were roughly the same age as we were. They were Mom's side of the family we knew the best during my childhood.

The Keefes, on the other hand, seem to be at every street corner in Eugene. At the top of the heap were Granpa and his two brothers Mike and Ed, my Great Uncles. Ed ran the bus company along with a shady partner we never saw. Mike worked at EWEB, the local utility company, and was an esteemed member in his conservative Protestant church.

They were the unlikeliest siblings: Granpa irreverent, philosophical, musical; Mike, the middle brother, soft spoken, spare, religious; Ed, the youngest, boisterous, sneaky, alcoholic. But somehow they got along. They and their wives—Gramma, Maureen, and Alice—lived within a stone's throw of each other in Eugene.

I came to know these three brothers and their wives and offspring—numerous first and second cousins and uncles—while growing up in Eugene after the war. And as the clan grew and grew and more and more cousins came into the world, opportunities arose and some of the families moved to nearby towns and cities to seek their fortune.

Mom said Dad was a different man when returned from the war. Quieter, brooding, he didn't know what to do. Then, coaxed by Mom and his older brother Dan, who already had two years of college under his belt, Dad enrolled at the University of Oregon. He had a talent for drawing, was good with his hands, making model airplanes as a kid, and could cut hair. He soon discovered architecture. Six years later at age 33, with the winds of the GI Bill pushing him along, he graduated, being among the first generation of Keefes who would graduate from college. The GI Bill was his ticket to the middle class; not that many years before Gramma and Granpa were failing dirt farmers in North Dakota.

2

In the beginning I remember sounds, sights. I was sitting on Dad's lap on a warm summer night when the doors and windows were flung open and hearing the roar of the crowd cheering for their favorite baseball team at nearby Washington Park. Banks of lights atop tall telephone poles lit the fields and I remember taking in the glow of these brilliant lights, how they made day out of night, how the light gradually gave way to the overwhelming darkness above, and how the intermittent cheering punctuated the otherwise quiet night like waves crashing against rock. But it was a disembodied sound for I saw no people make it. Did Dad explain it to me: the strange constant light, the strange fitful sound, the darkness above? I wanted to stay up as long as possible but soon it was my bedtime and against my wishes I was put to bed.

It was a quiet house on 20th because Dad spent his time studying for classes at the University of Oregon. Perhaps that is why the roar of fans at Washington Park remains with me since it was such a departure from the hush and silence, Mom's constant efforts to keep us out of Dad's hair. For example, I remember crawling into Mom and Dad's bedroom one night when the door was ajar, somehow eluding Mom's ever-present watch. Dad was sitting in a chair, one leg crossed over the other, reading a book. *A solitary figure reading a book.* He looked up and smiled while at the same time Mom swooped from behind and swept me away.

✳ ✳ ✳

"There's something wrong here," Dad said one day while moving his upright index finger slowly across my line of vision left to right. "Watch." He was talking to Mom. My right eye tracked his finger on the mark, following it like a hawk, but my left eye, showing a splendid independence, rolled the other way, focusing on what could have been any of Dad's other fingers.

"This is not right," he said. I was age 2.

Mrs. Crowder, our next door neighbor, whose own son John was recovering from his third eye surgery, was soon visited by my rattled and nervous mother.

"See Dr. McCallum," she told Mom." He's the expert."

At the appointment Dr. McCallum asked Mom if there was a history of crossed eye in the family. Because the family was so used to it and barely took notice, and because it was never talked about, it came as a surprise when Granpa's name came up.

"Jerry's grandfather has a crossed eye," Mom answered. And "No, he doesn't see so well out of it."

It would be years later when I'd read in Granpa's memoirs his account of what happened, his particular reason for the crossed eye, long after the rumors among us kids had been forgotten and long after he had passed on. He was legally blind in it.

From this came glasses and a patch over my good eye to strengthen my weak eye. I looked like the promiscuous issue of Captain Jack and

Edith Head. Over the next year follow-up appointments tested my progress, but it was tough going, the patch apparently didn't work, my eye resisted conformity and in fact insisted even more on its independence. It was hard to tell what I was looking at in any given moment.

Soon I was under Dr. McCallum's knife.

"Back then," Mom said, "that eye surgery was a hit and miss proposition. Sometimes the muscles didn't get tightened up properly, and there were follow-up operations, like with John Crowder." John, I was told by Mom, didn't fare too well in the long run.

Mom and Dad discussed the options beforehand and fretted about the outcomes—would I look like Granpa for the rest of my life? Like John Crowder? To do, or not to do? In the end they decided for surgery.

Days later, after the operation, Dad tested my eye again by moving his finger in front of my face.

Both eyes steadfastly locked on to Dad's finger, moving in conjunction like a couple of marionettes. My left eye no longer had a mind of its own!

"Dr. McCallum hit it right on the button," Mom said. "Later, when I took you to the doctor in Olympia, he already knew about you because Dr. McCallum wrote a paper in a medical journal about the operation." The operation didn't keep me from wearing glasses. Though my left eye was now focused, it remained weak and I would wear glasses for the rest of my life.

I don't remember those days—Dr. McCallum, the patches, the glasses, the surgery. It passed me by in a haze of other activities that were part and parcel of any child's early life. Wasn't everybody born with a crossed eye? Didn't everybody wear glasses? Dr. McCallum moved out of my life, but years later his son and I would serve together as class officers in high school.

* * *

From early on I remember Gramma and Granpa's attic.

"Watch out," Granpa would say, as I stood at the top of the stairs, gazing at the strange place. "Come over here." I followed the narrow wooden path to his desk, unsure of my tiny steps, unsure of what was going to happen next. It was a musty dark place atop a steep staircase.

Was it for the living or for the dead? I wondered. Granpa kept various musical instruments there—violins, trumpets, Frenchhorns, violas, and clarinets—and his primitive roll top desk and Underwood typewriter. And there were Gramma's antique porcelain dolls and 78 RPM records, ancient books and assorted building materials, a feather bed where later Bill and I slept during visits from Salem and Olympia, drawers brimming with ancient buttons and other sundries for sewing clothes. The unfinished attic exposed beams and rafters and sub-roofing. A single naked light bulb dangled from a rafter above Granpa's desk. In its dark corners I was certain savvy spiders and spotted beetles lurked ready to make a meal of me. It was a furnace in the summertime.

The feather bed was the most comfortable bed I'd ever slept in, the mattress so soft and forgiving that I feared disappearing into it when I lay down. The bed cover, of thick heavy quilt meant for harsher climes than Oregon, added to the bed's pure opulence and abundance. In total it was like another country. When Bill and I slept in it Granpa would come up and play his violin to put us to sleep. He'd pull up his wooden chair next to the bed, violin in hand, the naked lightbulb glowing above his head, and play Strauss waltzes and Greensleeves and Turkey in the Straw. His playing exhibited more passion than expertise, which included squeaks, burps, false starts, and missed notes, so that these pieces were difficult to get drowsy by. We did our best acting job, however, Granpa playing until he was convinced we were asleep. Then he would click off the hanging light and tiptoe down the creaky stairs and close the door gently behind him. When out of earshot Bill and I would giggle and punch each other—much to our relief—for now we could get some real peace and quiet for sleep.

Granpa didn't spare the rod raising his three boys Bobbie, Danny, and Jimmy, though perhaps with Dad he held back some, Dad being the youngest and sickliest and Gramma's favorite. But by the time Dad was 26 when he entered University, he was a man's man who'd spent four years in the Navy prior to the war and four years in the Coast Guard during the war. He'd criss-crossed the U.S., sailed around South America, hunted Japanese in the Aleutians. University, at the outset, seemed as foreign to him as those places he'd seen on the far side of the world. Not only were the university subjects baffling, but what good were some of them?—sociology, psychology—they appeared trivial after what he'd been through. Furthermore, he'd never been a good student, had never distinguished himself in tests in high school or in the Navy or Coast Guard. Especially baffling were the math courses he desperately needed to pass for architecture. Luckily, Dad's older brother Dan, a math whiz, came to his rescue, tutoring Dad through refresher courses in algebra and geometry, priming him enough that Dad could handle the upper division courses dealing in complex equations for building construction later. I have some of Dad's architecture notebooks and working papers from this time, written in pencil and filled with equations and formulas, drawings and renditions, calculations for mass of concrete and beam stress, page headings such as "Tension Compression and Shear", "Modulus of Elasticity", and "Negative Bending Moments". Written crisp and precise, they are void of cartoons or doodling in the margins, and detailed in Dad's distinctive style, a kind of "architectural standard" handwriting of the period which I later imitated. I have some of Dad's textbooks from those days too, three by Harry Parker, M.S., Professor of Architectural Construction at the University of Pennsylvania, the reigning author of architecture textbooks in those days: *Simplified Design of Structural Timber, Simplified Engineering for Architects and Builders*, and *Simplified Design of Reinforced Concrete*. I also have Talbot Hamlin's *Architecture through the Ages*, and Ramsey and Sleeper's fascinating *Architectural Graphics Standards*, a book of common configurations for stairways, chimneys, stone walls, floors, and a hundred other things. One of these textbooks was likely one I saw Dad reading when I crawled into his bedroom.

According to Mom, the family's schedule in those days was both rigorous and routine. "Your Dad worked part time for EWEB [Eugene Water and Electric Board] as a draftsman in the morning, went to classes during the day, home for dinner at 5:00 p.m., then later, when he was accepted in architecture school, he went back to school at night so he could use the drafting tables there. No one could afford their own drafting tables then, so they used the school's. On Saturday he worked at EWEB, so Sunday was our one day he had free."

Until Bill was born in 1946 Mom worked full time as an operator at the local telephone company. But she often fell sick during the pregnancy and missed work, so friends and family like sister Jean and Gramma and Mrs. Crowder, who had given birth to children before, helped see her through it. Mom worked part-time during her second pregnancy with me because the phone company needed her help changing to a new system. By 1951 she'd stopped working outside the home altogether, when she had Ann, the daughter she'd hope for after two boys.

Mom was indefatigable, driven, possessed by a whirlwind. Her work both inside and outside the home, her three pregnancies, her marriage to Dad, all were of a piece pointing to higher hopes for Dad's studies and career and to a better standard of living than she had before in South Dakota. She zeroed in on the practicalities of life, drawing from her experience in South Dakota, never forgetting where she came from and how far she'd come. By then South Dakota must have seemed like China. Her beloved single mother now lived with Mom's sister Grayce and her husband Bert in Bismarck, North Dakota. Her older brother Bob lived in Minnesota. Her younger brother Jim had joined the army and was stationed in Korea. Her father, whose name she could barely utter without disgust and antipathy, lived somewhere in California.

They wanted to stay in Eugene after Dad finished his degree in 1952, but he found no work there. He looked in Bend, Oregon, but like Eugene it was saturated with draftsmen and architects. He went north, skipping Portland, the state's biggest city and economic powerhouse, because, according to Mom, "he didn't want to raise his kids there." He'd seen enough big cities during his tours of duty in the Navy and Coast Guard to know he wanted nothing to do with their crime, dirt, and frenetic way of life. In Olympia, Washington he found work with Woelob and Woelob, a father and son architectural and engineering company. Though it was the capital of Washington State, it was in those days a small town suitable for Dad, and full of promise. We moved to Olympia over Christmas, saying goodbye to Gramma and Granpa and the rest of the family and friends from the university. It was a bittersweet goodbye, breaking Gramma and Granpa's hearts to see us go.

Mom set up house. Bill enrolled in first grade. Ann learned to walk. I peered at the world through glasses. For Dad several years of apprenticeship lay ahead before he could take the state exams to become a full architect.

We were among the tens of thousands of other families in the country with dads and new careers thanks to the GI Bill, hitching our wagon to his budding career and heading off into the post-war sunrise. We were a family, and a nation, on the move.

Little did we know we had set in motion a seven-year sojourn that in time would take us full circle back to Eugene. Much would happen in between. Mom would say later that those postwar years in Eugene "were the best times of my life. Everybody was in the same boat. Nobody had anything, so we shared a lot and made sure no one did without. If someone was low on cigarettes, we'd make sure they'd get a pack. We'd get together on weekends for dinner and cards and gab all night long. We were all the same then. All startin' out new."

3

OVER THE NEXT two years we rented three houses in Olympia and nearby Lacy, the first two I vaguely remember, but the third, because I was a year older and we lived there the longest, I vividly recall. It was a dangerous place in the country between Olympia and Lacy. A two-lane highway fronted the property, and between the highway and house unfurled an expansive front lawn that appeared to my young eyes to be a park. The lawn was bordered on both sides by a gravel driveway that circled around the back of the house where the garage was. Dad would come home from work in our '48 Plymouth and let me hang from the open driver's window while he parked, I hanging on for dear life while he eased the car into the garage, my legs and feet dangling below me while the gravel passed rapidly underneath, Dad saying "Don't look down!"

The house was ranch style with two bedrooms. Bill and I shared one bedroom, as we would until he entered college, and Mom and Dad slept in the other bedroom with Ann beside them in her crib. The kitchen, dining, and living-rooms were all of a piece, one flowing into the other, and the front entry door was adjacent to a broad picture window that opened to the front lawn and the cars and trucks speeding by on the highway nearby. The place was different from our house in Eugene. There were no sidewalks. You could step outside and see the enormous sky. I remember being alone in an instant.

There was a forest in back where Mom took us blackberry picking. We'd walk past neighbors Mel and Bernie's lazy-eyed cow named Biscuit, grazing behind a wood fence, and soon be in a wilderness of yellow jackets, bumblebees, giant ferns, scrub, thorny berry bushes, and towering evergreens. On stormy days the thick firs and pines would twist and writhe like an angry god, threatening to unhinge themselves and come a marching. The blackberry patch was not only a long way to hike for my short inexperienced legs, but it was also a place gotten to through a perilous path riddled with holes and boulders and stinging nettles. And the smell of rotting vegetation, and the buzzes and slithering of unseen things, and swinging branches loaded with deadly thorns. These accompanied Mom and Bill's warnings about snakes, wolves, bears, ticks, bees. I was on guard against these vicious things, constantly on the lookout for signs of them in trees, bushes, grass, poised in a heartbeat to bolt. I saw bees and flies and gnats, visible enemies against which I felt I had a fighting chance. But against bears and wolves I hardly knew what I was dealing with other than what Bill told me. And what he told me was that at any moment I was fresh meat for a hungry bear or wolf. This was enough to keep me hiding behind Mom's apron during the march, while Bill—fearless and free—ran in front, ran carefree, ran to the sun. We'd pick enough berries to satisfy Mom, her aluminum bowl overflowing with the large sweet berries as we walked back to the house. Later she would bake blackberry pies and take one over to Mel and Bernie's.

Our neighbors Mel and Bernie took Mom and Dad under their wings, and like Gramma and Granpa treated us as if we were their own kids and grandkids. Their house next door shared a driveway with ours, and the house itself was a larger ranch version of ours. Mel had built both houses, and I believe we rented from them.

Mom and Bernie soon became close enough that their daily visits covered everything from cooking, child rearing, picking berries, and the best stores to shop at. Dad and Mel talked about home construction, guns, hunting, flying. Mel had a single engine Cesna and took Dad along sometimes. There were shared dinners and picnics during long summer evenings.

One day I heard the ring of a gunshot from Mel and Bernie's house. It was like nothing I'd heard before: the loud intense explosion, the first echo through the woods, the interminable reverberation into infinity. Both frightened and curious at the sound, I froze in place—I was in our house—hesitant to move for I sensed imminent danger. Then, as the echo died down and I heard no further shots, I slowly made my way through the kitchen and garage to the driveway. The smell of fresh baked bread wafted from our oven.

I was met by a horrible sight. In the driveway a carcass hung from a tripod. It was split open top to bottom exposing ribs and innards of indescribable complexity and bloody foulness. Blood, dripping from the carcass, formed in pools underneath on the ground. The eyes of the beast were filmed over, empty and blank. Was it dead? It certainly looked like it. The simple wall of my world cracked. I reeled backwards. But it wasn't just the horrid image that rocked me on my heels but also the pungent smell, welling up, putrid and rotten; it quickly enveloped my whole body like a blanket I couldn't get out from underneath. Panicky, I turned and ran back inside the house. Mom was pulling fresh baked bread from the oven. It was too much. The smells of the bread and beast collided like crosscurrents of prevailing winds, one good, one bad, and I stumbled to the bathroom just in time. Mom ran after me. There I vomited into the toilet until there was nothing left inside of me. I felt like the beast itself.

Dad and Mel had killed Biscuit and were butchering it for steak and hamburgers. While I took flight, Bill stood watching, fascinated; perhaps he had a turn at the butchering.

Granpa and Gramma visited us at Christmas. For a week Gramma and Mom baked cakes and cookies, filling the house with the sweetest aromas, and on Christmas Eve, after Granpa had his traditional clam chowder, which we kids were loath to eat, we'd pile into their giant blue Packard and go looking for Santa. We'd drive down dark country roads with our eyes pressed to the windows hoping to see a sign of him in the night sky. Though we'd see red lights in the sky, claiming it was Rudolf and his nose, there was never conclusive proof. "That's a radio tower," Dad would say, or "looks like an airplane." Then Christmas morning came and we'd awake to the miracle of presents spread beneath the tree that were brought by that same Santa we tried so hard to find the night before—did anyone hear him and his reindeer on the roof last night? "Now, now," Mom would say as we'd make a mad dash for the presents and begin ripping and tearing. "Let's do these one at a time."

That Christmas Gramma and Granpa gave us a popcorn popper, the latest "all-in-one" model with a three-legged metal bowl and built-in heating element, a bona fide space age marvel to our eyes. We kids were soon arguing over the marvel popper and the finer points of making popcorn. I remember the pop of corn and sudden cacophony of chromatic cracks, splits and bursts, the lid rising while underneath white kernels appeared like brains oozing out, the decelerated popping and quick decanting of popcorn into the voluminous aluminum bowl, the glob of butter sizzling and melting and changing form at the bottom of the popper, the oh-so-careful pouring of butter over the popcorn in democratic fashion, the salting and long butter knife plunging into the bowl churning and mixing the popcorn/butter/salt into one final integrated opus.

Despite what Mom and Dad taught us, over time Bill, Ann, and I made perfect popcorn differently. Was it our Keefe disposition? It soon became a floating body of knowledge—never written down—that ranged far and wide regarding the best way to make it. At what point during warm up do you apply the glob of Crisco? How much Crisco do you put in? Do you let the Crisco melt and sizzle before pouring in the popcorn? Exactly how much popcorn do you pour in? At what point do you pull the plug before burning the last kernels? When do you apply the salt and how much (before or after the butter)? How much butter to melt? What pattern (circles or crosshatching) to pour the melted butter over the popcorn? What stirring method assures a democratic distribution of butter and salt? These questions were monumentally important to us, so much so that in view of our fevered theories and drawn-out pronouncements, our stubborn assuredness over these earth-shattering matters, a standard method of popping never saw the light of day. Mom and Dad watched with narrowed eyes from the kitchen door, mindful of the dangers children get into with electric appliances, ready to pounce in case we dare blow ourselves up or burn the house down. Over time each of us landed an idiosyncratic method that by our teen years made us professional poppers. I honed my style to haut cuisine: salty, but not overstated, buttery, but not overpowering. It was a source of both pleasure and aggravation in the family lasting decades.

* * *

A pulsating light filtered through the front window curtain of our house one night. In those years the country at night was so dark that against the sky you could see millions of stars, some of them, according to Dad, outlined bears, lions, and even a water dipper. The only light came from other homes down the road or from occasional street lamps at intersections. So what was this strange light silhouetted against our curtain, beating like a heart, at once white, then red, then white again? And what was that high-pitched sound we heard beforehand, throbbing up and down and splitting the quiet of the night? Mom and Dad told us kids to stay put.

They rushed across the front lawn into the pulsating light. We saw them do this after tip-toeing to the window and pulling the curtains apart. It was the strangest sight. On the highway was parked a vehicle with a blinking light on top: red, white, red, white it turned. We could see several people, now including Mom and Dad, standing nearby and talking and pointing. A couple of others dressed in uniforms were bending over something on the highway. A car was parked nearby on the shoulder. More strangers appeared from the darkness. We watched bewitched, noses pressed to the window. That something lying on the highway was now covered in white and put in the back of the vehicle with the blinking light. Several people did this. The men in uniform got into the vehicle. Then with an engine surge it pulled out and roared off, the high pitched sound returning, the pulsating light continuing to break the fabric of the night. After a long moment the vehicle disappeared into the darkness, its siren and light now a faint memory, and the rest of the people began to disperse .

Mom and Dad returned with serious faces. We were eager to know what happened. What was the strange light, the screaming siren? What was the white thing? Who were those people, especially the ones in uniform?

"It's the boy across the road," Mom said. We knew about him, had seen him here and there. The phrase "off in the head" had been used and we were not encouraged to play with him. There was something about the family too. They were different. "Poor" was another word I remember describing them. And where was the father? The boy had been wandering around outside in the dark that night. He'd walked onto the highway. The man driving the car never saw him until the last moment. The boy was on the way to the hospital.

"This is what happens when you go into the road," Mom and Dad chimed together, themselves a bit unhinged by what they'd seen. This could have been one of their kids! They used the incident as an object lesson for us kids, repeating the perils of passing cars, how fast they go, and this goes for all sorts of things like hot stoves and fires and animals and guns. "Keep away from the road" they said again and again.

Days later the boy returned from the hospital. Mom baked cookies and together she and I took a plate over to his house. We crossed the highway and Mom pointed at the spot where he'd been hit. Her other hand tightly held mine. The boy's mother greeted us at the door. She appeared frightened, shy, shriveled. She led us up narrow creaky stairs to his bedroom. Through the door the boy lay motionless in his bed, swathed in white linen and white pajamas and looking pale, tired. A scared look crossed his face. It was a haunting scene. He appeared as if he'd returned from some place other than the hospital—a place otherworldly, ghost-like—though I could hardly articulate this at the time. His mouth was all that moved on his body. He mumbled the few words he spoke, barely audible. Mom made small talk, presented him with the plate of cookies. His eyes moved to them, brightened, then went dull again. I was antsy and wanted out of there. We didn't stay long. Walking back home hand in hand with Mom, we checked both ways down the highway to make sure it was clear of cars before we crossed.

* * *

Near the end of our second year in Olympia the Woelob and Woelob Company broke up, for reasons undisclosed—there were rumors the father and son had a falling out—and Dad wasted little time in finding new work with Jim Payne's architectural firm in Salem, Oregon. In a moment's notice we were on our way again, headed to our fourth house since our move from Eugene.

We said our good-byes to Mel and Bernie and promised to keep in touch. Though we were going to miss them, we were happy heading south since it was back to Oregon and closer to Gramma and Granpa. Was this part of some grand scheme? How long would we live in Salem? Would it be a permanent stay or a hotel on our way to Eugene, or some other place? With his time in Olympia, Dad now had real life drafting experience. In Salem he would began taking sections of the state boards to get his architect's license.

We soon found ourselves in a house near the state capital. Bill was in the third grade, entering his third school. Ann was running. I was starting kindergarten.

4

OUR FIRST HOUSE in Salem, on Winter Street near the state capital, was a remarkable departure from our previous homes: colossal, a castle in our young eyes, big enough to rent one of the rooms upstairs. A craftsman style with planked stairs leading to an elongated covered front porch, in the entry lobby there was a stairway that wound upward with a guardrail that I used to slide down. To the right through an archway a spacious living room, flooded by light from the picture window nearby, opened to the rest of the main floor. The next archway led to the dining room with its built-in hutch for plates and serving dishes. The narrow kitchen in the rear, where I first washed dishes, led to the back yard. Two bedrooms and a bathroom completed the main floor. Upstairs was another world. At the top of the stairs was the master bedroom we rented. Then a long hallway led to two other bedrooms, a storage room, and a second bathroom. Bill and I slept in one of the bedrooms. Being so far from Mom and Dad downstairs, where Ann slept too, seemed unimaginable at first, and I'm sure it took some coaxing to get me to sleep there in the beginning. Off the kitchen was the stairway to the unfinished basement where Mom kept her canned foods and Dad his hunting equipment. In back was a yard that stretched to an alleyway and a one-car garage. With its multiple bedrooms, long hallways, expansive living and dining rooms, multiple bathrooms, a basement, the house was easy to get lost in, or so we imagined. Bill and I, and increasingly Ann, made this house our fantasy home complete with caves, tunnels, secret passageways, jail cells, cliffs, ledges, and battlegrounds. It was the house we never wanted to leave. I remember once wearing a cape believing I was Superman, and jumping off the front porch and landing with a thud on the hard lawn. My legs felt like they'd been crammed into my rib cage. I cried and cried from the pain, rolling on the grass in a fit of agony believing I'd never walk again. Mom soon came to my rescue, checking me over and assuring me nothing was broken. This house of wild proportions made you do things like that.

By then Mom and Dad were in their mid thirties. A good looking couple, Mom with her shapely figure set off by brunette hair, penetrating black eyes, and perfect white teeth (from the chlorinated water in South Dakota, she claimed), Dad with his curly red hair and pale blue eyes, broad shoulders and light Scotch/Irish skin, they loomed larger and larger in my life. At this house I began to run afoul of them, beginning innocently enough with vegetables, a class of food I hated for its taste, texture, smell, and shape, though what I knew then was why not eat dirt? The rule was I couldn't leave the dinner table without finishing them. Thinking I was clever, I'd chew the detestable green beans or peas into a measly pulp and, using my tongue, move it surreptitiously into the corner of my mouth. Then I'd pretend to swallow it. Later I'd pretend to have to go to the bathroom and there spit the detestable mess into the toilet,

　　　　DREAM FAMILY ♦ A MEMOIR

flushing it down with glee. How clever I was! But who was I fooling? Dad let me get away with this sham a couple of times before he put his foot down. "No, you're not going to the bathroom right now," he'd say. I'd sit at the table for 15, 20, 30 minutes believing I could outwait Dad. It was a showdown. He kept his eye on me. He put his stern face on, signaling that if I didn't eat the vegetables I'd get a licking. Eventually I'd swallow that last bit of green bean with a horrified twist of my face, letting him know in no uncertain terms the torture he put his little boy through.

My first run-in with Mom involved a recording. That first year in Salem she enrolled me in the Happytime Kindergarten across the alley in an annex of St. Mark's Lutheran Church. Our teacher Mrs. Clark sang and read stories to us, took us on field trips, including a trip to nearby Albany on the Southern Pacific "Shasta Daylight" train. For that I got my photo, along with the rest of the class, in the local newspaper.

One morning Mrs. Clark played a 76 RPM recording of a commercial airline flight. From the first seconds of the recording I remember being mesmerized. I heard pilot commands, the roar of the engines as the airplane took off, the flight attendants talking to the passengers while serving snacks and drinks. I was there—everywhere!—in the cockpit, serving the passengers, on the wings, in the engines—flying at 25,000 feet! I couldn't get the record out of my mind. Mrs. Clark said it was available at the local record shop.

I returned home that day intent on having that record for myself. I couldn't live without it. I told Mom where we could buy it, per Mrs. Clark, claiming to know exactly where the store was. Since we lived near downtown—Salem wasn't *that* big—we could get it in no time. Mom took me up on it.

We climbed into our Plymouth. Sitting in the front seat barely seeing above the dashboard, I pointed in various directions certain at each juncture the store was just around the corner. We drove and drove, stopping at various record stores where each proprietor said the same thing: they'd never heard of the record let alone have it. It became apparent I didn't have the faintest idea where the store was. Furthermore, Mom wondered if there was ever such a record—who ever heard of a recording of an airplane flight? She soon threw her arms up at wasting an afternoon chasing after...nothing! She made me feel dumb. I was miserable, not only for failing to find the record, but for making Mom angry.

But the record was no illusion—I'd heard it and wanted to hear it again—the drone of the engines and the pilots' voices and flying in the sky while looking down on the world. I was quite worked up about it. Mom promised to talk to Mrs. Clark about it.

The record appeared a couple of days later. I was happy beyond belief. For days on end I listened on our phonograph to the drone of the airplane engines and pilot commands, the easy talk among the stewardesses and passengers, each time pretending I was the pilot, or a passenger, flying above the world. It drove everyone crazy in the house. It would be a long while before Mom trusted me with directions again.

* * *

One day in that castle of a house Dad told me to go to the basement and tell what was down there to put its tongue back in its mouth.

"Don't worry," he said, "it won't bite you."

It was an unfinished basement with exposed beams and cracked concrete floor; a couple of daylight windows let a trickle of light in. I inched my way down expecting what? I had no idea and a bit unnerved. It wasn't like Dad to put me in harm's way, at least at this point in my life. When at the base of the creaking stairs I saw it I drew a quick breath. Hanging by its neck from one of the rafters was a four-point buck, its body shrouded in a white sheet, its head and snout tilted upwards. From its mouth hung its long dark gray tongue, limp and dry.

Did I sense this was a test? Did this have something to do with Biscuit? I stepped forward.

"Put your tongue in!" I demanded. The deer, whose head with its dead eyes and body shrouded in white seemed from another world, ignored my request.

"Put your tongue in!" I repeated, a quiver now in my voice. The deer remained still as before. I said this several times, hoping for some kind of response to share with Dad, even shaking my fist at the beast to get a wink or a nod. But the deer hung there motionless, its tongue limp and dry, refusing to do as I said. I turned and ran upstairs. I told Dad the deer's tongue still hung out.

"I'll be darned," he said, shaking his head.

✳ ✳ ✳

Our castle of a house was set in a busy urban section of Salem. We rented the second floor master bedroom to a young lady, a secretary—did she work at the State Capitol?—who had a boyfriend named Igor who would take his shoes off before entering the house. They went square dancing on Friday nights. Later we rented the room to a short plump shoemaker—Mr. Caulkins—who had a store nearby. Both tenants came and went quietly, rarely showing themselves during the day, and at night, despite Bill and I listening at the keyhole hoping to hear something, a word, a rustle, hardly a peep or movement was ever heard or seen from either of them.

Each morning Bill was off to Garfield Elementary School just beyond the corner. From time to time Mom let Bill and I go there to play on the merry-go-round, bars, and swings. Bill soon learned to ride a bike, and it was at the playground that Bill convinced me to hang from the parallel bars while he rode his bike underneath me. At the right moment, he said, I should let go and land on the back of his bike like a cowboy on his horse.

"It'll be easy," he said.

"What if I miss?"

"Don't be stupid."

"What?"

"Don't be stupid. You won't miss."

I climbed onto the bars and grabbed the first rung and swung out, legs dangling below me. "Hurry up!" I yelled, feeling my fingers slipping. I watched as Bill leaned his bicycle into a wide arc and headed towards me, gaining speed along the route. His hair was flying. Soon he was below me.

"Now!" Bill yelled.

I let go.

I was neither keen to the laws of motion nor trained in the tuck and roll method of falling. When my chin hit the asphalt first Bill was several feet beyond the bars, looking back in disbelief. He quickly turned around.

"You didn't let go when I yelled!"

"I did too!" I cried.

Blood spurted from my chin, dripping in globs on the asphalt and drenching my T-shirt. Bill rushed me home. I tried but couldn't stop crying. Mom, thinking fast on her feet, and sensing the wound needed more than a simple Band-Aid, fetched our neighbor next door, a state payroll clerk, whom Mom knew to be up on her First Aid. I remember her being very gentle, her hands carefully feeling around the bloody gap in my chin, mindful in light of my tears not to hurt me any further. She applied disinfectant and stopped the bleeding, and using special butterfly Band-Aids and gauze she closed my chin. I had a goatee.

Through my tears I gave Bill a weary glance.

"You didn't let go when I said, stupid," Bill said later.

"I did too!"

Today I feel the scar under my chin.

* * *

In addition to Bill's school a block away there was a Catholic school nearby where the boys and girls wore the same colored clothes: the girls in blue pleated dresses, white blouses, blue sweaters, black pumps; the boys in white shirts, blue sweaters, black pants, black brogue shoes. Along with the nuns, who dressed in black and white habits and arching head covers, and who led their students on daily field trips, we found them all intriguing, strange, like animals passing by from a traveling circus. We plied Mom with a hundred questions about them: Who are they? Why do they dress like that? Why do they go to that school? Do we have to go to that school? They looked just like us.

These questions came on the heels of our first venture to the First Methodist Church of Salem. Bill and I went to Sunday school, Ann to the nursery, Mom and Dad to the main service. Bill and I learned about the Bible and Jesus, the disciples, the crucifixion, Heaven and Hell. A sense of gravity and seriousness framed everything our Sunday school teacher talked about. And too, I remember her as a pleasant person, much like everyone there seemed to be. Mom said "that's what going to church is all about—being nice to people." No one made loud noises, or fought, or moved from their chairs. But the classes were excruciatingly long and boring, lasting a full hour that I couldn't wait to escape from. Furthermore, stories of God and Jesus living in the sky while the Devil lived in Hell below spooked me. I laid awake at night thinking about it.

It was Mom's idea to go—she'd been raised Methodist in South Dakota—and between Sundays Mom read to us from The Story of Jesus, by Lloyd Edwin Smith, whose pages are filled with wonderful illustrations of Jesus' life—I still have the book—and are as familiar to me today as they were then. Like questions about the Catholic children, Bill and I raised more questions about God and Jesus: what if I'm not nice? What do people do in Hell? Does God know what I'm doing *all* the time?

Life after death sounded o.k. to me, but what troubled me was death itself, or more precisely, dying. To go to Heaven (or Hell, God forbid), I had to die, and what I knew of death didn't look too good to me: pictures of Jesus nailed to the cross, Biscuit hanging from the tripod, the buck hanging downstairs. At one point among those first weeks of Sunday school the weight of these images pressed down on me. I was thinking only of myself. I was going to die sometime—everybody did according to the Sunday school teacher—there was no escaping it. Growing old didn't bother me as much as the dying part. How bad was it going to hurt? To make matters worse, rather than Heaven or Hell greeting me on the other side, I imagined an enormous black nothingness, darker than a well hole, with no up or down. This frightened me more than Hell. That my life would simply end, kaput, in this blackness was more than I could stomach. One Sunday night, in the blackest of moods, I whined and moaned into the wee hours about these things, especially about the dark nothingness while Mom and Dad took turns patting my heavy head, reassuring me that my fears amounted to nothing. I was too young to worry about such things they said. It didn't help.

Children are intuitive enough to recognize if someone's not buying into the program, and Bill and I sensed something amiss because unlike Mom, Dad rarely spoke of Jesus or God or anything else religious (unless he took the Lords name in vain!). Mom wanted him to go because Dad at church was good for the family and good for business. So he attended in body only. Many years later when I was a teenager Dad revealed to me his true feelings about God and religion. Sometimes, he said, he felt there was a God and a reason for life. He'd had exquisite moments. But they were fleeting and few and far between. Most of the time he felt there was nothing, that life was meaningless.

I have a photo of us posing in our Sunday best around this time, Bill and I dressed in sport coats and bow ties and shiny shoes, Ann and Mom in cotton dresses and dress coats, Mom wearing high heels. We looked like the All-American family. Having taken the photo, Dad was not in the picture.

✳ ✳ ✳

For a year we lived in the castle we never wanted to leave. Then one day trucks and men appeared and jacked up the house, put it on a long bed, and carried it away to a vacant lot across town. A year later a church was built in its place, a stained glass reminder of the castle we once lived in. Mom and Dad thought seriously about buying the house on the new lot, but for some reason it didn't work out. We were heartbroken. Years later the roof caved in and killed the owner's son.

We moved to a two-story bungalow on High Street one block west of South Salem High school. Though less spacious than the Winter Street house, it was larger than our other previous homes. On the main floor was a living room with fireplace, a dining room overlooking the back yard, a kitchen with breakfast nook, a TV/bedroom, and a bathroom. Upstairs were two bedrooms and an attic. Below was a ¾ daylight basement where Mom did washing and held Cub Scout meetings. The house sat on a slope that exposed the basement to the backyard which flattened in lawn to the gravel alley where the single car garage stood. A Doug fir towered over the south side of the backyard, and below it sat a sandbox the neighborhood cats pooped in. A white picket fence surrounded the backyard. "When we were going together," Mom said later, "your Dad said he wanted a house with a white picket fence for his dream family." He had it now. We lived in the High Street house nearly four years, making it the longest stay for our family in one house.

I soon began first grade at McKinley School up the street and continued there until Christmas break of my fourth grade year. Because McKinley rose so high above us on High street, floating like a temple in the sky, it seemed to me to be the most important place around, even more important than the modern looking South Salem High School a block away. From our house I could see its concrete front stairs and double doors, its brick facade and first and second story classrooms, its towering flagpole with the Stars and Stripes waving in the wind. On each side and in back of the main building were playgrounds of 4-square and tetherball courts, baseball diamonds and jungle gyms, merry-go – rounds and parallel bars.

Walking up High Street to McKinley each school day was a slow ascent to the Promised Land, past lazy tree lined streets, slow moving cars, the family grocery store halfway between, then up the broad concrete stairs to the magnificent entry doors. Mrs. Stingly's first grade class was at the end of one of the lengthy hallways on the first floor near the front of the building. On the long wall opposite our room, reaching from floor to ceiling and extending to the end of the long hall, were shelf after shelf of books of every size, shape, and form, more books than I'd ever seen before: it was McKinley's library.

Our classroom was a bright place due to the natural sunlight that came through the row of tall windows along the west side; and spacious too, with a high ceiling, and chock full of desks where we sat in pairs. But it bordered the nearby playground where we saw other kids playing at recess. This constant distraction as Mrs. Stingly stood at the blackboard each day teaching us the alphabet and arithmetic, with the kids playing dodgeball and tetherball and baseball within arm's reach, made us want to bolt and join them at all moments. The letters thumb-tacked above the blackboard in both cursive and print didn't hold our attention as much as the balls bouncing outside.

The principal of McKinley—Mrs. Rea—was a woman Bill told me in no uncertain terms to avoid. By the time I started first grade he'd already had trouble with her. In spite of Mom and Dad's partiality to us kids, defending us even when we were wrong, their defense of Bill during his troubles, which I was never privy to, crumbled in the face of Mrs. Rea. An imposing figure of tight bundled hair, rimless glasses, high-neck blouses, and floor-length skirts, Mrs. Rea could melt steel with her scornful and wilting demeanor. She resembled Gramma in physical appearance and dress, but the similarities ended there. There was nothing soft about Mrs. Rea. In the mornings when we arrived at the lower steps in front of the school, she'd be standing at the entry with her arms folded smartly in front of her, personally enforcing her first rule of the day: until the bell rang we early arrivals could wait on the lower steps but not the upper steps, where she stood. No one dared to cross that imaginary line. So we waited, talking among ourselves and listening for that first bell, periodically glancing at the compelling figure of Mrs. Rea from the corner of our eyes.

* * *

"You don't know how to read or write?" Bill said to me the night before starting first grade.

"No! Why?" I said.

"Because you have to to get into first grade."

"How do you know?"

"Because I'm a fourth grader stupid. I've been there! If you don't know they put you back in kindergarten."

This was unwelcomed news on the eve of first grade. Up to then I had looked forward to starting at McKinley, a real school in my estimation. How was I supposed to know the requirements? I certainly didn't want to do kindergarten over. Panicky, I grabbed our Walt Disney's Davy Crocket book that Mom had read to us and started copying it word for word in a tablet. I figured by doing that I'd know how to read and write by night's end. Make no mistake, it was hard work. My fingers, held tight around the pencil and unaccustomed to writing, soon ached. I found the letter "g" almost impossible to write because of its squiggly curves. And making all those letters look uniform was difficult too. But racing against time, focused like a light beam, I trusted everything would sink in. I copied a full page.

I asked Mom "could you read this so I can hear the words?" I handed her my tablet. Did she think I was getting a leg up on my new classmates?

She read my rendition of Davey Crocket just as she read it many times before in the book. The words flew out of her mouth while I matched them to what I'd written, except nothing connected. I stopped her and had her start over. Mom was patient. She explained to me how letters represented sounds of words and gave me examples. She could have been talking to a Martian for I understood nothing.

"What am I gonna do?" I cried.

"About what? Mom said.

"About not being able to read or write!"

"That's why you're going to first grade tomorrow. To learn how to do that."

"Bill said I have to know it now or I'm going back to kindergarten!"

"Bill said that?"

"Yes."

"Well, he's wrong."

"Really?"

Later Bill said: "Mom said that? What does she know! She went to school a thousand years ago."

Not sure who to believe, I kept writing from Davy Crocket.

I entered a dark night. Torn by whom to believe, and making no headway learning how to read or write, I threw myself into a funk so pronounced and desperate that I wished the next day, which I thought would be so different, so exciting, wouldn't come. I wanted to die. Nothing Mom or Dad said helped. I sobbed and stewed over the bad things soon to be thrust upon me. Bill surely fueled the fire. I would be sent to a corner wearing a dunce's cap, ridiculed and laughed at by all. I would repeat kindergarten and be forever held back in the shadows of my friends, never to catch up.

Bill must have laughed his head off.

Of course Mom was right. To my amazement and relief no one else in the class knew how to read or write either. Bill *was* wrong. Mrs. Stingly, a teacher molded by patience and grace, was an angel sent from high. She moved us first graders through those early lessons with the ease of a seasoned magician. The knot in my stomach left. Going to class was fun. In the class photo Mrs. Stingly is standing over her flock wearing black horned rimmed glasses, a frilly white blouse and dark knee length dress, brunette hair to her shoulders, a smile on her face. And we classmates sitting at our desks hands folded in front grinning at the camera like cherubs from a Bible book.

The honeymoon was short lived, however. Mrs. Stingly was soon on the phone with Mom. In secret meetings things were discussed. I was having severe earaches that plugged my ears and Mom and Dad feared I was going deaf. To compensate in class I began reading Mrs. Stingly's lips, which is why she called Mom. Next I was off to an ear doctor who lanced my plugged ears with a needle, a procedure painful beyond imagination. Afterwards the nurse gave me butterscotch candy as reward for the torture I'd just been through. I went to this doctor several times over the next few years, dreading those appointments knowing what was in store, but went with Mom under little protest. On our way home from the first appointment I said to Mom, "this car is loud!" She burst out crying realizing my hearing loss was only temporary.

I was moved to the front of the class and I heard whispers.

On the heels of that came the Salem ophthalmologist's diagnosis of "lazy eye". Since my operation a few years before in Eugene, Mom and Dad made yearly appointments to keep track of my left eye's progress, especially now that I was starting first grade. The doctor found the eye drifting and I wasn't using it to read. Like before he fitted a patch over my good eye which I had to wear at school.

This was too much. I protested loudly. Being singled out as the deaf one in class was bad enough. I wasn't going to be the blind one too. I agreed to wear the patch only after school.

I felt embarrassed and demeaned hearing those whispers when I was moved to the front of the class. It would not be the last time this would happen in school because of my hearing. But there was an up-side to this. My poor hearing and "lazy eye" forced me to concentrate on Mrs. Stingly's lessons at an intense level, a level I otherwise may not have reached under normal conditions. I simply had to hear and see what she was teaching. The downside, God forbid, and per Bill, was kindergarten, which I promised myself, if only to disprove Bill, wouldn't happen.

* * *

I forged on. I fell into the structure of things. We lined up for everything: recess, assemblies, lunch, visits to the library, spelling bees, bathroom breaks. We pulled the shades and turned the lights out to watch "film clips" of the planets in the solar system and the wild animals of Africa. At midmorning pints of "morning milk" were brought to the class by a sixth grade student, the bottles carried in green wooden crates and sealed at the mouth with paper pull-tabs. By the second and third grades there were girls I noticed who I secretly hoped would write something special on their Valentine cards to me.

Two things were revealed to me when I began school at McKinley, both latent up to that point: first, I had a competitiveness that seemed in place from the opening day. Bill, and perhaps Mom and Dad, must have warned me that we students were to be tested against each other from time to time. It was a free-or-all so don't lag behind! In fact, be first! Second, I had a curiosity kindled by the newness and variety of the subjects we studied. Flabbergasted each day by arithmetic problems, new words, strange places on the giant map, I couldn't get these things out of my mind. Bound and determined to distinguish myself by not being the last or the dumbest, I raised the bar, raised my expectations. I dreaded the horror of an ill-prepared lesson, or of being called upon and not knowing the correct answer, or handing in homework late. Having kids whisper behind my back because I couldn't hear or see was bad enough. The added indignity of being considered dumb was impossible.

I couldn't help but notice things because I couldn't stop thinking, even in my sleep when it filled with incomprehensible dreams. With no knowledge of my brain, of how it ran or how it thought, it seemed to me a wild intangible thing. School reigned it in. Whereas before I looked at things that became part of my interior and imagined world, with school I began looking at things knowing I was looking, an observer observing things. Structure emerged behind the surface of the world, making sense to me. The sun caused the shadow from the cherry tree.

So in time I fell in with the routine of school, eager for each day's events to unfold: the pledge of allegiance, the lessons, the spelling bees, the recesses, the assemblies. My days were filled. After school, when the weather was good, we remained and played baseball, four-square, and kickball on the playground. I made new friends and had my eye on girls.

Girls: there was always one in class I watched from the corner of my eye. I made mental notes of who she talked to, what she wore, which way she walked home from school, even where she lived. Was there something forbidden or wrong in this? What did the Sunday school teacher say? And Mom? Were my thoughts naughty? I scarcely understood what my yearnings and heartfelt moods meant, but I sensed something forbidden and mysterious at the heart of my enchantment.

Two incidents I recall were efforts to break through this shroud. The first occurred in our High Street basement. Bill and his friends were playing there one day after school, including a girl. I was there too, off to the side, by myself. At one point Bill and his group filed into the laundry room and locked the door. Under no uncertain terms was I allowed to go in. But once I heard the lock click I ran to the door and put my ear to it. Holding my breath, I listened carefully, curious to know what was happening on the other side. I heard giggling, whispers. My heart pounded. Minutes later the group filed out of the laundry room, pushing and shoving each other, still giggling, the flushed look of excitement on their faces. They promised secrecy among themselves. Later Bill told me what happened and warned me that if I told anybody, especially Mom or Dad, I was a dead man. The girl had lifted her dress and pulled down her underwear for Bill and his friends to see. Indeed this was sensitive information! I kept my mouth shut.

The second incident occurred one afternoon while playing hide-and-go-seek with neighbors, including a girl (was it the same one?). At one point we hid among the laurel bushes bordering our alleyway. Then one of the boys decided to go to the bathroom. In the next instant we were dropping trousers and shorts and urinating into the bushes, the girl included. We giggled like the giggles I heard on the other side of the laundry room. The girl had to crouch to go. Had I not seen this before camping with Mom and Ann? Nevertheless, I sensed we were walking along the edge of a cliff that could easily fall away. Done with our business, we zipped our pants up and scattered to play more hide-and-seek.

Though it spanned a mere minute of tens of thousands of minutes in those days, this escapade refused to leave my mind. Was this furtive and seemingly ephemeral event, like the previous one in the basement, both bound in secrecy, a blessing or a curse? Whatever it was, it promised no escape, ever, from my thoughts.

These were highly charged events at the time—otherwise how could I recall them so many years later? At the time I could not explain the paradox of finding them both exciting and shameful; in retrospect they appear more normal than I would have imagined.

A backdrop to these events was Mom and Dad's contradictory views about our "private parts". Mom's pointed comments about our "pots" being inexplicably bad things that must be kept clean and covered at all times were in stark contrast to Dad's rolling jokes about our "dinkers" and "rumps". He liked to sneak up behind Bill and me and pull our pants down (getting "pantsed" it was called). In turn Bill loved teasing me about my "dinker" when I got dressed for school, or for bed, laughing and jeering and pointing while I pulled up my skivvies. I'd get red in the face. Whether it was because of Mom's shaming or Dad's joking or Bill's jeering is impossible to tell, but from early on I was modest and reluctant to run around naked or half-dressed. Somehow this was connected to girls.

During one of our visits to Auntie Jean's in Eugene, we kids were told to go outside and play and leave the adults alone in the house. Soon a doctor drove up in a car. He emerged and carried a black bag into the house. Mom wasn't to be seen, and Dad and Uncle Buryl and Auntie Jean were wearing serious faces. We knew something was up and I remember being worried about Mom dying. I kept asking if she was o.k when Dad came out to check on us. Later, after the doctor had left, Mom remained in bed and was not to be disturbed. Dad explained Mom had a miscarriage. Whether we understood this is doubtful in light of our age and ignorance of how babies were made. And I don't remember Mom and Dad announcing beforehand that we were going to have another brother or sister. It came out of the blue. But Mom's fourth pregnancy, terminated as it was, turned out to be her last to my knowledge. The three of us siblings were the alpha and omega for Mom and Dad.

Perhaps due to what happened to Mom, the talk of "pots" and "dinkers," Bill's and my episodes with girls, there began a meager beginning to my understanding of what went on between boys and girls, between men and women. But it would be a long long time before I really knew everything. Until then it was endless conjecture.

✳ ✳ ✳

In addition to school and girls, sports on TV began at High Street. Until then TV held little interest for us kids. We'd gotten our first black and white Zenith in Olympia and watched Saturday morning cartoons and Wanda Wanda, and later the Mickey Mouse Club after school. But when we began watching the Yankees on Saturday mornings during baseball season things got serious. In those days the Yankees were King. They seemed to win the World Series every year with stellar players with the best and funniest names: Yogi Berra, Whitey Ford, Moose Skowron, Bobby Richardson, Tony Kubek, Mickey Mantle, Roger Maris, Elston Howard, Joe Pepitone. The coach, the ancient Casey Stengel, was a man worth watching on his own account. He had the weirdest body motions, one minute his index finger is buried knuckle deep in his elephant ear in search of what—the holy grail?—then in the next minute his rubbery face turns pure horror, pulling his finger from his ear, flailing his arms about like a giant windmill, apparently disgusted at a bad call against Maris or Mantle. When he'd walk to the pitcher's mound it looked as if he had a pebble in his skivvies.

Bill and I soon learned a lexicon of dazzling new words and phrases from Dizzy Dean and Pee Wee Reese, announcers for the Yankee games: slider, knuckleball, heater, sacker, full count, change up, hot box, rhubarb. Dizzy called pop flies "Texas Leagers" and errors was pronounced "eras." He'd break out in a southern rendition of "She'll be comin' round the mountain..." when Mantle hit a homer. In those days every kid wanted to be Mickey, or Roger, or Yogi, and I was no different.

I soon tried out for a team. My first baseball glove, autographed by Jerry Coleman, a minor Yankee player, I took to the Hoyt Street baseball diamonds a mile from our house. Bill and I rode our bicycles, and for uniforms the coaches spray-painted team names and numbers on white T-shirts. That first summer, across the front of my T-shirt, was emblazoned "Tigers" in bright red. I'd made a team!

My love affair with baseball, however, was short lived. Constantly getting beaned in the batter's box—in the head, on the shoulders, in the rib cage—while trying to get a hit, I simply couldn't judge where the ball was going once it left the pitcher's hand. I'd return home with bruises and bumps and aches as if I'd been thrown off a cliff. Soon I was bailing out at the slightest hint of a close pitch, which I swore was every time. When the pitch was a strike, I'd take a last ditch swing, hoping for a piece of the ball, but by then I was standing so far outside the batter's box that I could have been swinging at a ball from the next field. "Nice air!" someone would yell. Was it all an illusion? My bad eye? Striking out became my specialty. Baseball was turning out to be not as much fun as it looked on TV. I complained loudly.

Finally Dad had had enough of my bellyaching. After dinner one summer evening he gathered our baseball gear and together we walked to the baseball field at South Salem High, a block away. Bill, I'm sure in protest, was not included. At the field Dad handed me our Louisville Slugger and told me to stand in the batter's box. He walked a slow gait to the pitcher's mound, glove and ball in hand. Then, like Whitey Ford, he wound up, lifting his left leg high, then wind-milled his right arm around and let go the ball. Pitch after pitch came from his hand while I stood there at the plate, bat in hand, ducking every one.

He told me what to do each time: "plant your right foot," "step into it," "keep your eye on the ball." I swung but whiffed dozens of pitches. "Hang in there," he said, "I'm not going to hurt you."

On and on this went, but in time I started hitting Dad's pitches, albeit ticks and fouls at first, but before long I was nailing Texas leaguers beyond the infield—solid hits from the meat of the bat. It was easy! What made it so hard before? We kept at it until long after the sun had gone down and it was too dark to see. "Good job," Dad said at the end.

Walking home that evening from the field, Dad next to me, I carried the Louisville Slugger over my shoulder like I'd seen Maris and Mantle do on TV, alternately squeezing and letting go the grip, getting its feel. I had a game the next day.

I hit a triple the first time up. My Tiger teammates were amazed: "Way to go Keefe!" I singled twice after that.

"You eat a couple bowls of Wheaties today, Keefe?" the coach said, patting me on the back. He moved me up in the batting order.

From then on I spent long afternoons practicing. Using an old tennis ball, I threw pitch after pitch against the garage door to batters like Willie Mays and Al Kaline. I walked some of them, others singled or doubled against me, but most of them struck out after full counts. My windup was slow, precise, measured. If a runner was on first, I'd glance over my left shoulder with my eyes mere slits, warning the runner back. I'd scope the catcher's signal below his pancake mitt—one finger for fastball, two for curve, three for knuckleball—and nod my head for the curve. Then lifting my left leg and cocking my right arm, I'd begin the pitching motion, bringing my forearm over leading with the elbow and flicking the wrist on the downward pull. The ball would roll off my fingertips and rotate sailing down the strike corridor appearing as if it would sail wide, too wide, look out batter! But it was a curve ball, mind you. With the physics of the toss, the ball arched back into the strike zone in the final quarter of its trajectory, smacking the middle of the garage door and rattling its hinges. "Streeeeike one!" I'd yell to the crowd. On the garage door appeared a tell tale mark from the dirty tennis ball, one among many.

Our Tiger record that summer was 10 wins, 4 losses. Two teams were ahead of us at 14-0 and 12-2. Since they were mimeographed and handed out to us players each week, the scores and standings I found to be a fountain of fascinating arithmetic combinations. I studied the other team's win/loss records, the various scores, pondering why on any given day a good team might struggle, or even lose, to a bad team. I recall the arithmetic of the Tiger's record. There were eight teams in the league, and we played each one twice during the season. We'd lost to the two higher teams twice each, the second place team had lost twice to the first place team. I spent hours mulling these things over realizing in a seminal way there was more to baseball than just the playing.

In the Fall after the World Series was over we turned to sandlot football. A group of us from school would converge at South Salem High School in the end zone of one of the practice fields after school. Nearby the varsity and J.V. teams drilled, and I remember how old and mature those 15-16 year olds looked in their oversized uniforms as they ran laps around the field, chunks of grass hanging from their shoulder pads, sweat running down their faces. One player had blood in his teeth. We'd pick teams and play until it was dark, whereupon we'd scatter to make it home in time for dinner.

At Christmas I got a red football helmet. From my infatuation with the horns painted on the Ram's helmets (that's why I liked the Rams more than other teams), I absconded with Dad's black electric tape one day and cut out various horns, wings, flames, and stripes, sticking them on the new helmet signifying my own made-up team. The helmet, I hoped, would strike fear in my opponents. Trying out these designs I used up Dad's full roll of tape. Days later Dad asked "What happened to my tape?" narrowing his eyes upon my newly decorated helmet.

Like it did with baseball, TV loomed large for football. On Sundays we watched NFL games on TV, with the LA Rams and Baltimore Colts, or the NY Giants and San Francisco 49ers. Norm Van Brocklin, quarterback of the Rams, who also quarterbacked the University of Oregon Ducks when Dad went there, was my favorite player. A savvy playmaker who never failed to have the cleanest jersey on a muddy afternoon, he threw his heroic passes to receiver Elroy "Crazy Legs" Hirsch, another favorite player. Y.A. Tittle, quarterback of the 49ers, a smart blue-collar player who, unlike Van Brocklin, often had a torn jersey or a shoulder pad hanging out by game's end, was Bill's favorite. The teams were rivals and Bill and I would argue endlessly beforehand about which one had the best quarterback, which team had better defense, offense, and in the end, which would win.

But if there was disagreement about the Rams and 49'ers, there was complete agreement about our favorite college team: the beloved University of Oregon Ducks. Beloved because they came from Eugene, beloved because Dad graduated from there, beloved because their bitter rival was the Oregon State Beavers, a rabble of sod-busting cowpokes with 50 -word vocabularies from nearby Corvallis ("Cornvalley"), who hadn't that long ago crawled out of the primordial ooze. Indeed, Oregon State was the state's first agricultural land grant college. So what did you expect? The annual Civil War game (there was nothing "civil" about it) was widely anticipated and ferociously fought, and a win, regardless of the season record, would make or break the year. A loss to the hated Beavers was a fate worse than death, throwing the family into a funk lasting days. Only time and a sandlot game afterwards, where we'd replay the game and the Ducks would change the tide and miraculously win, could heal the wound.

* * *

One evening at High Street Dad called us to the front lawn and pointed to a corner of the night sky. Soon we picked up the tiny bright dot as it streaked across the heavens from west to east. Then in moments the dot was gone.

Prior to his departure from the Coast Guard after the war, Dad spent time training Russian sailors on how to operate U.S. Coast Guard Cutters. They were being turned over to the Russians on a lend/lease program as part of an agreement for Russia entering the war against the Japanese. He found the Russians sailors tough, crude, void of compassion. Their capacity for drinking vodka was beyond belief, even for a hardened sailor like Dad.

"I hope we never go to war with those guys," Dad told Mom when he returned home. He was not thinking so much of himself going to war with the Russians as he was of later generations, like his own sons. He had a premonition about future U.S.-Russian relations.

Nonetheless, in the immediate years after the war the Russians were considered a second rate backward people ruled by communist dictators, their country far behind American in terms of standard of living and technology. They'd never catch up.

Dad had pointed to Sputnik.

For us kids it was the first symbol of what we would later come to know as The Cold War and the space race. There had been Korea, the Iron Curtain in Eastern Europe, plus, arguably most alarming of all, the Russian's recent detonation of an atomic bomb. At school we learned to duck under our chairs and cover our heads in case of an attack. Magazines and newspapers had articles on how to build civil defense shelters in your basement. America, the preeminent world power after the war, a country moving forward with confidence and purpose, a country exploding with new material and intellectual wealth, a country full of unbridled and unrepentant pride, was suddenly rocked on its heels, seemingly under siege, shocked by the dot in the sky. How could a second rate country like Russia beat us with Sputnik? Maybe second rate Russia wasn't so second-rate after-all. Dad, remembering his time with the Russian sailors, could only shake his head as he looked at Bill and me.

The Russians, he noted later, never paid for the Cutters they got from the U.S. Coast Guard.

Salem, Oregon mobilized. Through the neighborhood spread word that a rocket was being launched by students at the football field at South Salem High. That was the spirit! It was a Saturday morning, I remember, and arriving at the field after the short walk from home, I could feel the air of nervous anticipation hanging over the crowd of onlookers already there.

We watched one of the students insert the rocket into a long tube that pointed upwards like a cannon. The rocket, slender and silvery, three or four feet long, came with fins at the bottom and a long nosecone at the top. Impressed, we thought: was this going to be the breakthrough for our national space program? We lived in a small world.

The fuse was lit. A tailing of smoke fluttered in the air as it burned closer and closer to the tube. Everything else—and everybody—seemed frozen in place, and quiet. Then the burning fuse vanished. Holding our breaths, we waited and waited.

The rocket hurled out of the tube faster than our eyes could track, accompanied by a swooshing blast. A cloud of billowing smoke hovered above the tube and then disappeared into the air. The crowd gasped. All eyes turned up.

The rocket climbed upwards and upwards, now we could see it plainly, gaining speed as it rose higher and higher, leaving a smoky squiggly trail. Then it was a dot in the sky. Straining to see it, a moment later the rocket vanished into thin air. We continued looking upwards, craning our necks, hands shading our eyes, hoping to glimpse the rocket one last time. Motorists passing by might have thought Jesus had appeared from between the clouds.

The next day Mom and Dad showed me the photograph on the front page of the newspaper of the rocket launch and the crowd watching. I'm sure the article congratulated the students on their success, it being a step forward in our new battle against the Russians—indeed we could launch a rocket too, even in little Salem Oregon! The space race was on.

For my part, and under Dad's tutelage, I constructed my own rocket for the McKinley science fair using an empty MJB coffee can. Turning the can upside down, we first fashioned a long pointed nose cone using a thin sheet of cardboard. Inside the coffee can, at the top, we attached a Popsicle stick that hung to near the open end of the can, where we attached a firecracker. We painted the rocket gray and placed four balsa wood fins at the bottom. In thick black letters we painted "USA" on the side. I drew a picture on a white sheet of paper to show how the rocket worked, outlining and coloring flames and smoke and jagged concussions to indicate the force of the exploding firecracker and how it would propel the rocket high into space, not unlike the rocket at South Salem High (or even Sputnik!). Certain to win first prize, I was disappointed to find no ribbon attached to my rocket on award day. Sure that my genius was not recognized or fully appreciated, I left rocketry like it was yesterday's fad. There were other things in life. Little did I know I was not quite done with rocketry, or with the Russians, not yet anyway.

* * *

Along with watching sports on TV, we gathered around to watch the Ed Sullivan show every Sunday night (Dad called him Said Ellivan) before bedtime. On stage appeared a variety of ventriloquists, jugglers, dancers, comics, all endlessly fascinating and enthralling to our young eyes and ears. But one night a young man appeared that would change my life.

"Ladies and gentlemen," he began, "could I have your attention please? I like to tell you we're going to do a sad song for you. This song here is one of the saddest songs we've ever heard. It really tells a story friends. Beautiful lyrics. It goes something like this." He grinned and chuckled, snapped his fingers. There were screams from the audience. He paused, then launched into "Hound Dog."

He was dressed in a sport coat and tie, black loose-fitting slacks and white dress shoes, his thick black hair accented by sideburns hanging like stirrups. One of his backup musicians played an arpeggio on his guitar. He surveyed the crowd, at one point shading his eyes from the stage lights. Gyrating on his tip-toes, knees bent, arms awhirl, hips pulsating, head rolling from side to side, eyes ping ponging from wide to narrow to sultry, his fat bodied acoustic guitar hanging from his shoulders, he was some kind of electric dynamo writ large. It wasn't dancing and it wasn't baseball, so what was it?

Camera pans of the audience showed grown ladies screaming and crying and holding their faces, jumping up and down in their seats, reaching out to touch the very air he breathed. Even the guys were going crazy.

He finished "Hound Dog" and took a bow, handed his guitar to another backup musician and shook Ed's hand, the audience continuing to scream. Then he and Ed chatted. The audience, like me, was in rapture, noticing his polite, shy, nervous, perhaps affected, demeanor. His answers to Ed's questions were short and inconsequential. His upper lip seemed pinned to a clothesline. It was all of a piece, but there was something happening, something there, something invisible, something powerful, something reaching out and rubbing against a raw nerve in me while I watched him. I didn't avert my eyes for a moment. Was it a force or spirit, a revelation or epiphany? I didn't know. Whatever it was, it reached out through the Zenith and touched me in the most inexplicable way.

I knew then and there I wanted to be Elvis. I wanted to sing and play guitar and shake my hips and make the girls go crazy. Was it sexual? I was only eight! What did I know about such things? All I wanted was whatever Elvis had, there were no words for it, plus I was impatient, couldn't wait: I needed to be Elvis now.

I begged and begged Mom and Dad to buy me a guitar. "We don't have the money!" they said. Each week we were donating our meager weekly allowances to a boat fund, putting our coins in a Kerr jar in the kitchen cupboard, only to find out much later Mom was using the fund to buy groceries.

But somehow performing a miracle, Mom and Dad scraped the money together to buy me a Stella acoustic six string, the Volkswagon of guitars at the time, but to me a Cadillac Eldorado with its dark sunburst finish and silver strings and pearly tuning keys. With it came a booklet of songs and instructions on how to play.

Since Mom knew the melody of one of the songs in the booklet—"My Bonnie Lies Over the Ocean"—I choose it for my first song, fully expecting to learn it in one night: the words, the melody, the left hand chord fingerings, the right hand strumming. Why not? Elvis glided through "Hound Dog" without trouble. I practiced and practiced until late, until my fingers bled, or felt like it, and until my voice barely emitted a croak. Harder to learn than I thought, I wondered how Elvis made it look so easy?

"It's like reading," Mom said. "It takes time."

"I don't have time!" I howled.

There was more to the story. A few weeks before a classmate had played his ukulele for the class. I remember him standing at the front of the classroom strumming and singing flawlessly, all eyes focused on him while he sang his plaintive song. I watched him closely, envying him, noticing the other students doing the same. But as good as he was, I knew he was no Elvis, far from it, and from my secret knowledge of Elvis I was certain I could outdo him. Elvis plus "My Bonnie..." was a certain winner.

I kept at it, practicing night after night. A few days later I declared myself ready, and the next day I headed off to school with my Stella slung over my shoulder, a jump in my step, my hair combed like Elvis's, determined to set the world on fire.

On the way everyone marveled at my guitar.

"Can you play it?" they asked.

"Yep. And sing too."

By the time I arrived at school I had a following. I could tell I was on the right track in getting what Elvis had.

Because of my classmate's previous performance, there were high expectations for me, especially in my own mind. All morning long kids asked what I was going to sing. I acted like Elvis—nonchalant, confident, curling my lip. But underneath I was a churning volcano of doubt. Over and over in my mind I repeated the words and the chords to "My Bonnie..." I could concentrate on little else.

The platform for my performance was "Show and Tell," a time when our third grade teacher Mrs. Woods permitted any student to come forward and share something special with the class. Soon in front of the class, I found myself adjusting the guitar to the right height for best fingering, the blackboard at my back, my Stella now hanging by a string from my neck, before me the eyes of the class on me. I took a deep breath. I strummed the first chord. A moment later I started singing.

"My Bonnie lies over the ocean..."

From the first words I uttered I knew something was different. My voice sounded as if it was coming from somewhere or someone else, its timbre reedy, pruned, sharp, almost a shrill. My heart raced, and soon a small panic set in as I mentally fumbled, losing track of the words. Then, as if an avalanche had begun, I forgot the chords too. My fingers pressed the wrong strings on the wrong frets. Little did I know I was playing my first "diminished" jazz chord, or something like it. Far from acting like those in the audience on the Ed Sullivan show, my classmates in front of me sat frozen, perplexed, some even looked down. I threw in a sneer like Elvis and gyrated my hips, hoping for cheers.

Silence.

What is the matter with these people? Why aren't they going crazy for me? Too many things were happening at the same time. My head filled up like a water balloon, feeling huge, and cool and hot at the same time—flush on the surface while icy inside.

Thinking of no alternative, I stopped playing and started over. By now I was a ball of nerves. Wading through "My Bonnie...," I continued missing notes and flubbing words. I threw in another sneer and a gyrating hip. I was determined to finish "My Bonnie..." like my classmate did with his song on the ukelele.

You could hear the wind rustle through the Doug Firs outside when I finished. No one moved, no one uttered a word. After what seemed like an eternity, Mrs. Woods said "Thank you Jerry" and began clapping. Like obedient sheep, the class began clapping too. It was a courteous clap, controlled and subdued, like you see on the Sullivan show after a circus act, not an Elvis clap.

Was it the end of the world? "You stink" might have been the nicest thing said to me afterwards. My embarrassment was understandable, but deep down I was mad too, a silent seething rage raced through me. Why didn't it work? Where did I go wrong? What can I do next time? Who can help me? Weren't good things supposed to happen to people who practiced! My mind spun out of control. But somewhere in the garble emerged this: If Elvis can do it, so can I.

Again, as if by magic, the money appeared out of nowhere, for shortly afterwards Mom found a teacher and I began guitar lessons. Once a week we'd pile into our '52 Plymouth and drive across town to the teacher's house. Mom sat next to me in the recital room, and the teacher, a rotund man with goatee and black glasses, must have been amused looking at my puny fingers and my Stella. "I want to be Elvis," I told him. Nobody could convince me otherwise. I was on a mission. The teacher had something else in mind.

Playing the guitar, like playing baseball, was more complex than it looked. The teacher soon had me practicing scales and reading music. It was like pounding nails with a whip. It wasn't getting me any closer to Elvis. Soon bored with the lessons, much of which was over my head, hating to practice each day, and hating Mom making me practice each day, I quit, first the lessons and then playing the guitar altogether. I never went back to class to play. If that was what guitar playing was all about, I wanted nothing of it. The Stella was put in the closet to gather dust, and years later it would see the light of day again, but for now my quest for being Elvis was put on hold.

✳ ✳ ✳

My first nightmare at High Street—my earliest recollection of a nightmare—found itself powerful enough to visit me again and again in the years to come. I'm in the backyard playing alone. I hear the crunching of gravel. Looking up I see walking down our alley from the south end a gorilla, or a beast resembling a gorilla, tall and covered from head to toe in black mangy hair, and held in its huge rounded head are two penetrating bloodshot eyes which quickly holds me in its sight. I turn to run but can't because an invisible weight on my feet keeps me anchored to my spot. I scream, but my efforts are for nought—something is caught in my throat—and neither utter nor cry escapes my lips. The beast, holding me with those bloodshot eyes, continues walking towards me, now under the plum tree in the corner of our yard. Frantic, I struggle to run, to scream, to do anything, but I'm trapped inside my skin. The beast approaches the white picket fence and is about to climb over it. A few feet away I suddenly understand I am doomed, there is no escape from this beast and I prepare to die for it can only happen that way. It is then I wake up, sweating, flailing in the dark, recognizing I'm in my own bed. Oh my God that was real, so real I couldn't tell the difference! But it's just a dream, a silly dream. Many years later, with similar nightmares, my wife says my body quivers in the bed sheets and I mumble incoherently, and she's afraid to reach out to touch me for fear of causing a heart attack.

✳ ✳ ✳

At High Street Dad taught Bill and me a variety of games using our hands. It was our first glimpse into Dad's magic. The first I recall was with the yo-yo, and long before we formally learned about geometry, physics, Space, and Time at school, we got our first lessons in them compliments of the yo-yo. Dad taught us how to "Walk the Dog","Rock the Cradle", "Round the World". With a flick of the wrist he would throw down for the "Rock the Cradle," the yo-yo spinning in place (or "free wheeling," or "sleeping") at the end of the string, his free thumb and forefinger grabbing the string midway down and hooking it over the thumb of his yo-yo hand. Now spreading the string horizontally with his thumb and forefinger, he created a triangle with the yo-yo rocking back and forth from the top. It all happened in a flash.

String tension was the key—the twist of the twine—how loose or tight the yo-yo needed to be for "free wheeling", for with the right tension and toss you could do any trick provided you were quick enough with your hands. Bill and I practiced these tricks for hours, endless variations of circles, triangles, and oblongs, and factoring in speed, friction, and resistance. We repeated each trick over and over to make them perfect, wanting that feel you get when the trick unfolds naturally without thinking about it. I'd practice the "Round the World," then just before reeling in the yo-yo I'd add a couple "Loop de Loops." The more I worked on the tricks the more I could improvise, add tricks on the end. The shape or geometry of the trick would change, but the physics remained the same—one variable, one constant. Hitting that sweet spot was the key.

After hours of practice the middle finger the yo-yo string was tied to would have a deep groove around it, and be inflamed, and I'd massage it to ease the pain and work the groove out. Over time calluses appeared, and combined with the bump from writing with a pencil at school, the finger began to look deformed compared to the other fingers on my hand.

In short order Bill mastered these tricks Dad taught us, soon doing routines of three or four tricks simultaneously and later winning contests at the local neighborhood grocery store.

Dad next taught us cards and marbles. Card playing, and the aura surrounding it in our family, began with learning how to shuffle and deal, the values of face cards and suits, how to hold your hand. Dad had funny names for the cards: "Mopsqueezers" for Queens, "Cowboys" for Kings; there were special cards to keep in mind too: one-eyed jacks, Ace of spades. During visits we learned Solitaire from Gramma Keefe and Gramma White. Poker opened the world of chance and risk, betting and bluffing. What was I willing to wager on the hand I held? Card playing helped us to add and subtract faster, helped memory by recalling what cards were played and what remained to be played. We learned the different values of poker hands: royal flush, full house, flush, straight, three of a kind. In all, card playing combined hand/eye dexterity with the brain's capacity for memory and calculation, plus a set of inviolable rules for each game. We wore serious faces while playing, breaking out of character only between hands when we celebrated or lamented our wins and losses.

Compared to cards, marbles was the wild west; open to fudging and negotiation, lawlessness was its bunkmate. It did not take Bill and me long to learn the essentials from Dad: two or more players drew a circle in the dirt and the first player would lob his marble into the center. Second and third players would follow. The object was to knock the other opponent's marbles out of the circle using your marble, thus winning and keeping them. Unlike cards, the equipment varied: "boulders"—giant and weighty ball-bearings—were used for mass destruction, " be-be's" were used to diminish yourself as a target; there were cat-eyes—agates— and "steelies" too. The artistry of some of these marbles were precursors to the psychedelic 60's with their multicolored and swirling interiors and surfaces of reds, greens, yellows. Depending on the number of players, circles were both large and small, and rules changed depending on who was in charge (usually the oldest, toughest kid). You could substitute your marble prior to attack—i.e. put a "be-be" in place of a boulder— or declare 'Bombsies"—thus hovering over the top of your opponent's marble and dropping your own. The risk was if you missed your marble ended up next to your victim for him to take you out on the next shot.

Like he was with yo-yo's, Bill's talent with marbles was beyond belief, having more dexterity and delicacy with his hands than the next kid, he soon had a bag full of marbles compliments of the neighborhood and me. Gramma was a big marble fan too, but as a collector, having a gigantic fishbowl of old marbles she kept atop the dresser drawers in her bedroom which Bill and I looked upon with envy. Some were Dad's old marbles from when he was a kid, their colors mixed together and floating among each other like a dense shoal of tropical fish.

In all these games, in spite of Bill's virtuosity, Dad reigned supreme: he taught us the rules of play, covered various strategies, acquainted us with the tools. Even after years of practice and play, after hundreds of rounds of cards, marbles, and yo-yo, neither Bill nor I could come close to besting him. And it was not a matter of pride for Dad to beat us, for he cared less about winning. But in these games he was magical with his hands, like when he looked at something across the way and in a moment made the connection between his brain and fingers and drew it on a napkin. It was like breathing to him.

At High Street Dad figured that sooner or later Bill and I would be getting into fights and he didn't want his boys coming home bloodied, or worse, beaten up. This was another extension of his magic hands. He'd been the youngest of three boys and in plenty of tussles as a youth, so he knew the terrain, plus he'd boxed in the Navy and had a fundamental knowledge of punches, tactics, strategy. He didn't encourage us to fight—quite the opposite—but his view was that if you had to fight you're better off knowing how. He bought us gloves and soon we were learning jabs, upper cuts, and body punches, and how to circle the weak side. And watching the eyes, Dad said, always watch the eyes.

He had his rules, the first was: "If you decide to fight, get the first punch in. If you deck the guy and he doesn't get up, then the fight's over and you're done. But if the guy gets up, then you have your work cut out for you. You better be ready."

Dad's second rule, which was more a code of conduct than anything else, was: you always come to the aid of your mate, no matter what the situation, and in our case this meant your brother. This boded well for me because in years to come bigger bullies in the neighborhood knew they had Bill to deal with if they picked a fight with me. And it wasn't below me to play this card on an ignorant pompous idiot giving me shit when I'd tell him to kiss my ass knowing Bill was nearby.

Boxing, however, was not altogether good to me. Though I practiced with Dad and learned the punches, Bill often took me on out of view. Not only bigger and stronger than me, he was fiercer too. Sparring with him was like sparring with Floyd Patterson, the heavyweight champion at the time. I took my share of lumps and bruises and discovered boxing to be, after all, an exhausting, debilitating sport, for a minute of it was like playing an hour of football. As the years rolled on I went to great lengths to avoid fights, choosing instead to talk my way out of them. Bill, on the other hand, was constantly punching it out with someone, using what Dad taught him, giving and taking his share of blows at school and around the neighborhood, often getting in trouble with teachers and principals like Mrs. Rea. His fierce temperament held sway over his conciliatory side for many years. But on High Street we boys got our first whiff of the streets, of bullies, of pecking orders; we would be facing a world of brutes, savages, barbarians.

* * *

And so it was for Dad's magical hands that he became our barber in those days, buying an electric clipper that came in a rectangular box with a variety of attachments and combs. The attachments, snapped on the end of the clippers, were for cutting especially thick hair, or bushy hair, or even thin hair, but Dad, a purist, didn't use them, choosing instead to use the clippers as it came out of the box, its tiny cutters blurring back and forth at the end, making a soft buzzing sound like a bumblebee.

On the kitchen chair Dad stacked telephone books and encyclopedias so when I sat down my head would be at his eye level—he needed a comfortable angle for a good cut. Upon getting settled, from the box Dad unfurled the white apron he'd drape over me, tying it in back.

"Be still," he warned me, "or you'll get a hat."

Oh no, not a "hat"—the worst possible outcome! If I fidgeted too much, wanted to play baseball in five minutes, or was generally anxious as I often was, in the mirror afterwards I'd find myself looking like Mo of the Three Stooges, appearing as if a bowl had landed up-side-down on my head. I couldn't go to school looking like that! So I kept still.

In those next minutes Dad and I were physically close, his hands running through my hair as he lined up his cuts. His face hovered close to mine. I could smell his breath and hear his breathing. I never felt threatened or intimidated by this, his hands gentle in those moments. Normally we were not a physically close family.

"How does it look?" he'd asked, holding a mirror in front of me.

"Fine," I'd say. "No hat."

A pile of hair lay on the apron and the floor. From the box now came a soft bristled brush that Dad whisked my neck and shoulders with, getting the excess hair off. Then, untying the apron, he'd pull it off and flick it in the air, more hair floating to the floor.

"That's it," he would say, and I'd jump from the stacked books to the floor. He'd grab a broom and start sweeping.

"No 'hat' today," he'd say.

The final thing Dad did once everything was cleaned and put away, when I was trotting out the kitchen on my way to whatever was next on my childhood agenda, was in pencil make a hash mark on the cover of the clipper box. He did this each time he cut hair. The hash marks were grouped in fives—four vertical marks finished with a slash. He cut Bill's and my hair through high school when by then the box was covered on all sides in hundreds of hash marks.

* * *

I was riding a wave of success at High Street. By fourth grade my teacher Mr. Powell was selecting me Boy of the Week nearly every week. Reading books—I read whatever I could get my hands on—created images in my mind that were as distinct and clear as the trees and houses I saw walking to and from school. And I was handling numbers as easily as seeing and breathing, adding and subtracting faster than my classmates and later even faster than Bill. I was not cognizant of this interior life—that would come later—but my mind was prone to stimulation and animation that I relied on and pushed, even provoked, in order to figure out difficult problems and puzzles. What delight I felt when I figured out how to multiply and divide, or how to write a complete sentence. I'd run home humming a tune. I'd quiz Mom and Dad on odd things: "Do you know what an auk is?" Each morning I was eager to go to school again, refreshed, nourished, a sponge walking through the classroom door.

How splendid I felt returning home each Friday and telling Mom and Dad I was the Boy of the Week again. I could see how proud they were. By Spring each year I was like everyone else, eager for school to end, but in truth the summer honeymoon lasted only a few days, for even with chores and beanpicking and baseball, even with camping and visits to

Gramma and Granpa's, there were long stretches of time when I was bored in the summer, I had few other diversions. I wouldn't admit it to my classmates, and certainly not to Bill, but each Fall when it came time for school to begin, I was ready and eager. While others lamented getting up early, facing the new teachers, the homework, I was secretly rejoicing.

* * *

I remember one day Dad getting the mail and opening a letter and a moment later he was crying. It was the Fall of 1958 and I happened to be in the living room with him when he opened it.

In the years since he graduated from university Dad, like many of his colleagues, had taken the state architectural board exams. He'd passed most of the sections but not all, and each year or two he'd mount another assault on the tests, studying for weeks beforehand those sections remaining for him to pass, and each time he'd get befuddled and fall short. It was wearing him down. Would he ever pass and be a licensed architect? Or would he end up a lowly draftsman the rest of his life? He had his doubts.

I watched as he pulled the letter from the envelope, unfolded it, and watched his eyes move as he read the lines. Then he walked to the arm of the davenport and sat down. The letter dangled from his hand. With his other hand he covered his face. For a moment I wondered what was going on: what was this letter about? Why does Dad have his face covered like that?

His crying came in thick watery sobs from somewhere deep inside. He hunched down, one leg dangling over the arm of the davenport. I'd never seen him like this before and it unsettled me. Between sobs he muttered something which at first I didn't understand, but when he repeated it a moment later I heard the words clearly: "I did it, I did it."

From then on things changed quickly. In what seemed to be the span of a few days Dad quit James Payne's office and opened a partnership in Eugene with Dan Herbert, an architecture professor at the University of Oregon. He began commuting to Eugene on Mondays and returning on Fridays, staying with Gramma and Granpa during the week. His return on Fridays was like Santa coming on Christmas, for he always had a bagful of treats for us kids—mostly candy—with Gramma never missing an opportunity to add to the bounty.

A moving van soon appeared on our front lawn and over the Christmas break, not missing a day of school, we loaded up and moved to Eugene. Bud Blanchard, Dad's colleague from Olympia who followed Dad to Salem and had, per Dad, a genius for spacial relations, helped us pack everything we owned into the van.

Bill came unglued. Having lived in Salem for nearly five years and making his first true friends, the thought of moving yet again was inconceivable. Even the prospect of living closer to Gramma and Granpa didn't console him. He begged and begged Mom and Dad to come to their senses and not move to Eugene. I remember him lying on the davenport crying and blurting between sobs that he wasn't going with us after all, that he'd made up his own mind, that he was staying behind to live with his friend Alan Hadley. I would see him on the weekends when we visited. It frightened me that this was true. How did I know Bill was talking out of his head, half crazed, delirious with loss? The prospect of him leaving the family created a black hole in me, as if the ground had cracked and I straddled an abyss. There was turmoil for a week or so, more crying, more insisting he was staying behind, but in the end he certainly came with us, there was never a question of that. From the beginning we'd been together, all of us, and it being any other way was unthinkable.

Was it Bill's fiery episode that precipitated my final memory of that house on High Street? On Election Day in November, a few weeks before we moved to Eugene, Dad was home to vote. While sleeping that night Mom was awakened by an odd crackling sound. She woke Dad, who mumbled something, then rolled over and fell back asleep. A few minutes later she smelled smoke. Now alarmed, she rustled Dad from his sleep: "can you smell it?" She whispered. Arising, and convinced something indeed was afoot, Dad followed his nose to near where Ann slept on the nearby landing. He felt around the stairwell wall, an arm's length from Ann's head. In short time he found it, a place hot to the touch. Quickly we kids were awakened and rushed downstairs.

Through the front door firemen in floor length black rubber coats and flared red helmets dashed, delivering a horrific jungle snake to the zoo, but lo and behold it was a long thick black hose with a pointed nozzle. On the curb outside we could see the red fire truck with its gigantic black tires and its red light on top blinking on and off, on and off, like the blinking light from the ambulance in Olympia. Up the stairs the firemen flew with their hose. At the landing they took an ax to the wall, now bashing away, splintering it open in a flurry of blows. From the base of the stairs we saw the flames burst upon the firemen when the wall opened up, leaping and licking about as if alive and determined with purpose, now inches from Ann's bed. The firemen jumped back. We froze, incredulous. Wasting no time, the firemen attacked again, taking turns chopping and hosing the wall.

It seemed like an eternity watching the battle before us, the myriad dashes and spurts of activity, but it was probably a few minutes before the firemen had doused the fire and what remained above the landing was a gaping hole where the fire had started, charred and splintered around its jagged edges, as if an angry meteor had crashed through. A stream of water trickled down the stairway. The smell of smoke permeated the house and Mom opened all the windows.

By now it was time to go to school. Acting as if nothing had happened, Mom rounded us up and prepared to send us off. "Good" I thought, "I can tell all my friends about the fire!" When a neighbor stopped by to walk with me, in a rush of words I told him every exciting detail of the fire. Overhearing this, Mom pulled me aside and told me in no uncertain terms: "don't tell anyone!"

Later it was explained that the fire had started when the firemen broke open the wall, and not before, contrary to what Dad and Mom had thought. It was faulty wiring, the firemen said, simmering from dust settling on them over the years, and coupled with the rush of oxygen from hacking the wall open, the wall to burst into flames.

A month later we were out of the High Street house. Bill readily went along too.

5

WE MOVED TO a house on Lawrence Street two blocks from the house I was born in. Washington Park, around the corner, was less than 30 seconds from our front door. It was a three-bedroom ranch style that next to our previous two houses was a miniature by comparison, but being so close to Washington Park with its several playing fields and swings and basketball court, it more than made up for its small size. Bill and I shared a bedroom upstairs in a stretch—limo dormer which ran along the back roof of the house, added sometime after the house was built. We climbed steep stairs next to the garage to get to it. From the bedroom window during the summer I could see the bright tennis lights from the park and the chatter of the baseball players and fans on the lower fields like I remembered from 20th Street.

Bill and I shared bunk beds for the first time. Because he was the boss in my world, Bill slept wherever he wanted, so he chose to sleep on the bottom since he could snap the bed springs networked underneath my bed.

"Stop it," I'd hiss when he'd start snapping. "I'm trying to sleep!"

"Who and what army's goin' to stop me?" he'd reply, smartly, sarcastically.

At other times Bill wrestled me down by the shoulders, straddled me on the floor, then manufactured a mouthful of saliva and slowly squeezed it out in a long thin line, spaghetti-like, until it was hovering above my eye.

"Don't do it! I'm tellin'!" I'd scream, vigorously rolling my head from side to side to avoid a direct hit.

"You do and I'll kill you!" He'd slurp up the spit and start over. He had an uncanny way of making his spit bob up and down, sucking and squeezing it out in long viscous strands like a yo-yo string, driving me crazy because I didn't know when the surface tension would break and the mass land on my face. A quick direct shot would have been preferred to this slow torture, this creeping drool. I called Bill "slobatoris, " given this dinosaurian trait, claiming it to be the apogee of his evolution.

At Lawrence Street Mom and Dad let us kids stay up as late as we wanted on Friday nights and pop popcorn and watch movies on TV. I remember Sam Jaffe in *Gunga Din*, clad in what appeared to be a diaper, and a towel wrapped around his head, trapped with Cary Grant and Douglas Fairbanks Jr. on the parapet of the Temple of the evil Cult of Kali. Under attack and greatly outnumbered, the group discovers the mortally wounded Jaffe, as Gunga Din, climbing to the pinnacle of the temple where with his final breaths of life sounds his bugle to warn the oncoming British troops of the impending ambush. In the final scene, having saved the day, Gunga Din is given a fitting burial by the British Raj.

But the main event on TV that night, what kept us awake and full of expectation well past our bedtime, was *Portland Wrestling* on channel 12, hosted by Barney Keep, a bespectacled coat-and-tie man who broadcast the matches from his "crow's-nest" hanging above the wrestling ring. Over time we gravitated to favorite wrestlers, each with a shtick, and we hooted and hollered as they made their separate appearances on the screen: Shag Thomas, the beer bellied African; Haru Sasaki, the sneaky Jap; Billy Whitewolf, the red-skin fresh off the reservation (he wore full Indian headdress and performed war dances); Tony Borne, the white trash from the tracks. Among these favorites was "The Sparkplug", a short pudgy guy nicknamed by Dad because "The Sparkplug" was quick and energetic, constantly flitting and bouncing around the ring as if he were laid with live telephone wire. He wasn't above the occasional eye-gouge or head butt. We loved his stamina, his nervousness, his lowbrowness. He lost his matches to the good guy.

After each match Barney would interview the winner, but occasionally the loser would show up and start shouting and throwing beer cans, and Barney would get that look of desperation and suddenly duck out of the picture. Once one of the wrestlers was tossed overboard during a scuffle, and fell, we were led to believe, several feet into the crowd below.

Eric Paterson, a Steve Reeves look-alike who appeared, with rippling muscles, perfect hair, and royal stature, as if only God and his vengeful army could defeat him, was my favorite. But Eric's matches were well scripted for maximum drama: in spite of his superior build and wrestling acumen, he seemed not to know why he was there. From the first bell onward Eric got dropped kicked and grapevined and full-nelsoned by his opponent to the point of near death. This went on for several rounds and, as a fan, was difficult to watch. I'd grimace in despair. Then, when all seemed lost, when it appeared that Eric would lose after all, the other shoe would fall. One time an irate spectator jumped into the ring and busted a bass drum over Eric's head. Another time his opponent crunched Eric's head with a mean spirited piledriver. A strange shadow would cross Eric's face. We knew what was coming. In the next moment, with his eyes rolled back in his head and his jaw clenched and his teeth bared, he'd metamorphose into Frankenstein. This was what happened when Eric got slammed on the head. He'd fall into a trance of great hellish proportion, giving him supernatural powers, like Popeye and his spinach. Now, in the middle of the ring, Eric stood with his legs wide apart, arms uplifted to the heavens. His opponent continued attacking Eric with eye gouges and flying drop kicks, but nothing fazed Eric for he was impervious as the Rock of Gibraltar with the weirdo look on his face. Then, in a sudden turn of events, with quickness and method, Eric searched out his opponent (even with his eyes turned up) and would trap him in the corner of the ring. He'd slide around to the backside and apply a full nelson, a behind the body head-lock. "It's all over," I'd say in full confidence, unclenching my jaw. "It's just a matter of time." Eric's full nelson was no ordinary full nelson, for no one ever shook themselves loose from it. Oh sure, his opponents would flail and struggle for a moment or two and try to break away, but it was fruitless. Eric wouldn't let go, even after the count was done and the ref ended the match he kept bearing down and the ref and other ringsiders coming through the ropes would finally pry him off. "He's still in his trance, you idiots!" I'd yell. His opponent had by now blacked out from the full nelson, and now freed would flop to the mat in a pile of blubbery flesh, nary a molecule of life left in him. God bless that poor wretched soul. That's what we believed. In the final shot before the commercial Eric was back in the middle of the ring with his weirdo look, legs apart, eyes rolled back in his head, arms raised in victory. I mimicked him on the other side of the screen, getting a laugh from Mom and Dad. Then Eric was led out of the ring by the ref like a blind person unsure of his next step.

In the cut-away to the commercial Barney Keep would be straddling an airline fuselage with an "American Airlines" logo painted on the tail fin. He was living the high life with a martini with olive in one hand and a lit cigarette in an F.D.R. holder in the other. "American Airlines," he would say," the ooonly way to fly." He'd take a long drag off his F.D.R. cigarette and stare into the distance, looking for paradise on the other side of the moon, then while slowly exhaling the cigarette smoke, which curled upward into the spacious studio, a look of blissful satisfaction would fill his face.

I soon discovered these same wrestlers from Portland Wrestling were on their way to the Lane County Fairgrounds, a mere five minute drive from our Lawrence Street house. I couldn't believe this good fortune. I could see them live! I asked Dad if we could go, and if I could bring new friend Tim Dority too. But Dad was reluctant. "I don't think so," he said. "What's the problem?" I wondered, "did he not want to be seen there? Did he not want us exposed to it?" Undeterred, I kept at him, pestering him and making him feel guilty for not taking Tim and me. Finally, flustered against my constant barrage, he relented.

Days later the three of us entered the spacious auditorium and found seats in the portable bleachers surrounding the ring. A loud frenetic crowd of loggers and fist shaking grandmothers were already there claiming choice seats they'd certainly sat in many times before. Dad rolled his coat collar up. I had my pad and pen ready for autographs.

Though Eric Paterson wasn't on the bill that night, "The Sparkplug" was, plus all the other regulars. Tim and I, in a state of bliss, had never seen TV personalities live, so when these wrestlers appeared in the flesh and fought in their matches, we felt at the center of the universe.

When "The Sparkplug" appeared in his featured match, Tim yelled for me to hurry as I ran down the bleachers to get his autograph.

"The Sparkplug" had climbed into his corner and was stretching and strutting about, warming up for his match. He was wearing black skintight trunks and black high top wrestling shoes laced to the top with a ring of white athletic sock showing. With a sneer on his lips, rolling his head back and forth, jumping on his toes, he was ready for battle.

The elevated ring came to my shoulders, and when I approached and looked up, "The Sparkplug" appeared to tower above me like Goliath.

Cautiously, hands trembling, I reached through the ropes with my pen and pad in hand.

"The Sparkplug" had his back turned. A look of surprise crossed his face when he spotted me. I may have been his first ever autograph seeker. But quickly, reverting back to character, he grunted and sneered and strutted across the ring to where I was standing. A funny look came over him, a sudden mind change now manifest, a thought toying behind his eyes. Hovering over me, blocking out the rest of the world, he appeared far more than even Goliath in his menace and size. My heart thumped. I felt light headed. But I held my ground. Through the ropes I held out the pen and pad for him to take. He leaned over. But for his shorts and shoes, he was naked to the world, a raw human specimen of flesh, muscle, pure brawn. Sweat trickled down his face and chest. I caught a whiff of mustiness, stink. I wanted to flee.

"The Sparkplug" reached for my pen and pad. But at the last moment he pulled back, lifted his leg and kicked at the rope next to where my outstretched hand was. The rope reverberated from end to end, like a snapped rubber band. I reeled back in horror. Suddenly behind me boos were heard from the crowd, and catcalls. A cavalcade of thoughts rifled through me. Coolness rose up in my hot forehead, similar to when I played the guitar in the third grade. I took a step forward, approaching "The Sparkplug" again. I saw he was satisfied with his despicable deed, the sneer, the contempt in his face. Without thinking, more a primal reaction, I clenched my hand and raised it in a fist. In the next frame of this crystal clear memory I'm shaking it with every ounce of energy I had. Now my lips wore a sneer. The crowd, witnessing the event unfolding before them, booed even louder and louder at each emphatic shake of my fist. "The Sparkplug" faded from my view, for now I was at the center of my own ring, now one with the loggers and the fist shaking grandmothers. Putting pen and pad in my pocket, I turned in feigned disgust and headed to the bleachers.

Dad was apoplectic, cracked by my antics, laughing, eyes watering, head shaking from side to side in disbelief. "You've got lot of nerve," he chuckled. Tim patted me on the back: "Way to go!" he said, "You showed him!" It was the beginning of one of the most significant friendships of my childhood.

I want to believe, as the night rolled on and the TV stars wrestled through their magnificent matches, and Tim and I yelled and screamed for our favorite wrestlers, and booed the likes of "The Sparkplug," that by the end, when the crowd began filing out through the exit doors and heading for their cars in the parking lot, and we had had our fill, that by then Dad's collar was indeed turned down.

* * *

I enrolled in the fourth grade at Adams Elementary school, a mile west of us. In contrast to McKinley, Adams had been recently built in a

        DREAM FAMILY ♦ A MEMOIR

contemporary style with wood siding and long hallways and naturally lit classrooms. The expansive playground was a carnival of tether- ball courts, baseball diamonds, jungle gyms, soccer fields, and a ¼ mile track.

I was recommended to Miss Culbertson, who had taught my cousin Denny a couple years before; she seemed old with pale skin and wrinkly hands and silvery hair worn in a tight bun. Like Mrs. Stingly, my first grade teacher, she was steady and patient, keeping us students on task through sections on Lewis and Clark and multiplication tables. She was single and devoted to teaching, living quietly in a small house we passed in the summer on the way to Jefferson pool.

I applied myself in Miss Culbertson's class because I was eager to make an impression on her and the other students. Our moving from town to town and house to house was not easy on us kids, especially for Bill, who was now in the seventh grade and beginning his sixth school. Mom and Dad promised this was the last of our moves: we would stay in Eugene as long as there was work for Dad. He was an architect now, so he had influence over his work. I could make friends and expect to keep them for a long time.

My stature among these new kids depended as much on what I did on the playground as what I did in the classroom. I was more than willing to show my athletic prowess, or what I believed to have in comparison to the other kids, since it depended on the competition. I'd played football and baseball in Salem. But more than anything else, above all, I wanted to fit in. I aspired for a spot at the top but not necessarily *the* top. I wanted to be popular. I wanted friends. I wanted to know the answers to questions in class and be among the first chosen for the baseball team. It took little time to figure out the pecking order. You look at who gathers around whom at recess. You see who raises their hand first. You notice a gaze that fixates you.

6

In the days I became more acquainted with him after we moved back to Eugene from Salem, Granpa Keefe—"Granpa"—was by then in his mid sixties and appeared to be an ancient contraption that had seen better days. As mentioned before, his right eye was curved in; his teeth were missing; his right index finger was half gone. His wire-rimmed glasses, speckled and smudged, looked like he had fetched them from the garbage can. His wispy white hair was plentiful enough to comb a few strands over his head. He walked with a discernable stoop, betraying not so much a particular ailment as an accumulation of physical labor that had bent him over the years. On Wednesday nights when he wore his false teeth to Eugene Community Band practice, he did, admittedly, look ten years younger.

But in spite of his missing parts and disheveled appearance, Granpa was unusually bright and energetic for his age, showing off his vitality and mental prowess at every opportunity, like when shortly after we moved to Lawrence Street he demonstrated for me how to skip backwards downhill. Observing such things was interesting to me, so I was an easy audience for him.

He was hard to forget not just for his appearance but also for his myriad and off-beat opinions. Not one to hold back before letting you know you were full of baloney, even if it was a first encounter, he had a pathological aversion to agreement. Even if he secretly agreed with you he'd soon figure out a way to disagree, and this love of argument made you either love him or hate him. Early photographs of him show a stout man, all of six feet tall, smiling and confidant, attentive to his group.

Soon after moving back to Eugene I began taking guitar lessons from Granpa. He'd caught wind of my interest in the guitar—and Elvis—while we lived in Salem. He must have seen these lessons as a chance to set me straight regarding what real music was. To him, Souza, marching bands, vast orchestras of strings, brass, and woodwinds were his kind of music. To him Elvis was a fluke. Over many years he played a variety of instruments including violin, cornet, viola, and most recently, because it was the only thing he could play by that time, the upright bass. No doubt he loved music with all his heart and soul, was so entranced by it that when he played he curled the corners of his mouth up and down at a pianissimo, swiveled his jaw back and forth over a crescendo. He didn't know he did those things with his face. But his virtuosity, at least when I knew him, exhibited more passion than expertise, and for all the effort he put into his music over his lifetime, the thousands of hours he spent playing and practicing and studying music, there was scant payback in artistry. It was a labor of love. He had little talent for it.

Every Saturday morning I'd walk the five blocks to his house on Monroe Street with my Stella strung over my shoulders. That Granpa didn't play the guitar didn't keep him from thinking he could teach me a thing or two on it (the guitar in his opinion was a simple and second-rate instrument). We'd spend an hour together.

Little did I know what I was getting myself in to. In addition to teaching me the guitar, Granpa saw the lessons as an opportunity to teach me music theory. Aspiring musicians should learn it first off—right?—and for that I would have a deeper appreciation of the intricacies and beauty of music (and thus shake the Elvis infatuation). While in the middle of fingering a new chord, my fingers curled and twisted along the various frets, Granpa would stop me to explain how the sharps and flats in the chord made up different keys, or how lowered thirds made minor chords, or how, if I moved a finger up or down a fret, I'd get a diminished seventh chord. My God, I thought, I'm ten years old! What is he saying? It wasn't long before I was in over my head, the notes bouncing off each other like atoms in a hot soup.

How I got through those lessons is a miracle. I'd nod my head during Granpa's lectures, pretending to understand everything, picking up enough tidbits along the way to fake my way through Granpa's cross examination later on. Actual playing of my Stella was minimal. I learned "Red River Valley," my signature tune, and played it at family gatherings.

The lessons were the longest hours of my life and challenged my sense of time. Though Granpa was encouraging, and occasionally entertaining, no matter what he did contracted the seconds that turned to days and the minutes that turned to weeks. I couldn't wait for the hour to end—I was bored out of my mind—but felt trapped, one set by myself, for there was another reason I couldn't wait to finish: the prize at the end, which kept me coming back each week. And admittedly, for a period of time much longer than I would like to confess, I endured the lessons each week because of Gramma Keefe's sweet chocolate drops at the end. With the lesson done she had a dozen or so in a small white paper bag waiting for me on the dining room table. The chocolates were of such high quality, their rounded nose-cones of chocolate with white and orange and pink fillings, that they more than made up for the insufferable hour I had just spent with Granpa. By the time I returned home from the lesson, walking those five blocks with my Stella thrown over my shoulder, the chocolate drops were long gone and the delight of first bite replaced by the belly ache of youthful gluttony.

A couple years later, after the lessons ceased—by then I'd taken up the trumpet and was in the school band—we moved across the street from Gramma and Granpa and I got to know him in a different way. Each week I would poke my head in to say "hi," ostensibly to visit them both, but ultimately I'd end up talking with Granpa for an hour or more. He would be sitting in his lounge chair by the front door, face in a book, Gramma lying on the sofa across the living room reading the Registar Guard, the local newspaper. I'd sit in the padded rocker next to the heater, between them.

"What's that book?" I'd ask.

Which is all it took, for he would tilt his head, smile, close the book, then off he'd gallop and five minutes later whatever he was talking about probably had nothing to do with the book. Master of the bait and switch routine, he'd often feel me out on a topic, get a grip on my stand, then, regardless of his honest belief or conviction, would take the opposite point of view. He couldn't help himself. He had a fiery temperament, was stubborn, tough. He knew a lot. He grew up in that turn—of—the—century milieu where people constantly talked about politics and religion because the world was going to Hell. He had seen great upheaval. What were we to do? His stories were strange to me, about a far off time, of horse and buggies and wheat threshers and North Dakota blizzards, and my mind would stand at attention. Life was hard then, he said, but over time it got better. "Don't worry," he'd go on, seeing the worry on my face. "Life does get better."

When he passed away in 1971 at age 78, I was heartbroken. I tried to forget about our talks and his stories. Fortunately he had written some of them in the form of a memoir, and I remembered when he used to take me to the attic to show me what he'd done. Too, I remembered a handful of times when I was a teenager when the summer evening sky in Eugene was a vast decal of turquoise and terra cotta, when if I stood perfectly still on the front lawn of our house across the street and listened carefully, I could hear the tap tap tap of Granpa's ancient Underwood coming from the open attic window. He put the pages in a gray loose-leaf notebook.

It took some coaxing to get Gramma to loan me Granpa's memoir several years later, promising not to keep them long. By then I'd given up trying to forget about him and his stories. I read the memoir in one sitting, finding Granpa's writing rough—his formal education was minimal—but also finding that it brought him back to life, the pages somehow breathing forth his voice and the unique manner in which he lived his life. The narrative begins in the late nineteenth century. Indeed over the years I'd heard these stories before, in one form or another, during our talks in Gramma and Granpa's living room, and in the musty attic where I first saw his notebook. One of the first things Granpa wrote was considered a fib; or, more precisely, part truth and part untruth. He claimed he was born on Feb. 20, 1893 in Garden Court, Chicago, Illinois, and was christened Robert Edward. He claimed his mother was a Campbell of Scotch/English descent and his father of German Irish descent. That much was mostly true. Then he claimed that his biological grandfather was not Byron Keefe, as was believed, but a man named Baltz, and that Granpa's father Edward was the issue of Baltz and Granpa's grandmother, Mary Ann Kindelin. When Baltz suddenly died Mary Ann married Byron Keefe, and the infant Edward took the Keefe name. Even though he wrote this story in his memoir, there was no document as proof. What was known of U.S. Census records at the time did not prove or disprove Granpa's claim.

According to my Cousin Paul Keefe, who had done extensive research in the Keefe genealogy since the 1960's, the claim could not prima facie be true. He found in the 1870 and 1880 U.S. Census a typical Irish Catholic family of that time. He found no marriage, birth or death records showing Baltz's name. In reply to a letter I'd sent Paul years ago regarding Granpa's claim, Paul said he'd talked to his father and Aunt Florence—Granpa's brother and sister—about Baltz, and both denounced Granpa's story as "just agitating," which was vintage Granpa. Furthermore, there were other correspondence and sections of Granpa's memoirs which indicate he didn't really believe in the Baltz story. Paul found Granpa's mother was 100% Scottish on her father's side and probably English on her mother's side. That family (Jenks) arrived from England in the 1600s. Granpa's ancestors on his father's side were 100 % Irish—there were no German roots.

What also came from Paul's research is a question about Granpa's birthday. The 1900 U.S Census of Washington Township, Nodaway

County, Missouri shows that Edward Patrick and Mary Jane Campbell Keefe had been married 8 years (October 7, 1891 at Our Lady of Mount Carmel Catholic Church in Chicago) and that Robert Edward was 9 years old. This conflicts with Granpa's claim of being born in 1893. The 1900 U.S. Census also shows that Florence Keefe was 7 and had been in school for 3 months, meaning that she was born in 1892 or 1893—not 1895 as she later claimed. Are these revised birthdates a cover up for Granpa born out of wedlock?

Continuing his research in light of recent DNA breakthroughs, Cousin Paul beginning in 2014 did various DNA tests including with a descendent of a sibling of Byron Keefe. Had Edward been a biological son of Byron, the DNA would have matched Paul and the Byron relative. It didn't. Furthermore, Paul found in the 1865 New York State Census that Mary Kindelin's marriage to Byron was her second, his first, in 1863, and there were two children, Edward age 3, Willie age 1. Edward, born before the marriage in 1861, makes his birth either out of wedlock or from an earlier marriage or relationship.

Then Paul discovered Byron Keefe's will, probated after he died in 1894. In it he gives "$2,000 to Willie" and "$1,000 to stepson Ed". *Stepson.* This appears to be clear evidence that Edward was brought to the marriage by Mary Kindelin—she'd been married before—and had been adopted by Byron. But continued searches of marriage certificates and census data for a Kindelin/Baltz marriage, or of any children, with Paul scouring several county records in New York State where these events would have occurred, found nothing.

So Granpa is right on one count: Byron was not his biological grandfather. But who is Baltz, or whoever fathered Edward? It remains a mystery. Which means beyond my paternal great grandfather, nothing for sure is known about my Dad's side of the family.

* * *

In the early to mid-1890s Granpa's father ran one of the first electric streetcars on Halsted Street, in Chicago. He also sold tea and coffee from a horse and wagon, when Granpa was age four. Granpa's mother,

Mary Jane, ran a boarding house, where the family lived, and Granpa's earliest memories include the men who boarded there: "[There was] Mr. Warburg, a red whiskered streetcar conductor, [and] a man named Byers. He belonged to the German Hussars and had a very flashy uniform. He also absconded with many dollars of the American Looking Glass Co., and got away with it by giving it to his wife and pretending they were very poor by rooming with [us]."

When Granpa was age four his Godfather—Edward Wise, a Pinkerton detective—invited Granpa to stay at his home outside of Chicago with his son, who was the same age. For two weeks the two of them would have a great time playing together. All was set. But soon after arriving Granpa became homesick, and since there were no telephones "to inform my parents of the condition," he grew so inconsolable and grief-stricken that he cried for most of the two weeks. By then, according to Granpa, a terrible thing had occurred: his right eye had "weakened and crossed" to the point that soon after his return home he was taken to a doctor and a hasty operation performed. Granpa recalls the operation: "The chloroform smothered me awful. After I was asleep—my—the pretty flowers I could see. They were everywhere." The operation, however, was a failure; his eye remained crossed and his vision weak. Granpa's mother took him to a Catholic Priest who prayed for the eye, but that failed too. Then "father took me to another doctor and was advised to get out into the country where I could see long distances, hoping that would cure the eye."

Sometime before 1900, heeding the doctor's advice, and with Granpa wearing a new "pair of glasses that was rated 20 for the left and 250 for the right eye," the family, now including Granpa's new younger sister Florence, moved from Chicago to Nodaway County, Missouri, where they rented eighty acres on a school section, which included a small house "but no barn". Why they chose Missouri isn't clear, but there was a cousin Joe mentioned in Granpa's memoirs who may have been living in the area: "Father raised corn...and traded horses. He and his cousin Joe Keefe, a jolly fat little fellow...made money trading horses [with] the English buyers [who were] anxious to get fat horses for the Boer War."

As for the crossed eye, Granpa wrote "[the operation did] a lot of harm as time showed it could not be straightened owing to the cord being cut." Granpa later claimed that because people instantly looked away when they saw it, his crossed eye caused him an inferiority complex that he never got over.

In Missouri Granpa first noticed his father's excessive drinking, how it made his father mean spirited and put his mother "in a state of anxiety all the time". To Granpa, it didn't make sense in light of his father's devout Catholicism. Granpa wrote: "About this time I was taken to an old fashion wedding—Jim Malone's—which lasted two days. A typical Irish affair. Lots to drink and dancing. Mother and Father had many quarrels too. Pa was drinking awful and it made him mean. [Later Mother] walked seven miles to Conception [Mo.] to see the Parish Priest and tried to have him do something with Pa. But to no avail. I have wondered 'why have a Priest?' if he cannot help on matters of which he has an absolute control like this. Father feared a Priest and would obey one if it was in his power. It would have made a world of difference in all our lives if some gentleness was born at this time. But the thing grew till it blasted all of us to the last one, and still affects me in my attitudes..."

Other things Granpa remembers of this time were "of a frightful nature": sister Florence nearly gored by a demented bull, "and I surely will never forget how she ran and screamed," and "the storms were tremendous in their awfulness...wind, lightening, thunder, and deluge... would wash all the plowed land off the hill side. We slept in a cave a great many nights [where] one was safe..." And his father's continued drinking: "...once he got his thirty-eight revolver and loaded it and shot it into the floor and then waved it around and threatened to kill mother."

They lived in Missouri until early 1902, when they moved to North Dakota. According to Granpa, "in 1901 the Great Northern Railroad Co. started an immigration program, and an agent named Leedy [later Chief Passenger Agent] went through the country and interested a lot of people in the great opportunities in North Dakota...and Oklahoma. Father finally decided on Dakota." In March 1902 the family loaded themselves and their worldly possessions onto one of the Great Northern's "excursion" trains, their furniture, livestock, and farm equipment carried in an adjoining freight car while they road in a passenger coach. Ten days and endless miles later they arrived in Grand Harbor, North Dakota where they met Granpa's father's second cousin, Mike Allen, also "a hard drinker", who lived with his two children, "a boy that was an idiot and a girl not quite so bad..." Soon after arriving in Grand Harbor, Granpa's mother, following a difficult pregnancy, gave birth to her third child, a boy, on March 29th , christened Michael Joseph, a named picked "against mother's wishes".

Ten days later the family was in Minot, North Dakota, where Granpa noted it was "crowded with immigrants." There Granpa's father "had gone with the stock", and where "a bed was found for mother and babe and sister at John Malone's while father and I slept in a barn." Was this John Malone related to the Jim Malone who was married in Missouri?

The homestead was "thirty miles north of Minot and thirty miles from the Canadian boundary." It is unclear exactly what the arrangements were for the next day, but it appears that Granpa and his sister Florence were driven by wagon to the homestead while Granpa's mother and father and baby Michael went ahead in another wagon. Peter Phifer, "a very jolly fellow and a great tease," drove the wagon Granpa and his sister rode in.

Beginning their journey early in the morning, Granpa and Florence found the wagon stacked high with lumber for their homestead. It frightened them sitting so high on top of the lumber, thinking they could fall off with a sudden bump, or tumble with the lumber if it fell. "But that was not all." wrote Granpa.

"The Mouse River [which ran through Minot] had overflowed its banks and no bridge was left except a pontoon bridge which was probably 200 feet long. Each team would wait till the one before had left the bridge, then they would cross. The bridge sank as we started. Down and down it went. The water came up to the lumber on the wagon bolsters. [Water] was running swiftly, carrying sticks and floating objects in its yellow flood. [Mr. Phifer] watched a stake driven in the ground on each bank as a guide for him too. Two feet either side of the direct line would throw us off into the swirling current. After it seemed hours we arrived safe and sound on the opposite bank."

On the other side they found another obstacle to overcome: "A great hill lies on the north bank, and one team [of two horses] could not draw a heavy load up. So another team was hitched in the lead, so we had four horses [pulling the wagon] up this hill. At last we reached the top."

"What a sight greeted us [at the top]" Granpa wrote. "The city behind bustling with people and noise. The raging river [below us] with its yellow flood glimpsed between the tree tops, which were turning green, and before us, like a rising cloud, a great level space of ominous black as far as the eye could [see]. A great prairie fire had passed over the Fall of 1901 from the Canadian border, leaving nothing but ashes."

The road to their homestead wound "here and there...and missing rocks strewn over the great plateau by a glacier ages ago." There were small shacks along the way, "covered with black tar paper...and an occasional new building would shine out of the blackness, giving relief to the eye of the monotonous black of the earth and blue of the sky." As they forged on, Granpa noted, the three of them heard the occasional chirp of a bird, or "the cross between a whistle and chirp of the gopher." It was the only wildlife they came across that day.

To humor Granpa and Florence, Peter Phifer sang songs and told stories and teased them. Finally, at around ten o'clock that night, they arrived and "stayed with Jim Malone's." Again, it is unclear whether this is meant to be "John" Malone or the same Jim Malone from Missouri.

They stayed at the Malone's while Granpa's father built a barn, "the largest in the neighborhood. The new shiny boards was like a beacon light against the black background. It was so tall that braces were placed against the top so the wind would not topple it over. The early settlers used it as a landmark for directing strangers."

Being "used just like a man," Granpa, who was now age 9, worked alongside his father that first summer and Fall in North Dakota and planted thirty acres of oats, flax, and corn. At the nearest post office in Byeland, four and a half miles west of their homestead, the family ordered their clothing and "small goods" through Sears and Roebuck and Montgomery Ward.

Though no mention is made of how the crops did that first season, Granpa noted that by early November "the ground freezes and does not thaw out till April 1." Soon a house was built next to the barn, and in preparation for the cold winters to come, Granpa's father "hauled coal from Burlington, 26 miles, and put it in the basement. He threw it thro the opened window down the basement stairs. I piled it back. This was one of the hardest tasks I ever did. The dust would choke me, and the coal was so heavy my young back would seem about to snap off, handling the 6 or 7 tons of coal each year. I also carried most of it up again for the fire."

Granpa recounts the "Great Blizzard of 1902", which occurred soon after they arrived: "It had about a fifty mile wind, and the air was packed with snow particles. For three days one could not see three feet away from himself. Great piles of snow drifted through wall cracks, and key holes of doors let enough snow through to make a pile as high as the hole." Granpa also noted that "when going to the barn or outbuilding, one usually carried a string fastened to the house so that one would not get lost." On one mild and cloudless day it was 52 degrees below zero, "and not a breath of wind blowing. Sound could be heard great distances. A man could be heard speaking in a loud talk a mile or more, and dogs could be heard 3 or 4 miles" away.

Not all was toil and hardship. During the lengthy winter nights when the sun would set in the afternoon and not come up again until late morning, nearly sixteen hours later, there were cheerful times. "In the long evenings…the neighbors—[the] Elm boys, Bickettts…and John Rumming and Charley Olson, who liked their alcohol toddies—would drop in to play cards. At first High Five, but later Norwegian Whist. I and sister would bring up the apples and pop corn. Many nights it would be 3 a.m. before the friends would leave. Many happy hours were spent that way and close friendships were made."

In 1905, as part of a project to connect one end of North Dakota to the other, the Soo Railroad Company built a railroad "from Thief River Falls to Kenmare," Granpa wrote. "The road bed is just three miles straight north of the home place. A town was started there. Hurd it is called." This is the first mention of Hurd by Granpa, which later would play a significant role in our family's history. In time, Granpa writes, Hurd would have "two General Merchandise stores, a bank, Post office, Depot, lumber yard, and three [grain] elevators."

In 1907, when Granpa was fourteen, he was sent off to boarding school in Conception, Missouri "so that I would learn something of religion." The day before leaving, while shocking grain "on the Riley place", Joe Cunningham, another homesteader, who was helping, told Granpa something he never forgot: "Robert, your father works you too hard. He should be better to you and not so cross." According to Granpa, "it was given kindly, and I know Joe did not intend it to injur (sic) either father or I."

Granpa departed by train from Landsford, a town ten miles from the homestead, leaving his mother on the platform "crying as if she could feel that her boy was going out of her life forever...And in fact I did. Home and mother never held me again like before. She seemed to sense it." Sister Florence, younger brother Michael, and a new baby brother, Ed, born in June 1904, remained at the homestead.

Granpa cried during the train ride to Missouri, much like he cried when his eye turned in years ago. But by the time he arrived and looked over the school and monastery, he was elated. Compared to his bleak accommodations in North Dakota, what lay before him was a castle. The school, just completed, included "a large study room, gymnasium with lots of equipment, a pool room, wash room, library, chapel, and dormitory, all in the same building. Another building close was used for music." A hundred yards from the school stood the Monastery, "a large structure consisting of a church, Priest's and Monks rooms, administration rooms, a dining hall, and storage rooms. These were all built together forming a hollow square in which was a fountain and sunken gardens, [and] a promenade for the Priests and Monks. The building proper was...constructed of red brick...[and] two large steeples rose above the front of the church and held two wondrous bells which on special occasions would blend their sounds in a most pleasing and musical duet. [The bells] were enormous in size and weight...and could be heard for many miles."

What dazzled Granpa was the church: inside were "two rows of four foot pillars [that] supported the great arches overhead. The seats were arranged in three rows and five aisles. The center [aisle] was a great wide one so that plenty of room was allowed for processions and ceremonies. The Great Alter stood high at the nave end of this aisle. [There were] two gates opening from it [that led] to the choir and [another] alter. Through the alter rail a beautiful piece of carved woodwork...was of massive dimensions. Seven marble alters were located beyond the rail. They were chased in gold and carved with patient hands. A great organ was here also. Its thunderous tones seems to ring in my ears even now. This was the most powerful organ I have ever heard. It would completely drown the voices of the 30 monks, 25 Priests, and 50 students who were in the choir stalls. The most striking feature of [the church] was the beautiful painting on the walls and ceilings. The ten stations of the cross were all placed there by the hand of a master artist. Each character was a portrait in itself. The ceiling was a deep blue dotted with stars, and angel faces shone down on the massive interior of this earthly relic of ancient times. This is the most medieval [place] I have ever seen. The church was magnificent."

The daily rigor began at the six o'clock wake up call and continued until the boys retired at eight thirty at night. Time was given to religious instruction and worship: "We went to chapel three times each day. On Sunday or special days we went to the main church." There were classes in Bible History and Catechism, which, when tested, Granpa noted, "we must be exact." There were courses on Church traditions and "the proper way to act in church, and how to serve at the alter." Twice each week there were singing lessons. Granpa made his first Confession, and "went to Communion, and was Confirmed there." At this school Granpa took three lessons, "the only lessons I ever received," on his violin. Everywhere he went a Priest was nearby, watching, instructing, scolding, and breaking up fights.

"We had our play hours," Granpa recalls, "and many fights were had by all. Some [were] quite dangerous. The boys from the large cities would use chairs, pool cues, or anything they could grab. I received my share of both chairs and cues."

It is not clear how long Granpa attended the school. "I returned home sometime in April," 1908. He probably left for the school following the Fall threshing season the previous year, which would have put him at the school for six months. What he got out of the school he made very clear: "I believe I was fed too much religion in too short a period, like eating too much and even though swallowed, it may all come back without being digested..."

He returned to North Dakota to face "the same old hard grind. Long hours, and thrashing again in the Fall of 1908." The crops were good enough that year that Granpa's mother and father took a vacation to Michigan while Granpa stayed behind with George Newell, a family friend, to care for the stock. George "was a Baptist, while not a good one. He believed the Catholics were all wrong, and I just coming from school...endeavored to prove to him he was wrong. Thank God I played into his hand. With great patients (sic) he would take my [beliefs] and use some common sense and get me all tangled up. I would get mad. How I hated that man. All the time he was kind to me and would gently plant some more seeds for thought in my mind. [Because of him] I began inquiring...and reading books about religion. He shall never know what he started that winter [and] I believe God will reward him for it."

What George Newell started that winter would soon come to a head. Combined with Granpa's growing independence, his growing sense of the larger world, his daily battles with his father, who was drinking more than ever, by age seventeen Granpa knew he had to do something, but what? His decision, as it turned out, would have a profound impact on family history. "I left home," Granpa wrote.

7

TIM DORITY, THE boy I went to the wrestling match with, was my first best friend. Funny, smart, full of energy, he had light skin with a fist full of freckles thrown in, jet black eyebrows that arched upwards one at a time when he smelled a rat, and bushy black hair highlighted by a white patch just above his hairline, his birthmark he claimed. His dark eyes were squinty but lively. I first spotted him on the playground in those early days at Adams School after moving from Salem. He was in the other 4th grade class.

The following year we were in the same class and both fell in love with Ann Hendrickson, the most beautiful girl I'd ever laid eyes on. Bedazzling with her long black hair—sable-like—which gleamed in the sunlight, and which framed her flashing dark eyes, she was a looker even at that age and flaunted it.

Though she infatuated us both, we couldn't have been more different in our approach to Ann. Whereas Tim was openly talkative about his feelings and made no bones about being head over heels, I kept my feelings about Ann secret.

Nonetheless we became fast friends. When we walked to Ann's house after school I played the trusty sidekick bucking up Tim's nerve while he tried to lure Ann in. But secretly I hoped he would fail and I would have Ann for myself.

His house was on the way to Ann's, so I soon became acquainted with his family. His older sister hid in her bedroom and clacked away on a typewriter, a budding novelist I was told. His older brother fiddled with test tubes and microscopes and blew things up in their garage. The family was cerebral and bookish, pale of skin and reclusive, quite different, I could tell, from my family.

At Ann's we played tag, hide-and-go-seek, hop scotch, foursquare. During one of our visits when Tim was pulling out all the stops to gain Ann's affections, bragging about anything that might fascinate Ann while winning at tag and foursquare, he said he hunted fossils. She quickly changed the subject by asking me: "What do you like to do Jerry?"

"I, ah, I, ah, well, I don't really know." On the hot seat, I could do no more than stutter in the presence of this ethereal angel. "I guess I like to hunt fossils." In fact I had no idea what a fossil was.

Did Tim and I know that Ann had planned this competition between us? Did we know that by age ten she had mastered the art of stringing boys along so well that unbeknownst to us we were no more than a couple of greyhounds chasing the elusive mechanical rabbit? Drunk with love, helpless against her whims, we fell victim to her vacillating heart. One day I was her favorite, the next day Tim was.

In the meantime we got on with our friendship. The family had a small glassed greenhouse in the backyard where inside on wooden shelves were rows and rows of seedlings, shoots, and cuttings, planted by Tim's mom, and neatly labeled: tomato, tulip, parsley, green bean. Tim led me down the narrow isle to the far end. We stopped at the last shelf.

"What do you think?"

We stood facing what appeared to be a collection of rocks neatly arranged and labeled like his mom's plants.

"What are they?" I said, noting the strange shapes with rounded contours, grooves, and fluting, each sticking out of ancient rock.

"Fossils."

"What?"

"Chambered nautilus', razor clams, snail shells, trilobites, leaf imprints," he said. "Well, not exactly—rock impressions."

"How'd they get like that?"

Tim took a deep breath, smiled. What he said next was unbelievable. "Millions of years ago Oregon was an ocean and the sandstone we see all around was the sand at the bottom of the ocean." He told me that creatures living back then died and got buried in the sand. "This whole place is a graveyard turned to stone," he said. "These creatures don't exist anymore."

"What happened to them?"

"They died out. Didn't make it."

"How you know that?"

"Because paleontologists dig for fossils and discover the mysteries of life."

"The mysteries of life? Paleontologists? What?"

Tim gave me a conspiratorial look. "You'll see."

"What'd you mean?"

"Tomorrow we'll go hunting. I'll show you."

"With Ann?"

"No."

That night I laid awake thinking how much a million years was. "I'm ten now," I thought. "A million is ten with five zeros behind it. And Tim said some of his fossils were 250 million years old!"

From our Lawrence Street house the next day Tim and I bicycled a half dozen blocks up College Hill to a vacant lot that overlooked west Eugene. From the street curb the lot sloped upwards to a ten-foot wall of solid sandstone which spanned the width of the lot. The wall was jagged, pocked with cavities, and stratified with shades of reds, tans, and browns. At the top of the wall the lot leveled into a small field covered with tufts of wild grass. Someday someone would build a dream house there.

We grabbed our tools and threw our bikes down, then clambered up to the sandstone wall. I'd brought a hammer and a flat head screwdriver from Dad's toolbox. Tim pointed to a section of the wall for me to begin on, repeating his instructions: "A little at a time. No big cuts. Be ready for something that looks different. Yell when you find something."

* * *

That Spring of '59 was unusually warm and sunny and I remember walking home from school in the bright afternoons with my coat tied around my waist and breathing in fragrant cherry blossoms heavy in the air and seeing red and yellow tulips in front yards and purple rhododendrons bursting in whorls from their buds. The sound of birdsong came from telephone wires, trees, and rooftops, and bugs zigzagged from everywhere. Look out! It was that time of year.

Tim told me about prehistoric man, showing me books with pictures of Cro-Magnon and Neanderthal, Piltdown and Java Ape-Man. One was a hoax, with an ape's jaw and a man's upper skull.

"These are our ancestors," Tim said. "They lived 50,000 years ago, and more."

From one book Tim showed me a series of black and white photos of sweaty sunburned men digging at a faraway site, digging deep in layer after layer of soil and rock. One photo was of a partial skull held together by glue, sitting on a primitive wood table with some other bones off to the side—maybe a femur, a thighbone. These came from the site. The next picture, not a photo but rather a drawing, portrayed what the skull would look like if it had a face. It appeared neither human nor ape.

"The missing link!" Tim said. "It's evolution!"

"Evolution?"

"Yea, buddy. You're just a smart ape."

"We come from Adam and Eve."

"That's crap."

* * *

Under the warm Spring sun, hammer in hand, I began gently tapping the flathead screw-driver against the rugged sandstone face. Shards and flakes rolled down the slope to the street's curb. It was hard getting a footing not only because of the slope, but also because of the loosened rock underfoot. I was constantly slipping and readjusting myself to get a better angle to the wall, using my knees.

I watched Tim from the corner of my eye, trying to mimic him in every way: his hammer strokes, his chisel work, his close examination of the wall before him, as if something inside was making a noise or quietly moving around, wanting to emerge. He was deep into what he was doing. The shards of rock dug into my knees.

Tim and I were spending more and more time together, becoming closer, developing a secret language between us; we were Laurel and Hardy and The Three Stooges rolled into one. All we had to do was look at each other. Ann didn't know what was going on, and her strategy of playing us against each other wasn't working anymore. Though she still had a pull on me, and I still wanted her for my own, it wasn't as important as having Tim as a friend. Over several weeks, while Ann persisted in playing her games with us, Tim and I cemented our friendship. Time had run out for her.

It was a pivotal period in my life. The move from Salem to Eugene ended a seven year sojourn that started in Eugene in 1952. There was never time to set down roots in those years, for as soon as we began to make friends and get established, the moving van showed up. Returning to Eugene meant we'd reached the end of the trail and I could make friends without fear of soon losing them. I took this to heart. In Tim I saw a long-term friendship.

The fossil came from nowhere. I was lamenting my sore knees while striking a stratum of rock in front of me. Then I turned to look at Tim. When I looked back, perched on the stone wall was what appeared to be a snail shell molded of sandstone, dark brown in color, frozen in the rock like a partially completed statue. Did it shudder at the sight of me? I let out a cry.

"What is it?" Tim said, rushing over.

"It looks like a snail."

"Holy shit!" Tim said, laying eyes upon it. "Move over."

Using short chipping strokes with his hammer and chisel, he loosened the facing around the snail, mindful not to crack or nick it. The more he worked, the more the snail emerged from the rock in full, its spiral base becoming thicker and broader, until near the end he handed me his hammer and chisel: "Finish it off," he said. "Tap it right there."

My stroke was short. The snail popped out. Tim caught it in mid air like a fly ball, not a blemish on it.

"This is good," he said.

From my allowance I bought a rockhound's hammer with a perforated rubber handle and a forged steel head, blunt on one side and tapered to a point on the other. I bought a chisel too (no more using Dad's flat-head screwdrivers for me!). I bought a canvass rockhounds bag with separate compartments for fossils and equipment and a detachable shoulder strap I snapped on while riding my bike. Developing a variety of strokes, whacks, taps, and jabs, the hammer became an extension of my hand, perfectly suitable for breaking down whatever rock confronting me. The chisel became my finishing tool; whenever I suspected a fossil close at hand—an irregular shape in the rock, or smoothness along the rough surface—out it came, and with small compact strokes at varying angles, my eyes probing cracks and surfaces, heart beating fast, laboring without a sense of time, the chisel pursued like a magic wand. Whatever the hammer couldn't do, the chisel did. At the end of each day I cleaned the hammer and chisel and kept them safe in my rockhound's bag. I was a paleontologist!

In a short time I had a sizable collection, and like Tim I labeled my fossils and displayed them on my bookshelf in my brother's and my bedroom. The scientific names I got from books Tim loaned me. Walking into the bedroom was an exercise in contrasts: on Bill's side were model cars, deer antlers, baseball mitts, on my side fossils and books.

Weather permitting, each day after school Tim and I bicycled to the sandstone wall and chipped away until it was time for dinner. It was, for that Spring, our home away from home, our Garden of Eden. My world was getting bigger and bigger while I seemed to be getting smaller and smaller. Discovering fossils made me realize that I was no more than a drop of water in a vast ocean of time. A scary thought. But in talking it over with Tim, and now looking back and understanding we were still children at the center of our own make-believe universe, we felt empowered by this insight, this sense of long time, it was a secret no one else knew about, certainly no one our age. We had cornered the market on something secret and unique, like a couple of pirates stumbling upon a long lost treasure and feeling entitled to the loot. Too young for existential worries, we were going to live forever.

We were in Mrs. Fulton's fifth grade class together, forging our own world and fast spreading our wings beyond fossils. We didn't like the silly school newspaper, *The Adams Apple*, for its saccharine poems and humorless announcements, so we started our own paper, *The Truth*. Each week Tim and I published feature articles like "Fossil Hunting", want ads ("Needed: Hatchetman to bump off the Old Man"), and short stories written by Tim's sister. We advertised as detectives—the Dorkee Detective Agency (combination of Dority and Keefe)—for solving any and all school mysteries (we received fifty cents for finding Mary Johnson's missing coat). Tim's sister typed *The Truth*'s mimeograph masters from our rough drafts, then Dad and I would run dozens of copies on his mimeograph machine at his office and collate and staple the pages together. We sold *The Truth* to our class for 25¢ each, but soon a student from the other fifth grade class appeared at the behest of her teacher wanting copies too. Word spread. In short time we had ourselves a business, and each week Tim and I split the profits, making as much as two or three dollars apiece, big money then.

It seemed great fortune followed whatever Tim and I did, so it made sense when Gramma and Granpa bought the house across the street from them on Monroe Street for us to rent in the Spring of '60. It was two doors down from Tim's. The rent would be put aside for a down payment if we wanted to buy it later. We moved in soon after school ended, and Tim and I couldn't believe our good fortune—best friends living within shouting distance of each other. That summer there were more fossil hunts, sleepovers, bike rides, swimming at Jefferson pool, hide-and-seek at night with ropes and handcuffs (thanks to the big brothers), and tag team wrestling matches like we'd seen on Portland Wrestling. We had our spats too. Tim was a show-off and know-it-all, his family brilliant, he claimed. But wasn't *my* dad an architect, and, by the way, who took us to the wrestling matches! Sometimes he was flaky and didn't show up. I was better at sports though he tried too hard to win every time. Bill thought he was a kook, a weirdo, "lame". Once I refused to answer the door when Tim came knocking. But we never stayed mad for long.

Was it too good to believe? Was our friendship destined for a plunge? Ann Hendrickson, whose star had fallen, was by then no more than an asterisk in our lives. We never invited her to hunt fossils and never asked her to help with *The Truth*. At some point she must have decided we were a bit much, or vice versa, and took another road; there was no defining event that comes to mind. Years later Ann and I would go to the same high school after attending different junior highs, but I hardly remember her then. Under senior student activities in our yearbook nothing is listed for Ann—no music, art, sports, drama, dance team, student council. What did she do in high school? How does one go through high school without a single extra curricular activity? Did we ever talk about our old grade school, or about Tim? Maybe. Looking at her class photo poses more questions than answers—who is that person whose gaze by high school was tentative, whose smile restive, whose luminosity had all but disappeared from the person I once knew so well in grade school. She's never come to class reunions, never been news about her. What ever happened to her?

Behind the scenes malevolent forces beyond our control were at work. That summer Tim's father, employed by an insurance company, was called to his company's Seattle office for an important meeting. Was it a promotion? Then while Tim and I were scurrying between our houses enjoying the long summer, his father moved to Seattle. What was going on? By summer's end, in a rush of activity that seemed to happen overnight, Tim was suddenly gone too, swept away by the same winds that brought our family to Eugene a year and a half earlier. He didn't want to go to Seattle, cried at the thought of it, he so badly wanted to be in that sixth grade class with the rest of us. He'd been at Adams all those years—why couldn't he finish there? I remember, before he left for Seattle, walking with me to class on the first day of school. Did we talk about him living with us? As a going away present I gave him a pencil drawing of Neanderthal Man in profile that I'd worked on for hours, taking great pains getting the sloping forehead just right, and the flared nostrils, the unkempt hair, and the soft chin and the protruding jaw. Tim was grateful, said he'd keep it forever.

It was difficult seeing Tim go because I thought I'd made a friend for life. But in retrospect it must have been more difficult for Tim since I was used to losing friends and moving on. He was not. We kept contact with each other over a remarkably long time, writing letters back and forth—he was a much better letter writer than I was, chatty, funny, full of himself—and once he rode the bus to Eugene and stayed for a week in the summer prior to high school, playing football with my new friends John Hall, Dan Jones, and Wayne Dickson.

I owe a great debt of gratitude to Tim. I was approaching age 12 when he left, more knowledgeable about the world due to him, but no longer at the center of it: he'd blown open a world of broad vistas and imagination, of keenness and possibilities. No one else could have done this for me at that time of my life, not even Granpa. I had a different slant on life going into the sixth grade. When our new teacher Mr. Smith began our class studying the ancient Egyptians, then later the Greeks and Romans, I couldn't have been happier. It was the next logical step after spending a year and a half with Tim and fossils and Cro-Magnon Man.

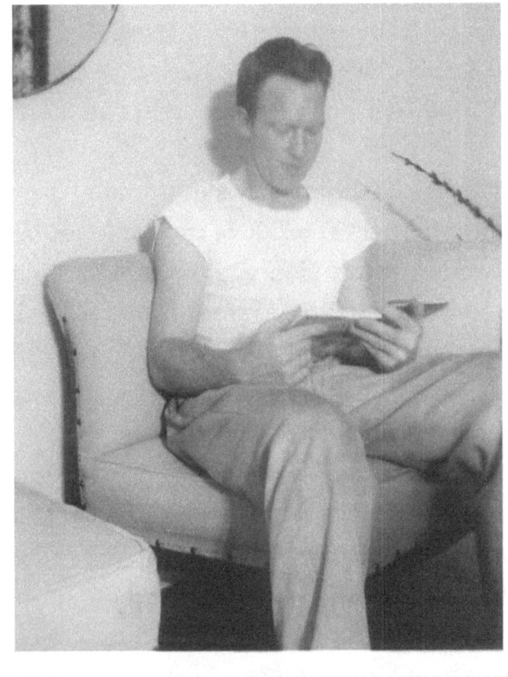

8

SINCE BILL PUT it in my head that I had to know how to read and write before entering the first grade, that's what I believed. And he said it not to forewarn me or to help prepare me for what was to come. He knew my nature and knew I'd twist over the fire about it—he was the big brother whose job it was to aggravate me. He was right—I did twist over the fire, at least in the beginning.

So I didn't start reading earlier than anyone else did and was certainly not precocious, but when I did start reading I took to it like shavings to a magnet. From age 8 or 9 on I always had a book going. In the beginning I read books from the school's library: pioneer stories, adventure stories, mysteries. I liked to read because I was gullible, believing everything I read as if it were happening right before my eyes. A good story would string me along for days and keep me guessing about what was going to happen next. I'd daydream about it while playing baseball or listening to a teacher drone on about long division. It never occurred to me to peek ahead and find out what happened in the end. I had to know everything that happened in between.

These stories were creating images in my mind like a movie, as if a film were rolling across the inside of my eye frame by frame. I saw the cowboy steal the gun, the dancer kick up her heels, the sailor yell "Argh!" in the storm. These images were as real as the baseball glove on my hand. I had very little control over it. And these images seemed both within my immediate grasp and beyond the furthest horizon. The piecing together of a few sentences did this to me.

Tim Dority was a voracious reader, so by the fifth grade, under his influence, I was reading books about fossils and Early Man. My favorite book that year was *The Mists of Dawn*, about a boy who goes back in a time machine and meets a tribe of Cro-Magnon. He gets trapped in a labyrinthine cave by a fearsome and growling cave bear, a giant of an animal, set to have him for dinner. Luckily, at the last moment, he is rescued by the Cro-Magnon, who scare the beast away with a newly discovered phenomena: fire.

I discovered science fiction around the same time, reading *The Rings of Saturn*, about a space flight to Saturn where the villains on board are set to sabotage the mission and take command, but are foiled at the last critical moment. So inspired by the story, and believing I could do something similar in short order, for it appeared so simple, I attempted to write my first (and, to date, last) science fiction novel. Mom agreed to edit my work, going through each sentence with a red pencil, making numerous spelling and grammatical corrections. Two or three pages in I began writing progressively larger and larger letters to fill up the page. I soon discovered writing was more work than I'd bargained for. Reading was much easier and enjoyable.

As I progressed, I found reading thicker books with several chapters similar to a long journey down river—I was looking both ways while the canoe slowly floated the current. At the end of each reading session I'd examine where I placed the book mark, noting if it was a quarter, or half, or three quarters through the book. When I was finally done, immediately following the last page, I'd sit (or lay, if I was reading on my bed) for several minutes thinking about the plot twists and weird characters, and fantasize about being the hero, or even the villain. I also felt a great sense of accomplishment.

Granpa read too. Each week he'd walk downtown to the public library and return with an armful of books. He loved anything about music and the Civil War. Sometimes when I'd visit he'd take me in confidence, beyond earshot of Gramma, and tell me about his newest book—*Andersonville*, for example—about the Civil War prison camp, filling me in on the plot and never missing an opportunity to shock me with grisly details. With a mischievous look he'd tell me I wasn't hearing any run-of-the-mill stuff. This was for men only. Could I stomach it?

Gramma, lying on the sofa across the room reading the newspaper, would occasionally crinkle it back and say "Now Robert, that's not true," after one of his screwball statements. She wasn't, after all, beyond earshot.

"Godammit Forrest!" he'd grumble, "it's true!"

Gramma would shake her head and go back to reading.

He recounted Civil War battles like Gettysberg, Shilo, Antietam. "War is Hell," he'd say, but I was in heaven. I loved the blood and guts, but hell for me was when he began ranting about his newest music book. Given Granpa was from the John Phillip Sousa school of music, the more military the better, any book giving legitimacy to jazz or pop, or to the new atonal orchestral music popular then, especially raised his ire. He'd start talking about music theory and raised 5th's and lowered 3rd's and resolution and we'd be back taking guitar lessons. I'd have no idea what he was talking about. To speed things along I'd simply shake my head in agreement and let him roll. He never caught on that my glazed eyes meant I was desperately trying to escape this hell, at least my version of it.

But it was nice having a soul mate close by because among my immediate family and my cousins and aunts and uncles he was the only one who read for the simple pleasure of it.

I remember other books from those days, some I still have: *The Story of Jesus*, from our Winter Street house in Salem, with a cover picture of Mary, Joseph, and three shepherds hovering over the baby Jesus cradled in a manger, a bright star in the background, the scene outlined in gothic arches and spires, retold for children by Lloyd Edwin Smith and illustrated by Henry E. Vallely. Some of the pictures in it, like the funeral series where Jesus brings back to life a young man from Nain, seem as familiar to me today as they were over sixty years ago. The pictures, all excellently crafted, though with Caucasian characters, are reminiscent of old woodcuts. Mom read this book to us kids on many occasions. There is Dad's *The Bluejackets* Manual 1940, the Navy's bible, containing information that "...would tend to make an able seaman and a thorough man-o'-war's man." I spent hours and hours thumbing through this utterly fascinating book examining the multitude of wonderful colored and black and white pictures, some of them pullouts, of subjects ranging from projectile types and seaman knots, to maritime flags (both man-of-war and merchant) and swimming strokes. There are chapters on how to fold clothes, respecting authority, methods of carrying the wounded, pay and accounts, courts-martials, sales and sailing, small arms, ground tackle, care of fiber rigging. I imagined this book not far from Dad's reach during his tours of duty. There are other books I recall: *Flight*, a WWII story abut ace fighter pilots; *The Story of Space*, with details on the first X-15 flights; *They Were Expendable*, a WWII story of heroism; *Paris Underground* (imprinted across the top of the binder are several links of a black chain, highlighted in tiny red swastikas, with one broken link; copyright 1943) about the French resistance, the author noting at the beginning that "A few details...have been recast...in order to make it impossible for any use to be made of this book by the German authorities against anyone described in it." I read the short stories of Saki. And in junior high I smuggled into the house Henry Miller's *Tropic of Cancer*, reading it in secret, and after each chapter hiding it in the closet so Mom wouldn't find it.

As much as I would like to re-read some of these books, I'm afraid they would disappoint me in some way, they wouldn't be as good as I remember, so they remain unread to this day, I don't even try to find them and conveniently believe them out of print. I prefer to keep them in the realm of memory like some radiant crown jewels, bigger than life, untouchable, incomparable, for I know I could never be in the same frame of mind to make them as good as they once were.

It strikes me how many of these books were about WWII. I especially remember the special *Life* magazine books we had that recounted the war from beginning to end, with page after page of photos depicting destruction and misery. Once, many years later during my first trip to Europe, I was walking along a street in Cologne, Germany, after crossing a steel bridge that spanned the Rhine River, and I suddenly realized, upon looking back towards the bridge and downtown, that I'd seen this view from somewhere before. In pressing my memory I recalled a black and white photo, but it was somehow different. Then it finally dawned on me: the photo I remembered was from one of the Life books that I'd spent hours examining, depicting a devastated Cologne recently bombed by the Allies, with its lone majestic Cathedral standing tall amidst the rubble, and the same steel bridge in the foreground, the photo taken from across the river exactly where I was standing.

Influenced by these war books, at Lawrence Street I once pranced downstairs with a black painted-on moustache and a red and black paper armband I'd colored in with a swastika. Standing in front of Dad, who was hidden behind the newspaper reading, I yelled "sieg heil," my voice shrill, my straight right arm extending slightly upward like I'd seen in books. Clicking my heels together, I thought I was being cute, clever. Dad folded the newspaper down. He looked me up and down. He threw me an irritable look. Then in an angry voice he told me that a lot of people had died because of Hitler and that everyone hated him. Did I *know* that? I quickly tore off the armband and ran to the bathroom to wash off the moustache.

My fascination with reading spilled over to maps. I'd spend hours hovering over them tracing the roads and noting the terrain. What was it about maps that pulled me in? The exotic names? The longing to escape? The getting from one place to another? On summer vacations we went camping in the Cascade Mountains, often going to Paulina Lake south of Bend, Oregon, off highway 97. I remember studying the Oregon State highway map then, tracing our route from Eugene up the McKenzie River, moving northeast through Leaburg, Blue River, and McKenzie Bridge, over the darker colored Cascades, then dropping down through Sisters and heading southeast through Bend. From Bend the highway angles south and southwest before forking off highway 97 between Sunriver and LaPine for the final push into the Paulina wilderness. On the map I noted the tiny curves and bends in the red highway line, how they followed the rivers, often crossing them, and dodging lava beds and lakes, or looping back and forth around towering mountains. Knowing the names of places was a big deal in our family. Gramma and Granpa talked about places in North Dakota with a certain reverence, places like Rolla, Bottineau, Williston. They had been there or knew somebody from there, and family members nodded their heads in agreement when a place was commonly known. I liked the way these places I'd heard of or saw on maps rolled off my tongue.

This fascination intensified while studying world maps at school. I loved those far away names: Samarkand, Belgian Congo, Yangtze, Madagascar, Rhodesia, Brasilia. What images they conjured up, so exotic and strange, so romantic and mysterious. I looked these places up in our World Book Encyclopedia, which Mom and Dad had bought for us in 1957, when we kids were by then all attending school, and there I found photos of colorful outdoor markets, crowds of dark people, strange buildings, temples, unusual dresses and coats, odd looking trees and bushes, animals with beards, China-men smoking long drooping pipes. The strange maps in the World Book indicated not only roads and mountains, but also agricultural products, minerals, and populated areas. It was an intoxication I was slow to emerge from.

The crux of this was that I was discovering through books and maps that the skin of the earth in its many layers was so deep and varied that it took more than a superficial look to understand anything. Things took on new meaning because I was seeing them through the prism of words, phrases, drawings. I must have liked the feel of my mind working, the smoothness and steadiness of it, while reading books and peering at maps. To a child the outside world is a frightening and turbulent place, to wit: the night before the first grade, Biscuit, fossils. The mind goes mad finding its way. I was beginning to see, because of a curiosity I had little control over, that reading books and gazing at maps were ways to make sense of a world that otherwise appeared to be at the whim of a wrathful and unpredictable god.

9

WE'D DRIVE TO Paulina Lake via the McKenzie Pass, winding through the Cascade Mountains through Vida and Blue River and Sisters, and any mountain we saw along the way that Dad didn't know the name of he called Mt. Thielsen. And any mysterious equipment on a truck he called a portable rock crusher. From Bend, Oregon, where we stopped for hamburgers and hotdogs, Paulina was another hour southeast. By then we were so far away from home and had been driving so long that we called the area Eastern Oregon, though in fact Bend and Paulina Lake are smack dab in the middle of the state. But since from early on our family considered anything east of the Cascades "Eastern Oregon", we never considered it otherwise, regardless of what the map said.

Paulina Lake together with its sister East Lake sits in the wide and broad Newberry crater, where thousands of years ago great volcanic eruptions of fire and molten lava ravaged the surrounding area, turning it into a geological Disneyland. On the way we'd see ancient lava fields next to the highway with their gaping grooves and razor sharp ridges and bulbous heads, frozen in time, and Dad would say how lucky it was the flows stopped just short of the highway since otherwise they would have incinerated the asphalt.

Packing for our Paulina trip took days; we were an army preparing for war, and a sense of excitement and adventure filled the air. Our abundant equipment: canvas tent that slept six, two burner Coleman stove with a tank on the front that you pumped when the burners needed a boost, Coleman lantern with two wicks hanging like basketball nets, sleeping bags, air mattresses, cots, fishing poles broken down and rolled together like bamboo, Bill's BB gun, which would wreak havoc on the camp's squirrel population, baseball mitts, bats and balls, swim suits, old tennis shoes for grubbing about in the streams and lake, books, mosquito repellent, an ax and hatchet, hats to prevent sunburn, extra grubby clothes that we didn't mind dirtying up, and much more. And the glorious food stuffed in coolers and boxes: steaks, cookies, chips, pop, potatoes, marshmallows, graham crackers, candy, (we kids each had our own stash of Snickers and Babyruths too). Somehow it all got stuffed into our white Ford station wagon, along with Mom, Dad, Bill, Ann, me, and this trip, cousin Denny. I believe that year we bought a gray metal luggage rack—a beauty—with four large suction cups on each corner, and tie downs with clips that fitted snugly along the rim of the car. Covering with tarp what we heaped on it, Dad secured it with rope crisscrossing the top using a variety of his Navy knots. Top heavy ambling down the road, we looked like Okies from the Grapes of Wrath.

The luggage rack was supposed to make more room inside for all of us to sit comfortably, but it only made things worse by making us think we had so much more. By the time we kids loaded into the back, sitting butt to butt, the car bursting from the load, the battle over turf had begun.

"The cooler's in my way!" Bill would scream, after sticking his butt into me.

Or: "I've got a cramp!" Ann would cry as she stretched her legs across the back seat.

This was before the days of mandatory seatbelts. We'd drive off. Jeers and protests, punches and jabs ensued and Mom and Dad would begin a slow burn; you could see them getting progressively agitated, Dad periodically glancing in the rear view mirror, Mom affecting great effort while twisting herself around in the front seat to glare at us with eyes that could creep out Frankenstein. We'd quiet down for a few minutes before starting up again. Dad would slow down the car. "We're goin' back!" he'd say. We'd pipe down and he'd speed up, and silence would reign again except for the steady hum of the car engine and the wind whipping by.

If it wasn't cousin Denny's first camping trip, then it was certainly his first time fishing on a lake. He was between Bill and me in age, around 13 at the time, handsome with a light crewcut and round eyes, full of energy and mischief, a perfect companion. Denny caught his first trout on this trip and Dad wasted no time instructing him on how to clean the fish— where to run the knife blade along the belly, how to scrape the guts out with the spoon end of the knife, how to wash it off. Halfway through this, with fish guts hanging in sinewy strands and blood running through his hands, Denny said: "Uncle Jim, I think I'm going to throw up."

"That's o.k. Denny, just don't do it on the fish."

At night Black bears came to the campsites and tipped over the garbage cans scrounging for food, making loud clanging noises. The Forest Ranger warned us to secure our foodstuffs before going to bed, and avoid keeping edibles in the tent, since the bears liked to barge in and help themselves.

"And eat you alive!" Bill added.

One night Bill slept in the car and convinced Dad to park it facing the garbage can. When a black bear entered our camp later that night and dumped over the garbage can, Bill flicked the headlights on the bear, fully illuminating it. In a moment Bill cracked the car window open and poked his BB gun out, firing one, two, three shots—who knows how many rounds flew, or how many hit the black bear; Bill quickly rolled the window back up and the black bear ambled off into the dark, leaving the overturned can where it was.

"You're goin' to get us all killed!" I said later.

"No way," Bill said. "You shoulda seen that wimp bear run when I hit it."

"Sure."

The bears got predictable enough that when the garbage cans started falling and clanging in the darkness, Ann, whose turn it was to sleep in the car (now parked next to the tent) cracked the window and called to us in the tent, her small voice echoing in the wilderness like a sweet folk song, "Here comes the bears!"

Denny was getting an eyeful.

The store on the south lip of the lake was opened in the summer. There we rented the skiff and re-supplied our bread and butter and milk, and we kids stocked up on more Snickers and Babyruths. There was much to see, hear, feel. I remember the rocky ridges trailing off the crater's rim, the pungent smell of the omnipresent Ponderosa pine, the pressing heat of mid-day, the blue green water of the lake, the blue jays raiding our camp for food, other birds singing in the early morning and waking us up, the dark pinks and whites of foxglove and trillium, the reddish browns and oranges of striated rock formations, the muted black lava fields versus the glossy black obsidian fields down the road.

I liked camping, but there were downsides. I got dirty at Paulina. I remember taking off my tennis shoes in the evening and my socks and feet and ankles would be dark brown from the day's muck and grime. "That's serious toe-jam," Dad would say. By then I was certain tiny organisms lived in my hair, burrowed deep in my skin, gathered in my nostrils. At night I could feel them crawling, creeping, slithering, and in those moments before slumber they especially taunted me when they grew mammoth size in my imagination. Indeed, I was a wildebeest with birds and horseflies living on me.

I hated getting up in the morning. Crawling out of a warm sleeping bag into the cold morning air—and sometimes there was frost on the ground—to go to the bathroom was a shock, taking years off my life. I felt like peeing in my bag to get it over with.

At Paulina we'd go fishing every evening while the fish were jumping. The skiff Dad rented was fitted with a 10 horse Evinrude. At five o'clock we readied ourselves to push off. The skies would be clear and blue, the sun's rays angling down over the rim of the crater and through the pine trees, and the insects—mosquitoes, dragonflies, horseflies—seemed to be everywhere, and in the right light, especially in the early evening, you could see millions of them swarming and bustling an inch or two above the lake's surface, which was smooth as glass and reflected like a mirror the trees and the sky and the crater's rim above. It was peaceful, like a scene from the Bible. On such an evening Bill, cousin Denny, Dad, Mom, Ann, and I prepared to push off, and except for Denny, we had done this many times before. All was set for an easy ride to our fishing spot.

"Put your life jackets on," Dad said, as we jumped into the boat after he shoved it from the bank. It was a trick vaulting in without getting your feet wet.

"And don't rock the boat," Dad added. We scrambled to find seats on the flat boards stretched across the skiff. Dad hopped in and moved to the motor. Looking at me he said, "do you want to steer?"

My eyes widened, "Yeah!"

"Well get over here and be careful, don't fall out."

"Dad!" Bill protested.

"Everybody's going to get a chance. Just hold your horses."

Dad tilted the Evinrude upright, primed it, and pulled the cord. Coughing a few times, it sputtered alive, then kicked into a soft purr. The steering handle vibrated as if full of angry bees.

"Point the bow in that direction," Dad said, "by that clump of trees, near the slide. See it? We'll drop anchor there and see if anything's bitin'."

It was easy steering. To go left, you turned the handle to the right, and vice versa. As we were crossing the lake to the far side, enjoying the easy ride and beautiful scenery, thanking our lucky stars to be there, thin white clouds appeared from the crater's north rim. Nothing to worry about Dad must have thought. We chugged across the lake to our spot—by then I was a pro at steering—where Dad threw the anchor overboard—a piece of jagged concrete attached to a rope. On the lake, Dad took great pains with Denny, Ann, and me in rigging up our poles, showing us the best lures to use, demonstrating how to cast our lines. I was clumsy with the fishing gear, forever tangling up the line or catching the hook on a rock or piece of wood. It was an act compared to what Dad and Bill did: they knew the best holes and what lure to use, they knew the best time of day to fish and what weight line to throw in, they knew when a hole was hot and when to move on. They seemed to possess a powerful magic that bolted through their fishing line and made fish stupid for their hooks. They always came home with fish. I, on the other hand, was a complete failure. By the end of a day of fishing I was bored out of my mind, my pole long retired, and was skipping rocks across the river or lake. But I was a good sport and went along. (I found out later the secret to some of their magic: according to Bill Dad used to sprinkle cat food to attract fish, called "chumming." It was illegal, but I don't remember him doing it.)

As we baited our spinning rods and cast our lines, we settled in for a long leisurely evening of mid-summer fishing.

The sun sank behind the crater rim and dusk fell. The wind began roughing up the lake creating small whitecaps, and Bill, who was at the helm now, steered the boat to another spot. The clouds, which half-an-hour before were sparse, began filling the darkening sky, and watching closely you could see their rapid movements and formations as they rolled in from above the surrounding crater rim and trees.

It happened all too quickly, however, for in a matter of moments the cloudscape that appeared innocently enough in the form of a few wispy puffs had metamorphosed into the largest, darkest, and most ominous I'd ever seen. And with it came a magnificent set of black/gray drapes—sheets of solid rain—that hung from it. First hitting the rim of the lake, the rain soon moved onto the lake and began pounding the water and beating it up. The wind was kicking up too, shaking the pine trees and further agitating the lake's surface. We were on the far side of the lake.

"Manischewitz" Dad said when he saw the clouds and rain.

He grabbed the anchor rope.

"Pull your lines in and get in the middle of the boat," he said. "And hold on. Don't be moving around."

"C'mom kids, let's get going!" Mom added, excited.

Dad pulled up the anchor and revved the motor. Turning the boat, we headed straightaway for camp.

The whitecaps grew larger and soon water began splashing into the boat. We were rocking and dipping and banging against the waves. We hung on tight while Dad revved the motor some more.

By the middle of the lake the dark curtain caught us.

"Ouch!" Ann cried, then another "ouch!"

It was not a sheet of rain that hit us. Perplexed, we wondered what was suddenly raining down upon us from that darkened sky. Now there were millions of them—thump, thump, thump—not only pelting us from above but also churning the lake's water into a roiling cauldron of chaos. A series of lightning bolts ripped the sky above us, one after another, jagged spears of intense white light that seemed to strike within feet of the boat, followed a second later by great explosions of thunder. Sinking into the black vortex of a battlefield, we could hardly hear ourselves speak.

"Huddle together!" Mom yelled. She draped her body as best she could over us kids to protect us from the tumult.

We were being bombarded by hail stones the size of a golf balls and larger.

By nature a composed man, Dad was rarely unnerved, but now his eyes were wide as the Moon and his demeanor as intense as a man condemned to die the next day. I see him in my mind's eye steering the boat, his right hand on the motor's throttle, his left hand held up in front of his face blocking the hail stones pounding from above as he navigated the waters. Dad was back in the Navy steering us through battle.

More lightning bolts struck from above, ripping and tearing and illuminating the gray sky as if car-sized light bulbs were blinking on and off overhead. Bill, Denny, Ann and I continued to huddle beneath Mom while she bore the brunt of the hailstones hitting us. We dared not move for fear of rocking the boat more than it already was. It was clear Dad was having great difficulty seeing through the storm. Dead reckoning he later called it—he hoped he was heading in the right direction, towards our camp.

Waves continued to break against the boat and more water washed over the sides, mixing with the hailstones that were filling up the bottom of the boat. It was like a bathtub of floating cotton balls and we had nothing to bail it out with. We hung on tight, roller coasting over swells and troughs—up and down and sideways, jerking and jarring us—causing butterflies.

Time seemed to stop. We were six people huddled in a small skiff with a 10 horse Evinrude at the bad end of a storm in the middle of a lake. Was this a dream? If it was, when would it end? All we could do was hold on tight and promise God Almighty we'd go to church if we made it back.

Barely afloat, Dad landed the boat on the little beach below our campsite. He'd done it, navigating the angry seas against insurmountable odds and bringing us back alive! We were wet and cold, teeth chattering while melting hailstones trickled down the inside of our underwear; this in spite of Mom throwing herself upon us. Jumping out of the boat, we scurried up to camp and inside our tent to strip off our clothes.

"Look!" Bill said. He was pointing to his bare back. It was covered in red spots, as if he had chicken pox.

"The hail did that!" said Mom. "Went right through your coat!"

The last of the storm passed. Dad built a giant fire. We warmed up. We strung our wet clothes next to the fire. We roasted hotdogs and ate Mom's chocolate chip cookies. Later, in the glow of the fire, dry and stomachs full, and out of Harm's Way, we talked. It felt great to be alive.

"What do you think of campin' now?" Dad asked Denny.

"Pretty cool, Uncle Jim. Pretty cool."

We went to bed. I was tucked deep into my sleeping bag, dry, tired, warm, thinking of the day and our good fortune, and how all was as it should be, when off in the distance a clang was heard, then another, and another. A sing-song voice floated in the dark, "here come the bears". It was Ann.

"And eat you whole," Bill muttered from the sleeping bag next to me, and for the second time that day I pondered my mortality.

In looking back, many of our camping trips were busts. There was torrential rain or no fish, or forest fire warnings that drove us out, or pesky mosquitoes sucking our blood dry. Often a dark shadow was cast over our vacation, sinking our spirits. But year in year out we suffered from group amnesia, for early each summer we'd start planning for our next trip to Paulina Lake or some other place, as if nothing bad had happened the year before. What awaited us next trip was going to be novel and pristine, especially tailored for us. There was fire in our bellies. Well, maybe not in Mom's, who would have preferred a cabin on the lake with a shower and kitchen.

"But that's not roughing it," Dad would say. Roughing it took ingenuity, stamina, toughness, and—the bottom line—was what we could afford.

* * *

When I was age 14 and 15 Dad and I used to go camping by ourselves in late August, leaving on a Friday afternoon after he finished work and returning home Sunday in time for dinner. We'd drive to central and eastern Oregon, and these trips were for an entirely different reason than our Paulina trips.

In those days—along with his fancy used Thunderbirds and Buicks—Dad had a four-wheel drive Ford pickup with an aluminum canopy on the back, where we slept on foam mattresses. One night near the John Day fossil beds we slept outside on the gravel parking lot, too dazzled by the multitude of stars to worry about rattlers crawling into our sleeping bags. I remember looking up into the pitch-black sky and marveling at the bright and bountiful stars—thousands of them pressing down upon us, seemingly within reach—and the concentrated band of the Milky Way stretching North and South. Shooting stars streaked across the night sky leaving an imaginary trail that lingered in my mind's eye for a second or two. The next day I found a fossilized Gingko leaf.

We were looking for deer in anticipation of the Fall hunting season, often taking back roads not found on the map. In those days vast sections of Central and Eastern Oregon were planted in alfalfa, farmers using it for fodder, pasture, and cover crop. Stopped next to these fields, with the pickup idling, Dad would "glass in" with his binoculars huge deer herds feeding and lolling in the distance, sometimes a hundred or more, and hidden in a clump of trees nearby he'd spot a buck lounging and watching over his herd, his "rack", a three or four point, outlined against the trunk of a tree.

"That's a nice buck," he'd say, licking his lips.

We drove many miles on those weekends with long silences while Dad and I scrutinized the landscape, me half looking for deer and half looking at the natural and uncivilized panorama passing before me. This was the wild west of a kid's imagination, for between the alfalfa fields were interminable sagebrush and towering mesas, rolling hillocks and twisted juniper trees, dried creek beds and stratified rim rock. I half expected at any moment for Geronimo and his warriors to appear on the next bluff on horseback and full regalia, faces painted, set to swarm down upon us in savage vengeance for encroaching on their beloved and sacred land. But that was me making things up. In truth no one was there, certainly none of my friends were there, and furthermore, it seemed to me, no one was there for hundreds of miles, which secretly scared me. In the midst of driving through one of these isolated landscapes that was giving me the creeps, I blurted "today is the Feast of the Assumption." Dad looked at me like I was some kind of genius. I'd seen it on the wall calendar.

When we hunted in the Fall it was a man's affair. Our hunting parties included Bill's friend Fred Beckley and uncles Jim White and Dan Keefe. Like for fishing, hunting was a tag-along event for me. I had mixed feelings about it: I liked the adventure and being outdoors, being with Dad and the guys, but I hated missing those early days of the new school year—the new classes, the new people, catching up with old friends, the football games and dances—and I hated falling behind in my studies knowing there would be hell to pay when I returned.

From Dad's and my scouting in August, we found hunting grounds in the high desert plateau near the tiny towns of Clarno and Monument, where the land is especially mountainous and rugged, the sagebrush shoulder high, the juniper trees crooked and bent from their fight for survival, the views vast and incomprehensible. Once Uncle Dan brought a U.S. issue Tommy gun that he let me fire off, and in one sweep I killed a dozen Nazis.

One year near Clarno we were hunting with business acquaintances of Dad's and we'd been out since sunup and now it was late morning and our group was rendezvousing to head back to camp. I was riding in a jeep with Bill and Dad. Suddenly from a draw below appeared several deer walking towards us in single file. They'd been bedded down by a nearby creek. Stopping and turning off the engine, everyone now quiet, we noted two deer in front with discernable racks. How many points were there? At two hundred yards out it was hard to tell. Signals were made among the men. Dad leaned to Bill and whispered "Take the first one." Pete Peterson, next to us, who worked for Dad, took the second buck. We watched the deer for several moments as they got closer, careful not to spook them or allow them to see us. Through his scope Bill sighted in his deer, bracing himself against the jeep for a steady aim. He and Pete held for the best angles for their shots. Then the deer veered off, quickly walking in the opposite direction from us. Had they caught a whiff of us?

"Now!"someone whispered.

Two shots rang out one after the other. In sudden pandemonium the file of deer broke apart and began fleeing in fright, except for one: Bill's buck. In an instant it crumpled to the ground in a heap.

The second buck was on the run.

Pete cocked his rifle and fired a second round. His buck kept running. He cocked and fired again. Again his buck kept running. In the meantime Bill had taken aim of the second buck and was ready to fire. "Can I shoot him Dad?" he asked after the first miss.

"No," answered Dad. After the second miss Bill asked again. "No," repeated Dad. Bill wrinkled his face. By now the second buck was running down the draw and away from us. After the third miss Bill said "Now?" Dad didn't hesitate.

"Yes."

Bill pulled the trigger. In the next instant the buck, now three hundred yards out on a dead run, ducked his head between his two front legs and nose-dived into the rocky terrain, flipping over several times before coming to a full stop. A cloud of dust rose above it.

"Nice shot!" someone yelled.

We began walking down the draw. Before us lay two downed bucks.

When we approached the second buck it appeared as if it was sleeping—lying on its side, head buried in its fur, deep in a dream—for there wasn't a mark of death on it. How was this possible? We saw it go down when Bill shot it. We examined the body further and found nothing. Then we turned its head over. Bloodied, splintered, and grossly deformed, its nose and snout had been blown away. That side of its face looked like something from a horror movie.

"That's not a kill shot," someone said.

"Yeah, it should have kept runnin'" someone added.

But the buck was dead, that was obvious. But what had happened? Why hadn't the deer gotten away?

We began gutting and cleaning the two deer, both four points. Bill would later mount the antlers in our bedroom.

"Hey! Look here," someone said minutes later, pointing. "Feel it. The neck's broken. The bullet must have forced the buck's head down making it stumble and snap its neck."

"That's how I aimed it," Bill would claim. "I didn't want to waste any meat." At age 16 he was all bluster.

"Yeah right," I said. But it was hard to argue otherwise.

That night, sitting around the campfire and retelling the story of Bill's shot, the two prized bucks hanging skinned and gutted from a nearby tree, looking not unlike the buck that hung from the rafters in Salem, it was clear that this was a different kind of camping than at Paulina.

10

"I WASN'T BORN in no hospital," she said, matter-of-factly, raising her chin in pride. I leaned over and turned the volume up on my tape recorder. It was 1978 when Gramma was approaching eighty that I formally interviewed her. It had been seven years since Granpa had died and she was living alone in the house on Monroe Street. She was frail and many pounds lighter than the rotund figure I remembered in my youth, but she was not intimidated by my cutting edge Sony reel-to-reel tape recorder I'd set up in her living room, a tall fat monstrosity of dials , switches, wheels, and gauges the likes I'm sure she'd never seen before. Logically I began by asking her where she was born (I thought I knew the answer).

"I was born in a small white house about six miles outside Sweetsprings, Missouri (she pronounced the last syllable of "Missouri" with a short "a"). [The date was] November 17th, 1898. It had just one bedroom and I shared it with my father and mother."

Her father was Joseph Lewis McDaniel from nearby Eustonia, who "was a little bit younger" than wife Ollie Belle, according to Gramma. "...they met at some parties...he was just a farmer. They didn't have occupations in those days like they do now-a-days."

Gramma was Joseph's and Ollie Belle's first child. Joseph worked odd jobs around the county, helping friends and relatives on their farms, while Ollie Belle cooked and cleaned and cared for their newborn. A few years later Ollie Belle was pregnant again, and it was during this pregnancy that a mule kicked Joseph.

"At the time he was working for my uncle," Gramma said, "when he was digging a pond and this mule kicked him right in the heart. I was three. He died within a few hours. I was awfully small when I lost my father. It was September he was kicked and killed and my sister Josephine, the only sister I had, was born Valentines Day the following year. That was nineteen and two. She never got to see her father."

Once Josephine was born the three of them—Ollie Belle, Gramma, and Josephine—moved in with Gramma's maternal grandmother, my great-great grandmother Scott, who lived three miles the other side of Sweetsprings. She took care of Gramma and Josephine while Ollie Belle began sewing for other families.

"People in those days had larger families," Gramma said. "It was nothing to have 8, 9, 10, or 12 in a family. There was no place to go, or at least that I knew of around in the small towns where you could go buy like you can nowadays. So practically all the families had lots of sewing to do, like shirts and dresses, and my mother took in sewing. She'd go out and work for people who needed her for a week or two weeks at a time. She stayed right there in their homes. They'd feed her and keep her. She always got cash. And then she had to pay almost all of this money to my grandmother to pay for us two children, except for what little she'd had to buy our clothes."

"Josephine and I thought Gramma was an angel. She was so good to us. She never laid a hand on us, never touched us, never scolded us, never said a cross word to us in all of our life. She was very religious.

Christian church. Every time there was church we was there. They had their meetings. Sometimes they'd have a couple weeks of meetings and once or twice a day we went. And always on Sundays."

In those days Gramma's attachment to Gramma Scott became so strong that "after I was married, if I had any problems, I went to my grandmother. I never went to my mother, which is a sad state of affairs, in a way, because my mother had such a hard time raising us two girls. And I feel now that I got older that I kind of failed her. I know now Grandmother kept track of all the bad things we did. And later mother had to lick us. So all we can remember when we were little of our mother is her switching us with a little switch. So that's why my Grandmother took priority. It wasn't that my mother wasn't a good person, because she certainly was."

They lived with Grandmother Scott until Gramma was age eight or nine. Then one Christmas her uncle Frank, Ollie Belle's oldest brother, arrived from North Dakota, where he'd gone homesteading after his wife had died. He made a proposal to the family. "...he had decided before he come that he had no family up there," Gramma said," and he needed somebody to cook his meals, take care of some chickens, and keep his house. So he made a proposition with my mother that if she would go to North Dakota with him and keep house for him and do the things that he needed done around there, that he would take care of us two girls. Send us to school, send us away to college, see that we got a good education, and do all this if she would come. So she gladly went. That was about nineteen hundred eight or nine. We went by train. I still have my trunk I carried. I had half fare. We went to Hurd, North Dakota."

But their stay at Uncle Frank's was short lived. Soon after Gramma left Missouri, Great-Great Grandmother Scott found she couldn't make a living with all her children gone, for Ollie Belle was the last one "... making any money for that house," Gramma said. "And so what did Grandmother do but sell out and come up and pile in on Uncle Frank. Then he had four people to take care of besides himself. So he was swamped. He couldn't keep that many people on a farm. So we didn't know what to do."

Three months later Ollie Belle's other brothers—Ed, Dan, and Ernest—made a similar offer to their sister: come to Williston, N.D., in the northwestern part of the state, where they would help her stake a claim and become a homesteader herself, provided she picked one of them to cook for. Ollie Belle chose brother Ed. She staked a claim next to his, whereupon Ed bought a cabin for the three of them to live in.

I asked Gramma to explain homesteading. Not missing a beat she said: "You get a parcel of ground 160 acres and the government gives it to you if you live on it. Now you can live on it, and I forget the amount, but it's a small amount that you have to pay in 14 months. You can 'prove up' on it and it's yours. Or you can stay five years and 'prove up' on it without having to pay a cent. A woman with two girls could certainly homestead, or a woman who didn't have any girls could homestead if she's twenty-one."

Gramma didn't remember what happened over the next few months, or what sudden realizations about homesteading occurred, but not long after they settled the homestead Ollie Belle began school in Williston and soon got a teaching certificate. "You was supposed to have a high school education [to teach]," Gramma said, "which my mother didn't have. But it was either a high school education or you could pass this examination. So she went to Williston, passed the examination, [and] got the school. She was very fortunate. She taught all the time she was there. She taught everything. Then she had plenty of money to help pay her way."

The school Ollie Belle taught in had one room and eight grades. There were a dozen kids. She taught all the subjects—arithmetic, geography, English, reading, art—and Gramma was one of her students. "It was a lot of fun settin' there in the second or third grade. You prit'ner knew your lessons better ahead of you than you did back of you. I don't know why. You're not interested in the ones under you, but you're interested in everything you don't understand. I liked drawing. Things to do with my hands. I still work with buttons, stamps, and coins with my hands."

Ollie Belle taught for three years then changed careers again. "Mother was a good cook," Gramma said, "[and she] thought, and knew, that she could run a little restaurant. [So] we went back to Hurd. By that time I was about twelve years old, and I still wasn't out of the [sixth] grade, but I started waiting tables by then. The restaurant was more or less a boarding house because we had about three elevator men, and the depot agent, and a banker, and a postman, and one or two extras at the bank and lumber yard who all boarded with us. And then the train crew on the freight trains ate with us everyday. And lots of times they'd telegraph in the morning and tell us what time they'd be there. Sometimes it would be two or three o'clock in the afternoon before they'd get there.

"We had beef, potatoes, vegetables, biscuits, cake or pie, lots of fruit—always canned—very little fresh fruit, and coffee or milk. We had good food. That's why the railroad men would wait till two o'clock to eat. They could eat anyplace, and anybody'd cook for them—everybody wanted them. But the trainmen always came to our place even though Hurd was the dinkiest place on the line."

"I worked there seven days a week. Mother never gave me no time off. We never thought anything about it. I never even got no pay. And she'd keep me out of school. Now if I come home at noon and the trainmen said they'd be there at two o'clock, I didn't get to go back to school till after the trainmen had eat. Now that was all settled with the teacher at the first of school. Lots of times I didn't even go back to school, so it made me a little bit slow gettin' out of school. I didn't like it very well, but I didn't say nothin'. There wasn't anyplace to go."

Though Gramma didn't like the long work hours at the restaurant and didn't like falling behind in her studies, her life up till then had gone pretty well. "We didn't have a lot of money," she said. "But you see my mother had nine in her family and there was nine in my father's, and we saw this after we grew up, there was eight and eight, we'll say sixteen people, they went out of their way to see that two little girls was very happy. We always had plenty of clothes. We always had plenty to eat. And we never knew what it was to even want for money. We didn't want for things. All it took to make us happy would be a sack of candy or a sack with oranges or a sack with bananas, or some material for a new dress, or just something like that we were happy. It doesn't take much to make a child happy. It takes very little. So that's why I think we had a happy life. In spite of the fact that we lost our father, there were so many people trying to make up to us for our loss, that it made it quite nice for us. We thought everybody liked us, and we were so tickled."

"I started going out with the boys real young—thirteen—because I didn't have no way to go," said Gramma. At her fifteenth birthday party her suitor at the time—Lloyd Tarvestead—introduced her to a friend of his, since "he had the nicest girl". Ollie Belle was happy Gramma was going with Lloyd and secretly hoped they would marry. "His dad was dead, but he was well to do [from] farming," said Gramma. "They just had everything. And of course my mother was real pleased that I had him." But Ollie Belle didn't know Gramma's true feelings towards Lloyd, or towards any of the other boys that she had dated. "...I wasn't serious about any of them."

Lloyd's friend was Robert Keefe, age 20. Gramma hadn't met him before her birthday party, but she'd heard of him and his family. Hurd was a small community, and rumor had it that Robert was treated badly by his father.

"Robert couldn't do much right. Everybody said he worked awfully hard. When he was eight years old he was driving a bundle team. This was wheat. They picked up them bundles and carried [them] to the thrasher. And he had to keep up his turn. You had to keep up with the men. For that Mr Keefe got paid a man's wages—he got paid for Robert, and he got paid for his team and his wagon. And of course Robert never got anything. And he did the work."

Ollie Belle was furious with Gramma when she started dating Robert. At least with Lloyd, Ollie Belle figured, Gramma's financial future was secure. With Robert it was not.

"Robert never had a dime," Gramma said, "[but] after Robert came, well that was it. I dropped Lloyd right away...I wasn't serious about any of them [boys] until I went with Robert...There was no complications with me. But I'll never forget it. I was kind of cruel to him in a way. I think about it now. But at the time I didn't think nothin' about it and cared less. I saw Lloyd after I was married to Robert. At my uncle's store there in Hurd he used to come up lots of times for two or three hours and talk to me and tell me how bad he felt. And he used to tell me he'd never get married. But he did. But it was a long time—it was many years."

In June following Gramma's birthday Robert proposed, presenting Gramma with a gold ring. Then, according to Gramma, "I asked my mother if I could get married to Robert, and she told me no. I told her if she didn't let me I'd run away. She pretty much let me have my way. I never really had a big argument there."

They were married on December 16th, 1914, one month after Gramma turned 16. According to Granpa's memoirs, the ceremony was held in "Landsford [a town ten miles from Hurd] about 8:00 p.m. Mr. and Mrs. John Olson were the witness... [and later] I bought the boys a keg of beer and the young fellows celebrated in Henry Rummy's elevator." Afterwards the newlyweds went to a movie and then "got a room at a private home." Many friends thought they had gone to the Landsford Hotel, the only hotel in town, which burned down later that night, and Gramma and Granpa were teased about starting the fire.

In spite of being just 16 and newly married, Gramma had seen quite a bit in the world. She knew her mind better than most people her age. Her round open face was set with intelligent eyes. She was physically sturdy. Her fingers were nimble. She was practical. And she knew how to live poor, which would come in handy with Robert.

Robert "got lots of ribbin' about robbing the cradle," said Gramma. "And Mr. Keefe [how Gramma called Robert's father] didn't like the marriage because I wasn't Catholic." He insinuated that Gramma was the reason Robert stopped going to church altogether. "[But] I had nothing to say about Robert quitting the church," she said. "He had already quit the church before I ever met him."

Granpa used to tell me about how the priests at his school would whack his knuckles for misspelling words or for adding numbers incorrectly. He fought against a persistent sentiment of guilt and paranoia: "I felt God was always looking at me from behind the clouds, making judgements about me. It seemed I couldn't do anything right." From his memoirs and stories he told me, Granpa's disenchantment with the church grew and grew until he finally broke away in his teens. I agree with Gramma and believe Mr. Keefe wrong in his assessment regarding Gramma. Before their courtship Granpa had left the church far behind.

Granpa and Gramma began their married life by renting Uncle Frank's farm outside Hurd, the same farm that Gramma had come to from Missouri seven years before. Uncle Frank was running the store in

Hurd, "so he told us he would sell us all of his horses and a few cows and machinery. It was all old because he'd been farming all those years. So he said if we would rent the farm he'd sell us this [horses, etc.] for a certain amount. I forget exactly the amount. We didn't have any money. [So] we couldn't lose, cause it was all his stuff, and we were farming for him and he furnished the grain, and all Robert did was furnish the work. And we had a good crop that year and we paid it off."

Gramma was soon pregnant, and ten months into the marriage son Bob was born. "Having Bob was like something I'd never experienced. I didn't know a thing about it. I'd say we had complications. I don't know if you talk about it in this day and age. We called the doctor out early morning of the 24th of October. He came ten miles from Landsford—it was the closest doctor. I remember distinctly it was on a Sunday. He came in a horse and buggy. My mother's birthday. And we thought, 'well, we're going to have our child on my mother's birthday.' And I was real happy about that. We all were. Well it wasn't born that day. And the doctor stayed right there. He never left. He worked with me. Now I would of had...a section, you know, caesarean, if they could have done anything about it. But they didn't do that in those days. There's no hospitals or anything there. So it wasn't born on the 24th. So the doctor was with me all day Sunday, all Sunday night, all day Monday, all Monday night, all day Tuesday. And Bob was born Tuesday morning. He was just about as black as my purse laying out there. What I thought was...it just look like it was a negro baby. He was so black. Well he's supposed to be dead. My grandmother said she saw many babies just laid out dead. He was just smothered till he was blue. He's just blue. But he did live."

Gramma was sixteen and not prepared for what was to come. She got help from Ollie Belle and sister Josephine. "Josephine spoiled him," Gramma said. "She had him so spoiled he didn't know which end he was sittin' on."

But in spite of the help life was hard. "The first year on the farm I shocked grain. I followed the binder and pushed the baby buggy at the same time. And kept up with the binder...that was a hard job. [But] we wouldn't have had any money if we'd paid a man. So in order to have money I had to do that. Then we got all the money."

Less than two years later, in August, 1917, Gramma gave birth to her second son, Edward Daniel (called Dan). She fretted that the birth would be like her first one—how could she possibly cope; would she even survive; would the baby? Fortunately, "...[Dan] was much easier," Gramma said. Though she secretly wanted a girl, it didn't matter. "... Mother used to say that when we were little, both Josephine and I...she'd dress us in starches like we come out of a band box. And then she said 'you'd come and get somebody's baby and get it swallowing and messing all over you and then you'd be all wrinkled up. You wouldn't look nice, and you was always taking care of somebody's baby.' We liked children. We both did."

My Dad, James Wilbur—"Jim"—was born next, in April 1919, and though the pregnancy and birth were successful, Gramma was so disappointed about not having a daughter that she openly declared to anyone who would listen that "I'm going to put a dress on him and call him my girl."

That same year the crops failed. In August, four months after Dad's birth, the family, now five in all, moved to Rolla, North Dakota, a county seat ten miles from the Canadian boarder. "...mother had a restaurant there, and uncle Frank was there too," Gramma said. Why Ollie Belle and Uncle Frank had moved to Rolla is unknown, but, unlike Hurd at the time, there was work there for Gramma and Granpa.

Grasshoppers had destroyed their crops. It was heartbreaking. In his memoirs Granpa wrote: "...our money was gone, and [a 1917 Ford] was all we had left out of nearly five years of work in which our hopes, our children, and our early marriage were centered. We were still very much in love, and I had learned to respect Forrest's judgement highly also. She had a stability and accomplishment far beyond anyone that I have ever known, and after all [this] she still would not admit that we had failed badly." It would be the last time—Gramma making a special point of this during our interview—they would farm.

They lived in Rolla six years, from 1919 to 1925. Gramma worked in the restaurant and Granpa did odd jobs around town. North Dakota's frosty winters are legend, especially on the U.S./Canadian border, and during that time Dad caught pneumonia three times, the third time a severe case. "We had such a hard time with [Jim]," Gramma said. "There was two doctors in town. [One was a Dr. Vetter]. They both come to see him. They'd come any hour of the day or night. They never even knocked. They just open the front door and come in and come up stairs to see how he was. Now Jim was that sick that the doctors both thought it was necessary. They never knew when each other was coming. They never did exactly meet. Nobody knows the hours Robert and I spent with him. One of us had to sit up all night long. Well, finally Jim did get well and [Dr. Vetter] told us we just had to get him out of there. And that's what we did. So we sold out and left."

Following doctor's instructions to get Jim into a warmer climate, the family prepared to move. In Rolla there was a public auction of their furniture and other belongings, which netted nearly $1,000. Ollie Belle gave them half interest in a 1924 Ford sedan. Then along with a tent, a gasoline stove, good tires, a roadmap, and "...the spirit of pioneers as we left Rolla," Granpa later wrote, the five of them set out West across the Great Plains and the Rocky Mountains, driving along rutted dirt roads and dizzying precipices, and up and down mountain roads so steep everyone except the driver had to help push. They arrived weeks later after many flat tires, after gazing at an amazing variety of landscapes, glad to be together and alive at the end of their long trek, the memory of North Dakota now but a whisper in their ears. They never looked back. Finalizing this chapter in her life, Gramma said: "Our kids were worth more to us than the house was or anything." They pitched their tent in Eugene, Oregon, a place where Granpa had lived for awhile when he had run away from home years earlier. He remembered the mild winters and warm summers. And it rarely snowed there. Gramma and Granpa hoped it was the cure for my Dad's fragile lungs.

11

WHEN WE MOVED into the house across the street from Gramma and Granpa's in the summer of 1960, renting it from them with the intent of buying it someday, the neighborhood now had four Keefe families living within a stones throw of each other: along with us and Gramma and Granpa, Great Uncle Mike and his family lived a block away on 19th street, and Great Uncle Ed and Aunt Alice lived four blocks away on 24th.

The bungalow style house had two bedrooms upstairs, a detached garage, a basement, a bath and bedroom on the main floor, and a spacious back yard full of walnut, peach, and apple trees (where I said we hung Cousin Jay), in all a step up in size and character from our Lawrence Street house. Upstairs Bill and I shared one bedroom and Ann had the other. Our bedroom had half walls on two sides that followed the slanted roof- line, giving us plenty of headroom in the middle between our beds. At the far end between the beds was a double hung window where our chest of drawers stood. Mounted on the wall at the head of Bill's bed were the deer antlers from the Clarno hunt; on it he hung tennis rackets, T-shirts, sling shots, binoculars, and dirty socks. At the foot of his bed stood his blue and white portable phonograph, the size of a cardboard box, which played 33 and 45 RPM records. We stuck plastic triangles in the big holed 45's and played "Hound Dog" and "Flying Purple People Eater" hour after hour. I first heard *Meet the Beatles* and Dylan's *Highway 64 Revisted* on it.

On the headboard of my bed I clamped a red reading lamp, and after long episodes of reading and studying the metal shade was hot enough to fry an egg on. Later I rotated in a sunlamp the dermatologist suggested for my acne, lying under it to bake and heal my erupting skin, but when I didn't pay attention to the time I'd find my face red as a fire engine except for my eye sockets, blocked out with halves of ping pong balls stuffed with cotton, leaving me looking like a mutated species of raccoon.

On the left of the bedroom door was a metal book shelf where I put black and white photos of JFK walking the beach at Hyannisport (the famous one with the sweater around his neck) and later RFK running the Oregon beach during the 1968 Oregon primaries, just before he was shot in L.A.. On the other side of the door next to the closet was a desk that Dad made from a hollow-cored door. It had no drawers, but even after I piled it high with books and fossils and notebooks and model airplanes, there was still room enough to push aside a space for doing homework.

In the summer I put my model airplanes—Spitfires, Hellcats, Stukas—on the dresser in front of the double windows, and when Mom opened them to air the house out each day the breeze would make the propellers spin around and around, and sometimes when the wind really kicked up these Spitfires and Hellcats and Stukas seemed as if they were readying for battle, their propellers whirling to near invisibility, the strong breeze inching the tiny fuselages forward in preparation for takeoff, the pilots inside the miniature cockpits pulling on throttles and checking their fuel gages, giving the thumbs-up sign.

There was a reason we used the desk chair to tie Cousin Jay to when we tortured him, because when Dad bolted up the stairs to find out what the ruckus was about, it was easy—since the room was so small—to throw the rope under the bed and put the chair back at the desk before he got to the door. By then Jay would be sitting comfortably on the bed acting like he was having a nice chat with his older cousins.

Bill and I shared this room until early in his college years when we remodeled the garage into a family/bedroom and he soon moved into it. In my own room at last—I was in high school then—I had no one to answer to regarding lights, noise, messyness, or space. With the light on, I laid awake late at night reading or thinking about things.

In those first years a giant green truck filled to the brim with sawdust came once a month in the winter, backing into the driveway and sticking its thick hose through the basement window to blow mounds of sawdust into the corner room. Mom tacked a plastic tarp around the room to keep the dust down, but even with that we'd find a thin layer of sawdust throughout the rooms, and the house would smell of fresh cut wood for days. It was up to Bill and me to keep the furnace filled, and using a 5-gallon bucket I'd transport sawdust from the sawdust bin to the metal holder sitting atop the burner, making several trips each time. The holder resembled an inverted pyramid, and was tall enough to keep me on my tiptoes while I poured the bucket of sawdust in. Sometimes we'd forget to fill it—we always blamed each other—and the furnace would burn out and leave the house cold in the middle of the night. I smoked my first homemade cigarette next to the furnace—crushed maple leaves wrapped in notebook paper—thinking the furnace would camouflage whatever smell I generated. At first puff I went into an interminable coughing fit that I shook only after spitting up a lung, or so it seemed, and I happily threw the makeshift cigarette into the burning sawdust to cover my tracks.

In all the years we lived at Monroe Mr. and Mrs. Blais lived next door, on the corner. They were Catholic and had two adopted children, Mark and Theresa. Mark was a year younger than I was, red headed, fair of skin, a stocky build. Theresa was a year younger than Ann, with jet black hair, pale of skin, and an aloof demeanor. Mr. Blais, who early each day went to work in denim overalls and cork boots, worked at one of the local sawmills as a sawyer. Tall and angular with a swarthy complexion, he wore rimless glasses, walked with a stiffness in his bones, and made the occasional effort to be friendly by cracking a joke (always unfunny and poorly timed). To the lumber mill each morning he drove his blue Ford pickup fitted with an aluminum canopy on the back. His wife Mrs. Blais was short and dark haired and wore hideous horned rimmed glasses. I cringed whenever I saw her, for her face was usually pinched and her thin colorless lips pulled down at the corners, her squinty eyes peering through those pointy framed glasses while her short bandy legs bounded like a monkey's. Her black hair became wild and frizzy, especially when she weeded in the yard. Her whole persona made me think I was in the presence of something dark and prehistoric, a hagfish of flesh and bones, and I suspected she harbored a secret grudge against life, each day vacillating between civility and evilness, her world populated by demons and traps that she used to bend Mr. Blais to her way of thinking. Her child rearing was Modern Reign of Terror that put both kids on a short leash. Over the years I knew Mark, when we played hundreds of hours of basketball in our driveway between the houses, he was constantly glancing towards his house to see if Mrs. Blais was spying on him from one of the windows or from behind the fence that separated our houses. He once pulled up his T-shirt to show me a black and blue mark on his back that was the perfect outline of a handprint. "My mom," he said. In those days I was getting an ear full from Granpa about him being raised Catholic and the useless and inhuman punishment he received at the hands of fathers and nuns and priests in the name of God. I now saw it next door. And as well as getting whacked by his mom, Mark said he was getting whacked by the sisters at Saint Mary's. To Mark the message was clear: if you don't follow the rules then you're going to get the hell beat out of you (because the devil resides in you!). In their perverse Catholic way I suspected Mr. and Mrs. Blais felt Mark and Theresa were their tickets to the Pearly Gates, for who could condemn or criticize their humanity for taking those poor lost souls in? And beating kids? No problem—they did it at Saint Mary's! I wondered if they'd have beaten their own biological children.

In the house on the other side of us lived a reclusive elderly lady we seldom saw. She passed on after a few years and Bill's friend Wayne Taylor and his divorced mom moved in. When Waynes's mom was out Saturday nights Bill and I would go over and play poker late into the night, often with older guys, even older than Bill, and there would be beer and cigars and talk of "shacking up [with girls]...that's the only way I'll live." One guy had been briefly married. At these poker parties, which were much different than the one's I had with my friends, talk of women zeroed in on how to get them to bed and the myriad heartaches they caused in the name of "love". To them women were strange alien creatures who held sway over men, who at whim could freely dispense equal doses of pleasure and pain. But signs of sentimentality were ridiculed among these guys because women were heartbreakers you had to be tough with. Then a week later Bill would tell me about one of these guys cracking up because his girlfriend suddenly loved someone else. "Pussy whipped" his friends would say, laughing nervous laughs, but knowing at any moment they could be next. And woe to him who got a woman pregnant, the worst thing that could happen to a young man, a slow numbing death. "Be careful!" was the catch phrase. This young-men's banter and bravado covered deeper-seated feelings and jealousies that only later I understood. For the moment it was a small vocabulary and a smaller sensibility, but it was fascinating nonetheless as I watched this among Bill's friends, wondering about it, acting like I was one of them, but in truth my amorous experience with girls was nothing more than fantasies in my head. My secret claim was in the bushes at High Street.

Our backyard ended at the alley that split our block in two. In my teens when we remodeled the garage, Dad in turn built an open-air double garage next to it with access from the alley. In those days Dad started buying used but well preserved Thunderbirds every two or three years, the first a tan '58 with fins and red bucket seats that gave the overall impression of a Cuban cigar. Nearly every night after work he'd spray it down with the hose then wipe it clean. We'd had decent used cars before, a '48 Chevy, a '60 Plymouth, often buying them from Uncle Buryl at Lew Williams Chevrolet, who always gave us a good deal. But this first

Thunderbird was a departure from the past and began a string of fancy cars that lasted until he settled on his Chevy pickups and "revolutionary rotary engine" Mazda after we kids left home. He bought two more Thunderbirds after the first one, a powder blue one that I backed into a light post, another one Bill totaled hitting another car at an intersection on College hill. But the car I believe he cherished the most among them was a burgundy red Buick Riviera with white leather interior, sloped roof line, streamlined body, which even to my untrained eye was a thing of splendor and beauty. I believe it was one of the first cars of that kind to have front wheel drive. Incredibly, Dad wasn't mad at Bill after totalling his Thunderbird. More importantly no one was hurt. He said "once something is done there's nothing to say about it", and generally he let us kids drive his cars when we came of driving age. Of course we had to have a good reason, but he never quibbled about it.

On Columbus Day 1963 the giant tulip tree that stood next to our driveway in the Blais' front yard tried to kill me. A world class storm had roared into western Oregon that day, swooping up the Willamette Valley like a swarm of hungry locusts and arriving in Eugene mid-afternoon. I was attending Wilson Junior High, and I remember principal William Williams announcing over the school-wide intercom for us to grab our coats and books and go directly home, for a deadly storm was on its way and there was no time to lose. By the time my friends and I emerged from the old brick school building the wind was lifting our coats shoulder high and blowing our hats down the street. We could lean into the gusts at odd angles, like Charley Chaplin in his movies, without falling over.

I took a different route home than usual that day. At 19th and Lincoln, Dan Jones and I broke off from our pack and headed across Washington Park to Dan's house, a couple blocks off my normal route home. Far from making haste like we were told, we took our time playing in the wind as if it were the first snow of the season. We threw our arms up and turned our backs to the wind, and the fabric of our coats and pants writhed and whipped over our stick-like frames. Above us branches waved and swished about in the frantic air, several breaking from their limbs and swirling by, buffeted by the gale force. Exhilarated by this onrush of visible and invisible elements, Dan and I forged on block by block while chaos raged on all sides: the flood of wind and flying newspaper, leaves awhirl of every kind and color, trash cans banging and rolling down driveways. The world was coming apart as we skipped along.

From Dan's house on 21st I walked alone north a block on Madison to 20th, then turned west to cover the gravel portion that led to Monroe. From there it was a short 100 foot trek diagonally across the intersection and the Blais's front lawn to our front door, cutting the corner where their tulip was. I'd done this a million times before. By now the storm was in full force, rearing its ugly head in such anger that it seemed as if all things large and small were powerless against it, and the world was merely a platform for its violent performance. Was this another planet that I'd studied about in astronomy? With all my energy and concentration I trudged ahead while holding tight to my books and coat and hat, even my glasses, hoping they wouldn't fly away.

I heard the crack as soon as I walked under the tulip. Mom was watching from our front window, on the lookout for us kids coming home from school. It was a 50 foot tree, maybe taller, dense and firm with a solid trunk and branches and limbs that spread over both properties and the street, and from which I raked many leaves each Fall that floated to our front lawn. I took it for granted as I approached it, focused more on reaching our front porch and avoiding being hit by a flying branch or garbage can lid. I had little control over what happened next. The crack was followed by a groan, then by a high screech and whine. I took off running, but not to our front porch, which would have been the natural place to flee, but rather at a 90-degree angle from it, across the Blais' front lawn towards 20th Street. I'd never heard the sound of a fatally cracking tree, but when I did there was no doubting what it was. It's like someone's first earthquake: it's never happened to you but you know precisely what it is. What occurred next I did without thinking.

Running faster than ever before, a sprint supercharged by the flush of adrenaline, my heart pounding out of my chest, I did not stop to look back. In a moment it was done. From over my shoulder I heard the giant whoosh and thud of a crash. The outermost branches hit the ground first, acting like a momentary buffer, then at full impact the tree and the earth shuddered as if a giant meteor had hit from the sky. I could not have heard myself speak. It was only then that I stopped and turned around, certain that the tree was down. My heart continued pounding in my ears like a kettle-drum. Surveying the scene I alighted at the spot where the tulip tree used to be: there now stood an upturned root system and a splintered and cracked base, the long tapered trunk lay flat on its side and diagonally across our driveway, its very top pressed against our dining room window. It lay in the path I was walking to our front porch.

With my heart still pounding and my face still flushed with adrenaline, I stood there afraid the tulip tree would reanimate and take another shot at me, like a deer feigning its death, so I walked in small steps around the felled tree, alert to ominous signs—an errant branch, a hidden splinter. I made my way to our back door.

Moments before through the dining room window Mom had seen me walking across the street and heading for the tree, then witnessed the tulip fall and had stepped back in horror as it angled towards the house. Panicked, she ran to the back door. I was there when she opened the door. "Thank God you're alive!" she said.

It grew dark. The city lost electricity. Severed electric cables crackled and sizzled on pavement and lawns. By night the worst of the storm had passed and Gramma and Granpa came over, and we cooked dinner on our Coleman stove and lit the living room with our Coleman lamp. The felled trees, debris, and live cables fascinated us kids, all in view outside our front window, and we begged Mom and Dad to let us roam the neighborhood once the storm had died down, but we were not allowed to go outside, it was too dangerous.

The next day Mr. Blais, Dad, Bill, and I cut the tree into firewood, a job that took most of the day. Had the tulip been a foot or two taller, we all figured, it would have broken through our dining room window where Mom was watching from.

* * *

I didn't like the people who moved into Tim's house because I blamed them for breaking up our friendship. How dare they! Furthermore, they spoke with accents! Kingsley Weatherhead came from England

and was a new professor of Literature at the university. His dark bushy hair formed a triangle atop his head, making him appear taller than he really was, and contrasted against his pale skin and five o'clock shadow. His perpetual smile gave him a bemused look, and dressed in his tweed jackets with pads on the elbows, he came off as stereotypically academic. His wife Ingrid was Norwegian; blond, fair skinned, tall and robust, on the clumsy side (I remember milk bottles slipping out of her hands and breaking in their driveway), she like Kingsley was intelligent and friendly and eager to make friends in their new adopted town. I remember Dad calling the English "limeys" from his time in the Navy, which gave me the impression he didn't like them either.

The first time I met Kingsley he was driving home from the university, not long after they had moved in, and I was walking home from school. He pulled over and rolled down the window.

"Hop in," he said, "I'm your new neighbor." He was smoking a curved pipe, in contrast to Granpa's straight pipe, which appeared to be a permanent fixture hanging from his mouth. The ride would be short—a block or so—so I thought why not. Right off he asked me if I enjoyed my school.

"Sure," I said.

"What are you studying?"

"Ancient Egypt."

"Wonderful!"

The car stopped in front of our house. He shook my hand like a gentleman when I got out. I couldn't help but think that he liked me.

Kingsley would often have Dad buttonholed on the front lawn and speaking in a low voice. This wasn't for anybody's ears—Kingsley loved jokes and stories—and then suddenly Dad was bowled over from Kingsley's scatological punch line and I could see the tears form in Dad's eyes from laughing, and Kingsley would be giggling and taking a puff from his pipe. I believe it was Kingsley who told Dad the story going around at the time about Sammy Davis Junior's reply about his golf handicap: "I'm a one-eyed Black Jew." Kingsley's father was a well-known theologian in the Methodist Church in England who'd published many books, and though he wanted his son to be a medical doctor,

Kingsley chose the couplet over the scalpel. He loved poetry and taught it, as well as other courses in English Literature, for many years at the university, and he too would publish many books in the years to come, including a memoir about his father.

Ingrid was just as charming, and she and Mom got on famously in those few years they lived in Tim's house, in part because as intelligent as she was, Ingrid (as well as Kingsley) was clueless about running a household for a family of five (they had three very young children). Mom's excellent practical advice about child rearing, cooking, cleaning, and shopping, much of which I suspect Ingrid was learning for the first time, was a godsend for her. I often babysat for them, being paid generously for doing nothing while their children slept; easy money I thought, but at night's end when Ingrid and Kingsley returned from their party they always gave me the impression that the success of their evening was in large part due to me, which couldn't have been further from the truth. They were the most generous, urbane, and charming couple I'd ever met.

So it was unusual when I saw Ingrid lose it one day while Mom was giving her a hair permanent in the kitchen. She was thumbing through that week's Life magazine and reading an article about West Germany possibly having an army again. I was getting a snack. "Those damn Nazis," Ingrid seethed. My ears perked up, for that tone of voice was uncharacteristic of her. "They are beasts, every last one of them. You just wait. If they get an army, watch out. They love war and can't wait to go at it again. They stole my childhood," she said. I found out the Germans were as cruel occupying Norway as they were in other countries they occupied during the war.

They moved across town a few years later to be closer to the university. We were sad to see them go, but we kept in contact with them, and during my senior year of high school I went to Kingsley for letters of recommendation for scholarship applications. He must have put pen to paper in the most glowing way because I got offers from the colleges I applied to. But the hole they left in our neighborhood not only underscored their unique friendship but also the bright light they held against the darkness of the hagfish and sawyer next door. From then on the families who would move in to Tim's old house in later years would never quite measure up to Kingsley and Ingrid, or to Tim, so we never got to know any of them well.

* * *

We grew rich at Monroe Street, at least in our own minds. By the mid-sixties our family was doing better financially with the new cars, the carport addition, and now a membership in the new Shadow Hills Country Club ten miles outside of town. This was Mom's idea, for in her eyes the membership was not only an avenue for playing golf and meeting new friends, but it also carried social status. She was bound and determined to raise herself from her humble origins in Mitchell, South Dakota. What better way to show this than a membership in a country club! Furthermore, Auntie Jean and Uncle Buryl were new members of the Eugene Country Club, the most exclusive club in town, "so why not us?" Mom must have thought. Determined to make her mark, she took to the links with a vengeance, becoming quite good over the years, her consistency her strongest suit while driving the tiny white ball 150 yards down the middle of the fairway each time, playing bogey golf on her best days, and quitting in her 70's only when strokes and arthritis befell her. In those first years at Shadow Hills each of us in the family took a swing at golf, and John Hall and I set personal records by golfing fifty-two holes in one day at Shadow Hills, part of a once-a-year infatuation with golf that lasted the few weeks between school and summer work. But my infatuation was short lived since unlike soccer or football or basketball, golf was a physically slow game of intense concentration. I didn't sweat playing it, and it didn't reap immediate rewards. Too antsy, I often blew my whole round on the first hole. Members looked down on John and me for throwing our clubs and saying "shit" and not replacing divots. "Screw this," I said after a couple years.

The Monroe Street house would be the house we lived in the longest as a family, and we eventually bought it from Gramma and Granpa. We never had to change schools again. Later, when we kids went out on our own after high school, we stayed close, Bill and I going to university across town and living at home from time to time to save money, Ann moving to Sacramento, but her job on the bus line often bringing her back to Eugene for short stays. Until the divorce, the doors to Monroe were always open to us.

12

"How **could they** do that?" we asked, for indeed America was shocked once again that the commies had beat us in space. In early Spring 1961 Yuri Gagarin became the first human to orbit the earth, his face splashed across the front page of the Eugene Register Guard. A few weeks later, in an attempt to take their thunder away, we shot Alan Sheppard up in Mercury. At Monroe Street we stayed glued to our radio early that morning listening to the countdown, but barely had Sheppard blasted off and reached space that he turned around and came back, the whole thing lasting a mere fifteen minutes! Were we bursting with pride? Were we now convinced of our superiority? Hell no, because it was a feeble effort compared to what Gagarin did, whose flight lasted over an hour and encompassed the whole earth. Not until the following year did

John Glenn orbit the earth, but in the meantime we Americans were pathetic and down on our luck, so in Eugene, like once before in Salem, we decided to take matters into our own hands.

It began with Dave Hodges during a recess at Adams Elementary School. He and his buddies had strung kite string between two wood poles stuck in the ground, and sliding along it was a CO_2 cartridge Dave had punctured. There was a loud fizz as the cartridge raced quickly forward like a torpedo. For us handful of kids gathered around that day, the "experiment," complete with its poles and string and its small tube to guide the CO_2 cartridge, impressed us. Hodges was testing his CO_2 cartridge as a possible power source for launching a rocket. He was on to something, I thought, but something wasn't right.

Dave's cartridge petered out several feet before the opposite pole, stopping as fast as it started.

"You'll never get a rocket off the ground using that," I yelled. "You need more power!"

I'd known Dave for a couple of years at Adams and knew a few things about him: he was smart, competitive, and dogged in his pursuits. He hated to lose. He was in the other 6th grade class.

"Wait and see," Dave growled.

A week later Dave and his buddies—he now had a full blown rocket club—were at it again, this time with the CO_2 cartridge fitted into a small rocket outfitted with fins and a nosecone. At recess dozens of kids gathered around "the launch" near the baseball field. My teacher Mr. Smith and other teachers stood in the background watching with eagle eyes, looking for any signs of danger, but also, I suspect, proud that Dave and his group were making this effort.

We held our breath as Dave punctured the CO_2 cartridge and ran back from the launch pad. The fizz sounded and the rocket lifted off the ground and you could hear everyone take a deep breath. But then the rocket began turning around head over heels at eye level, spinning faster and faster until it became a blur. Instinctively we kids scattered in all directions like frightened sheep, and in the next moment as we turned our heads we saw the rocket crash in a thud on the ground, breaking into pieces.

   DREAM FAMILY ♦ A MEMOIR

"Nice goin'" I yelled to Dave, jeering along with others in the crowd when we regrouped. "You're lucky you didn't kill someone!"

"Like you," Dave grunted.

He may have been down on his luck at that point, but knowing Dave he was already thinking about his next rocket.

And in spite of their failures Dave and his buddies were getting a lot of attention at school. Kids took notice and teachers were encouraging them to keep trying. Not to be outdone, three of us in Mr. Smith's 6th grade class thought we could we do better if we put our heads together: myself, Bob Walwyn, and Danny Adams, each agreeing to humble Dave Hodges and his rabble of dunderheads with an ambitious goal: not only to launch a successful rocket, which Hodges had yet to do, but more important, we wanted to launch a living thing into the skies. Now that would certainly turn heads and put Hodges in his place.

Fuel was crucial to our rocket. We knew from Dave Hodges that CO_2 wouldn't work. But what would work, what should we try? The next weekend in Danny's backyard, just over the hill from Monroe, the two of us cut the heads off a box of stick matches and ground them into a fine powder, then packed it into an empty CO_2 cartridge. Anchoring it down with heavy rocks to keep the cartridge from flying off, we laid a long fuse into the nozzle and lit it. Danny and I ran behind his upturned picnic table a few yards away.

Crouched down and peering between the table slats, we watched as the fuse's torpid burn crept along the ground leaving a trail of smoke like from a distant choo-choo train. Soon the burning fuse vanished into the end of the nozzle and we held our breaths and waited... and waited, but nothing happened.

"It's a dud," Danny said.

"Yea. It should have gone off by now."

"Let's check it out.

We took a couple steps from behind the picnic table when the blast, sounding like a .30 caliber rifle shot rather than the swoosh and fizz of CO_2, which we expected to hear, threw us backwards. We hit the ground face down, covering our heads, not daring to move for fear there might be another surprise for us; how did we know what a cartridge of powered match heads would do once ignited? Now a smoky haze hung over the cartridge along with the pungent smell of sulfur.

A moment passed. Gathering our nerve, we arose and began searching for the cartridge, tip-toeing along and finding the now scattered rocks, but the cartridge, blackened and mangled like an over-chewed dog bone, remained where we'd placed it.

"Look at my hands," Danny said.

"They're shaking. So are mine."

The cartridge was still warm to the touch. We rolled it around in our fingers, carefully examining it and rubbing the black soot off.

"It stinks, like someone farted." Danny said.

"Like a major fart," I laughed.

"You know, it's not going to work."

"I know. It's like a grenade. It'd blow up a rocket."

"No shit."

"What are we going to do?"

In spite of our failure, it was a beginning. Furthermore, we'd seen on TV Vanguard and Redstone rockets go up in flames seconds after liftoff. And hadn't Dave Hodges' rocket careened out of control and crashed to the ground? This was no time to get queasy about our quest.

* * *

Bob Walwyn was an unlikely colleague in those days. He had light hair cut in a crewcut, his rimmed glasses covered half his face, and his body was slight and willowy, his skin pale. But behind those heavy glasses were lively eyes: he was bookish, scientific, albeit clumsy. His dad was in the insurance business and was good with numbers. Bob kept to himself most of the time, but it was the shared goal of launching a rocket that brought us together.

Danny Adams, on the other hand, had been a friend through sports. He had sandy hair and a strong build, baby skin that blushed easily, wore a perpetual smile, was excitable, and bounded about under an endless supply of energy. His parents drove a fire-engine red Ford Fairlane.

The fuel flummoxed us. What to do? Ground match heads or CO_2 wouldn't work. We soon learned through books and magazines that sulfur and zinc mixed together made an excellent rocket fuel. Days after our match head experiment in Danny's back yard, I entered Hiron's Drug store at 18th and Willamette Street and approached the counter. In the back a man dressed in a white smock was filling prescriptions. He must have been standing on a platform because he towered above me. He saw me waiting. Could he hear my heart pounding?

The prior day, at mom's suggestion, and using the Yellow Pages, I'd made phone calls to chemical and fertilizer companies around town, but each time I was met with suspicion: "what do you want sulfur and zinc for?" One man suggested I go to a drug store for the small quantities I needed.

The pharmacist, now hovering over me and peering through his glasses, asked, "what can I do for you young man?"

"I want to buy some sulfur and zinc."

He held me in his gaze. "Sulfur and zinc, eh?"

"Yes, sir."

He paused; the hint of suspician crossed his face. "What do you want it for?"

"Just doing some stuff, you know, some science stuff at school."

"Like what, exactly."

"You know, experiments."

"Your teacher know about this?"

"Kinda."

"That a yes or no?"

"Well, he's going to know."

He bore down on me like summer heat, holding my eyes. "You building a rocket?" I looked down. "Are you?"

"Oh no, no sir," my voice trembling.

"I think you are."

"No, really. No sir." Blood rushed to my face, my voice now fraught with tension. "But never mind," I said. "That's o.k. Forget about it." My brain locked up, unable to advance the argument that I was asking for something that would make our people stronger and better than the commies. I turned and ran down the aisle and out the front door without looking back, fearing the pharmacist would see my face again and remember it. Eugene was a small town and you never knew whom you'd run into.

I wondered why I could buy cigarettes at the store with a note from Mom but could not buy sulfur and zinc to save the world from communism.But then Bob discovered while thumbing through his latest *Boy's Life* magazine an ad for a rocket kit, complete with fuel. Pooling our money we ordered one, and soon after delivery at Bob's house we had the rocket parts laid before us, we especially eyed the fuel packs: there were three in all, 5" long and 1" wide round cylinders with a nozzle on one end where the thrust was created, and inside was the sulfur and zinc fuel mixture (so said the instructions). At the other end of the cylinder was a separate cache of powder, apart from the main fuel; in the Boy's Life rocket this small cache pushed out a parachute that was stuffed into the upper body of the rocket between the fuel and nose cone, igniting after the main fuel was expended. The parachute would pop out at the top of the rocket's trajectory and float the rocket gently back to earth, the whole system intact, ready to be launched again with a new fuel pack.

But we had our own ideas. Furthermore, passing the *Boy's Life* rocket off as our own was foolish since Dave and his buddies would certainly catch our fraud in short order.

Using the fuel pack as a basis for our design, we soon began a series of tests and experiments. We debated long and hard over what kind of creature we'd put into space: flies, beetles, caterpillars, worms. Talking about this at dinner one night, Dad suggested an earwig. "They're the toughest insect around," he said. "And small enough too." There were plenty in our flower garden to use for tests. I soon picked one and held it captive.

The capsule for the earwig came from Danny, who one day brought an oval plastic container—with a prize ring inside—from a gum machine, which twisted open in the middle and was the perfect circumference for our rocket body.Like NASA did for its own astronauts, we put our earwig through a strenuous training program, testing "G's"—how many increments of gravity it could take—by taping the capsule with the

　　　　　　　　　　　　　DREAM FAMILY ♦ A MEMOIR

earwig in it (there were tiny air holes we'd drilled) to the outer edge of brother Bill's turntable and running the earwig and capsule through 33 RPM's, 45, and 78 RPM's. Next we taped the capsule and earwig to a kite, flying it on a windy day until it was no more than a dot in the sky, testing the earwig's acclimation to high altitude. Then using saran wrap and string we made our own parachute, attaching it to the capsule and tossing it out sister Ann's second story bedroom window onto our driveway, watching the parachute as it unfolded and billowed out in enough time to float the capsule the final few feet to the concrete. In case the parachute didn't open and the capsule fell directly from the sky, I threw the capsule on the ground, earwig inside, as hard as I could, winding up like Whitey Ford and giving it a hurl at point blank. Each time the earwig popped out the capsule and scurried around in circles, seemingly trying to catch its pincer tail, unfazed like Dad said it would be, alive and well.

Using cardboard tubing and balsa wood fins, Danny, Bob, and I fashioned a tall slender rocket very similar to the *Boy's Life* rocket, the plastic capsule fitting snugly on top and leaving enough room for stuffing the parachute and strings inside. We placed a tin foil gasket between the fuel pack and parachute to keep the saran wrap from melting, and along the outside rocket body we glued a narrow metal tube which fitted onto a three-foot vertical cable, part of our launch pad, helping to guide the rocket at takeoff.

Our first launch after school attracted a crowd of classmates, including Dave Hodges and his buddies, but the rocket didn't include the capsule and earwig—we were testing the rocket fuel, still an unknown at that time, and like NASA with its astronauts, we decided not to risk our precious earwig the first time out. We'd set up the launch on the baseball field at Adams School, and Bob, because he discovered the *Boy's Life* kit, and using a long stick fireplace match, lit the fuse. As the fuse burned and crept along towards the rocket we held our breaths, anticipating ignition and a slow takeoff into the skies. The fuse burned up inside the nozzle. Any second, we thought, any second. We waited. And waited. But the rocket stood there still as a telephone pole. After a minute we knew we had a dud. We tried again using another fuse, watched it burn into the nozzle, but still no liftoff. After several more attempts we realized the fuse wasn't' burning close enough to the fuel in the nozzle to set it off. So frustrated at that point, embarrassed in front of Hodges and his gang, who were laughing and snickering at us, and so determined to ignite the fuel, I remember grabbing the rocket in one hand and while looking straight into the nozzle, my face only inches away, I tried lighting it with the other hand. I dread the thought of what would have happened had it ignited.

"Nice going!" yelled Dave and his buddies, continuing to laugh. "At least ours went off!"

"Just wait and see," I said.

We'd failed miserably. An exploding rocket at liftoff would have been better than nothing at all. We packed our rocket and launch pad and walked home, dejected and humiliated, wondering why the rocket didn't work.

That night after dinner—it was springtime and there was plenty of daylight—I took the fuel pack to our garage and affixed it to a vise, placed a candle underneath it, and lit it. I wanted to know if the fuel pack worked. I figured if a fuse wouldn't ignite it, maybe a steady burning candle underneath the nozzle would, for sooner or later it would get hot enough to ignite the fuel. I watched as the candle's flame licked and flickered up into the nozzle, waiting patiently.

Rather than a loud crack or explosion like I expected, when the fuel pack ignited it sounded more like a swoosh that started slowly then suddenly shifted into high pitch and full throttle. I could see the red thrust from the nozzle. In an instant the garage filled with smoke, then as quickly as it started, it stopped, a moment passed, then a small puff came from the top of the pack, pushing out the imaginary parachute at the top of the rocket. All this happened in seconds.

"What was that?" said Mom, sticking her head out the window. She was doing dishes in the kitchen.

"I'm testing rocket fuel," I said with a cough, pointing to the fuel pack.

"You o.k.?"

"Yeah, no problem."

"What's with all the smoke?" Is there a fire?"

"No, no fire," I said as I glanced at the candle. "Definitely no fire."

"You shouldn't be doing that kind of stuff. You'll blow your finger off or something."

"Don't worry. I'll watch it. Promise."

I looked at the candle again. It had been wide and thick when I placed it beneath the nozzle, but it now had a gaping hole through the center where the thrust had burned through. It looked like a glazed donut. What I had just witnessed, the power of the thrust, would most certainly lift our rocket into the heavens.

For fear that Mom or one of the other parents would shut us down, things got very secretive from then on. Plus we needed to keep Dave Hodges and his buddies in the dark, especially about putting a live creature into space.

I reported to Bob and Danny the results of my test, and soon we modified the nozzle/fuse system to make certain the fuse burned completely to the fuel to ignite it. Within the week the rocket was finished, the launch pad ready, the earwig and capsule trained and set. We were ready to go again.

The morning we brought our rocket in word spread quickly throughout the school. It was a warm Spring day, partially cloudy, no wind. We kept the rocket in a shoebox, keeping secret our earwig and flight plan, but hinting a surprise was in store. Dave Hodges, now working on a new rocket, snickered at morning recess: "Won't get off the ground."

On the playground at lunchtime we set up the launch pad and rocket. Mr. Smith kept an eagle eye on our proceedings, keeping the other students at safe distance; he seemed as excited as everyone else—was he taking pride that his students, not some other teacher's students, were launching a rocket?

A gasp rippled through the gathering crowd when we pulled the capsule and parachute from the shoebox and placed them atop the rocket.

"There's an earwig in there," we proudly announced, producing another gasp.

"I'll believe it when I see it," Dave Hodges cried.

The fuse was carefully laid on the ground. Bob nodded at Danny and me, then lit the fuse.

In truth, the three of us had little idea what was going to happen. Our worst fear would be a repeat of last time with the fuel failing to ignite. In my imagination I saw the rocket lifting slowly off the pad like those Atlas 5's from Cape Canaveral, almost lingering in the beginning, inching up and up, gaining momentum and speed, moving faster and faster until the rocket was a speeding fireball in the sky.

When our rocket ignited it made the same swoosh sound I remember from the garage experiment. There was the familiar sulfur smell. I saw a quick flash of red from the nozzle and a puff of smoke. And then the rocket did something I didn't expect—it disappeared from the launch pad. An inch after liftoff it must have been hitting 100mph, or so it seemed, for it was like a bullet shot from a Winchester 30/40. There was no languid liftoff. Quickly adjusting our line of sight, we watched the tiny rocket as it rapidly climbed into the sky, shooting up and up and up, getting smaller and smaller, until...until... it vanished into nothingness!

For a moment we stood there in silence looking skyward, and it crossed my mind we'd grossly underestimated the power of the fuel. Only the launch pad remained as a material witness to what we'd done. But where was the rocket? Was it so powerful we'd actually put it in orbit? And what about our earwig? How was it faring? Had the shock of the thrust killed it, or the lack of oxygen at high altitudes? And if the rocket hadn't gone into orbit, where was it, and where would it come down?

We held our breaths.

A murmur ran through the crowd. "Where is it?" someone said.

In vain we searched the sky for a sign. If someone had driven by the playground they'd have thought we were witnessing the Second Coming. The seconds ticked on but it seemed like minutes, hours. There was no trace of our rocket.

On a run Danny took off downfield, quickly hitting full stride like a cheetah on the chase.

"There it is!" he yelled, pointing upwards, "there it is!"

Like a herd of Wildebeests we took off after him at full gait, mirroring Danny's every step while glancing upwards. It soon came into full view, and we could clearly see the capsule dangling by the strings below the parachute, rocking back and forth like a pendulum on a clock, floating. There was a gust of wind as we got closer, but Danny was fast. When the parachute and capsule were to hit ground, Danny arrived with outstretched arms to gather them in like a baby, his timing divine. Pulling up and crowding around him, the rest of us pressed in and stretched our necks to see.

"Open it!" someone cried.

Though everything had happened so fast and so differently from what I had imagined, thoughts of the earwig had never left my mind. The success of the launch depended on it living; a dead earwig would give Dave Hodges a thread of hope.

"Open it!" someone repeated. Danny fingered the capsule, twisting it apart. Cotton padding puffed out, and now Danny held the two halves of the capsule in each hand.

Dozens of us were bending over Danny like a giant football huddle, heads together, looking at the capsule, now split in two, looking for our earwig in the fluffed cotton that hopefully held it.

"Where is it?" someone said. "It's gone, disappeared!"

Then from beneath a tuft of cotton scrambled the earwig in a dart from here to there and then curling around as if trying to catch its pincer tail, by any measure the sign of an earwig as healthy as the day I caught it. Danny let it slip off the cotton to the ground where it continued darting about, unaware that it was the most famous earwig in the world. We put it in the shoebox.

By the end of day there wasn't a kid at Adams who hadn't heard of our feat. We were instant heroes. Mr. Smith cracked a rare grin. And any hopes Dave Hodges harbored of beating us in the space race evaporated that day. What could he do, launch a cat or a dog? He'd need a rocket the size of a Chevrolet! Days later he made overtures to join forces, suggesting building missiles to bomb the hoodlums from rival Francis Willard School. We declined. We were the good guys, Dave and his buddies the commies. We had no time for hoodlums.

Several weeks later at Washington Park at the baseball diamond we launched our most ambitious rocket, a two-stager that instead of the fuel pack pushing out the parachute with a tiny blast, it would ignite a second fuse and a second fuel pack that would launch a second stage. In theory it was the perfect idea.

When the rocket ignited and shot off the pad in a blur like our first rocket did, it rose a few feet then began twisting and spinning end over end. Then it shot horizontally and stuck into the chain-link backstop, its nosecone sticking out one side while the fins stuck out the other. Bill McCoy, one of the spectators, who lived near Washington Park and was a year older than me, ran over to pull it out.

"Get away!" we yelled. "There's a second stage!"

Undaunted, Bill reached for the rocket the moment the second stage fired.

It narrowly missed Bill's head and slammed into the dirt infield, skidding along and jumping around like a wounded robin.

"You idiot! You're lucky you're not dead right now!"

In a moment the rocket lay dead in pieces.

Bob, Danny, and I were furious. How could we fail after so much success? We took it out on Bill McCoy as if he were the one who caused the failure—how dare he try and touch our rocket! The rocket lay there smoldering—still, silent, broken. We gathered it up—both stages, the broken fins and nosecone, and put it in the shoebox. The smell of sulfur hung in the air.

One day around this same time our class was goofing around and not paying attention and Mr. Smith got mad and warned us that next year we'd be in junior high and we'd have a different teacher for each subject and they wouldn't care like he did if you succeeded or failed. And the classes would be harder. I'd never seen him so mad—his voice an octave higher and quivering, his face beet red, his eyes watery and bulging. We'd better get prepared now or we'd never catch up he said. By the end of his tirade we were sitting upright, quiet, stunned.

And so, our rocket lay in the shoebox until the end of days. We never went back to the drawing board, never built another rocket, never looked for another earwig to put into orbit. I think the whole business scared us after that, and with Mr. Smith's warning about junior high, our thoughts wandered into other areas.

It was time to move on: a 12-year-old doesn't articulate that so much as quietly slip into a new set of circumstances, unable to understand the deeper meaning of things. We loved launching rockets and later sentimentalized about it, but junior high was upon us with girls and model hot rods and basketball and pegged pants and hoods and rock 'n roll and strange science teachers. Our little earwig climbed back into the flower bed from where he came, into the dirt and root balls, indistinguishable from the other earwigs burrowing about. Someday in the near future he would die not far from the spot where I found him, his earwig travels on average covering no more than a few yards in a lifetime, but in his case he had traveled far and wide, the Marco Polo of his day, for he was the most extraordinary earwig that ever lived.

Looking back, I'm surprised at the hands-off role Mr. Smith and other teachers at Adams played while we launched our rockets. Always in the background but keeping an eagle eye on the proceedings, Mr. Smith never once said we couldn't launch our rockets or discouraged us because of the danger. Nowadays you could no more launch a rocket at school than invite a gang of drug dealers to first period band. It was different in those days. On the heels of national hand wringing over falling behind in the space race to the commies, it was all the rage to encourage science of all kinds, especially space aeronautics. NASA was started. Walt Disney's animated program on space travel was a hit. Everyone wanted to be an astronaut. No one worried about us losing fingers or getting blown up. And on the whole the teachers and parents left us alone to do our project and solve our problems. We preferred it that way, for we liked the camaraderie, the secrecy, the rivalry, the turn of events and surprises, the possession of special and prohibited knowledge, but most of all, we liked the fame. And beating the commies!

 13

Mom had $2.50 to her name when she arrived in Eugene the summer of 1940. That June she had graduated from Mitchell High School in Mitchell, South Dakota, a farming town of 10,000 tucked into the state's southeast corner. Mom's older sister Jean, who was living in Eugene at the time and newly married, had arranged for a married couple to drive Mom by car.

Her first trip outside the Midwest, Mom and the couple took turns at the wheel, driving through a Wyoming heat wave where to keep cool they taped newspapers over the windows except for long slits across the front and back. Mom saw the massive Mormon temple in Salt Lake City shimmering in the dark of a mid-summer night. Days later at dawn, after a night crossing of eastern Oregon's high desert plateau, they came upon the majestic Cascade Mountain range by way of the Willamette Pass. Mom remembers: "We had stopped at a scenic pull off...It was cool... Trees everywhere...Clear water...Lakes...It was absolutely gorgeous. After growing up back in South Dakota...I felt if there was a heaven on earth it had to be Oregon."

Mom lived with sister Jean and brother-in-law Buryl in a tiny upstairs apartment above the Rosebud Bakery on Broadway Street, between Willamette and Olive streets. Each payday the three of them would hop down the back stairway of the apartment and rush into the bakery "...and get these big pasteries. Bismarks we called them. Right out of the oven and we'd have 'em for breakfast". The delicious smells of the bakery, Mom said, "drove us crazy."

Soon Mom got a job ushering at the McDonald Theater, close to their apartment. The McDonald, along with the Rex and the Heileg, were the premier movie houses in Eugene. The pay covered her expenses, but no more. Weeks later Mom and other ushers noticed the Montgomery Ward store across the street expanding into the next two lots. "We just kept bugging them," Mom said, until "two of us got steady jobs out of it." For a while things went well until a business slump in the late Fall forced layoffs by Christmas. Mom kept her job. Then a rare ice storm hit, and Eugene, accustomed to mild rainy winters, lacked the equipment to cope with this sudden freeze. Mom said: "They called us and told us not to come to work. There wasn't any business. Nobody could get downtown. I thought, 'well I'm not going to sit around all day,' so I slipped and skidded down all that mess to the telephone company. I just walked in there and [Mrs. Brown, the personnel manager] looked up and she said 'what are you doing out on a day like this?' It was dangerous. People were out cutting the trees down to prevent accidents." Mom had heard the telephone company was a good place to work. Though she didn't get a job that day, she kept pestering Mrs. Brown like she had done with the Montgomery Ward personnel manager. Two weeks later she was hired as a telephone operator.

Years later, when Mom and Mrs. Brown had become good friends, they were chatting in the company lounge when Mrs. Brown told Mom that "the best workers [I] hired from those years were girls that came from the Plains states. You could depend on them." Then she added:

"Besides, I just got tired seeing your face walking in that office." Mom worked at the telephone company until the war ended five years later when an automatic operator system replaced the manual operators.

Mom went to Eugene under mixed blessings from her mother, my Gramma White, a formidable woman not one to quibble or joke with. Short and stocky, dark keen eyes, abundant silver hair rolled in a bun, a square jaw that once set seemed immovable, Gramma White demanded respect from the outset.

As mentioned before, she would visit us during summers for a week or two, often preparing dinners for the family and teaching Bill and Ann and I how to play solitare. In those days she lived in Bismarck, North Dakota with Auntie Grayce's family. I remember her knitting afghans while rocking in the living room rocking chair, hour after hour, beginning with multi-colored yarns and her long shiny knitting needles looping and tucking and sliding with machinelike precision, magically turning the yarns into stacks and stacks of six inch square rainbows of color, then lacing the squares together one by one to fashion a luscious blanket that we could wrap around ourselves several times while getting lost inside. She made one for each of us children, mine woven in dark maroon accented with reds and whites, greens and blues. Fortunately, Mom put it in mothball storage, and now, some sixty years later, still smelling like mothballs, it is stored in our linen closet in a zippered plastic box looking as new as the day it was finished.

Born in Nebraska, "She was brought up a lady", Mom said, "and she had a lot of—what we called later on—false pride. She was a very proud woman. She had such good morals, and she would settle for nothing less among us."

Gramma White married the Wyoming rancher Harry White and had five children: oldest son Bob born in 1912, daughter Grayce born in 1913, daughter Jean born in 1918, Mom born in 1922, and son Jim born in 1924.

Why Gramma White, with her education and common sense and high morals, married and had children with Harry White is a mystery. In Omaha, where she was brought up one of four daughters, her father and mother owned a neighborhood grocery store, but sometime during Gramma White's childhood her father fell ill and became an invalid.

Gramma White's mother (my Great Gramma Howell) knew that since the other three girls were already married, it was up to Gramma White to get an education in case she had to take care of her father. She was sent to business school. "She was a legal secretary when she met and married my dad," Mom said. "She was educated."

They met through a cousin of hers. Mom said "she was a city girl and she married this cowboy rancher, and went from a city girl out to the bare necessities." They began homesteading outside Lusk, Wyoming, near the intersection of Wyoming, Nebraska, and South Dakota. This was around 1910. Harry White's mother, two brothers, a sister and their spouses homesteaded nearby. "They had been farm people all their lives," Mom said, "and they made fun of her." When Gramma White put pillowcases on the pillows and curtains on the windows, her in-laws wondered aloud when she was going to have time to clean them. It meant more work on a scrub board, more work on top of work already needed to be done, but Gramma White paid her in-laws scant attention. "That's just a part of her she had to do," Mom said.

They raised chickens and cows. Each week Harry White took eggs and milk to Lusk to sell. When a blizzard came and he didn't make it back to the farm, Gramma White found herself alone for the first time. As the blizzard raged on, debris flying here and there, one of the riding horses broke out of the corral and bolted for the house.

"All of a sudden the horse was on the front porch trying to get mother's attention, "Mom said. "Following her from window to window to window. She'd get out there and try to shoo it away with a broom. It just stayed around the house until dad finally came home and took care of it. Just scared her to death. She didn't know horses seek out humans when they're sick."

Another time while Harry was in Lusk, Gramma White heard noises in the chicken coop after the chickens had roosted. She wasn't sure what was out there—probably coyote or wolf—but she was bound and determined to protect her chickens. A shotgun rested inside the front door of the house. "Mother never had one in their home [in Omaha]. She didn't know how to shoot it," Mom said, "but she couldn't stand the thought of something getting at her chickens."

I picture Gramma White grabbing the paper wrapped shotgun shells and wondering what end goes in first, breaking open the 12 gague double barreled shotgun like she'd seen her husband do, dropping the shells into the breach, her hands shaking, next snapping close the shotgun with a crack. Now she's running out the front door across the tiny porch, stepping down onto the dirt and taking aim over the top of the coop just 20 yards to the left, adjacent to the corral, cocking one of the two rabbit ear hammers and pulling the forward trigger. Like a fury the thunderous report echos throughout the countryside. I see Gramma White jerked from the recoil, her 5'4" 98 lbs. frame flung backwards in a split second blur. There is pandemonium in the chicken coop. Whatever was stirring up the chickens has quickly and quietly crept back into the night from where it came, perhaps with bounty hanging from its mouth. If Gramma White has fallen from the recoil of the shotgun, I see her getting up, brushing herself off like a lady, then cocking the second rabbit ear hammer and pulling the rear trigger, letting off the second round as a warning. Shortly, when the noise dies down in the coop, Gramma White fetches a lantern and takes a careful look around, but the chickens are too testy for her to count. She sees bloody feathers on the floor of the coop. She runs back to the house and bolts the door, wondering why on earth she ever came to a place like Wyoming.

Years later on July 20th, 1922, on a farm a few miles outside Mitchell, South Dakota, Mom was born on a kitchen table. Soon afterwards, the family, now six strong, moved to Mitchell, ending over a decade of farming that extended from Lusk, Wyoming to the Dakotas. In 1924 Mom's youngest brother Jim was born, the only one of the five siblings born in a hospital, and the last child Gramma and Harry White would have together.

Mom's earliest memories are of the family's house on South Duff Street, in Mitchell: "...I think I was three or four when we moved there. I started the first grade there. It was a brown shingled house in a fairly nice neighborhood. Gramma Howell, our mother's mother, lived with us. There were two large bedrooms. Two double beds in the back bedroom. My grandmother and I slept in one and Grayce and Jean slept in the other bed. And my brother slept in a little partitioned room off the front of the house, on a cot. That's Bob, the oldest. And Jim slept in a crib with my parents [in the other bedroom]. It was a one-story house with a basement. The furnace and laundry were downstairs. [The furnace was fired with] coal, black shiny coal. It was brought in and dumped. You had large trap doors in the foundation of the house, and they would back the truck up and dump the coal in. Great big hunks. Oh yes, in the winter it was very cold, but we were always warm."

Mom started school at Eugene Field Grade School under her first grade teacher Mrs. Graves, and recalls the new single storied red brick school as a short walk from her Duff street house and nearby Dakota Wesleyan University. In the third grade the family moved across town to an apartment, and Mom changed to Lincoln Grade School where she met classmate George McGovern, whom she'd go through high school with and later become U.S. Senator and candidate for President. On a swing through Eugene during his 1972 presidential race, Mom and I attended a speech George made at a local church. At the reception Mom shook George's hand and introduced herself as the former Gayle White from Mitchell, and added: "We went to school together, remember?" George's eyes lit up, and he said, "Of course I remember, Gayle." They exchanged pleasantries, and George added "Please write me a letter." Later Dad teased Mom that George didn't recognize Mom anymore than he recognized the town he was in.

Mom was age eight when her dad turned the world upside down. "He had a young girl friend just a couple years older than Grayce. And he was trying to break up with her. We lived in a one bedroom apartment then. Bob had left home. But six of us lived in a one bedroom second story apartment. And she came in the middle of the night banging on the door. Woke us all up. I can remember crying because my mother was upset. And my father was upset. Told my mother to go into the bedroom and he would handle it. I mean go back to bed. And I can remember seeing him dress in the shadows and leaving. A few days later I came home from school and there were suitcases out in the hallway in front of our door. And I went in and my mother was sitting in her rocking chair sewing and I asked her whose suitcases those were. That's when she told me our dad was moving out. She had had it. She just kicked him out."

"My dad was just no good," Mom said. "He gambled a lot. He gambled mother's egg money, and many times come home empty handed from town. [Older brother Bob] was kicked off the [baseball] team when the coach found out dad had bet against our high school team. He liked wine, women, and song. That old phrase. That was my dad. He liked wild horses and when he was on the farm he was a wild, wild young man and he never quit."

Harry White's carousing and fast life was no secret in small Mitchell, where people gossiped and passed judgement. "I was never ashamed of my mother," Mom said. "I was just ashamed of the things my dad did that everybody else knew." They didn't divorce. "[It] was a sin in those days. You stayed together whatever."

A "legal separation maintenance" agreement was drawn up between the two with the children staying with Gramma White. Harry White continued gambling and carousing around town, frittering away money he should have given in support, and years later a divorce was finally decreed.

In retrospect Mom sees the damage to the family. "The circumstances leading up to their separation gave us an inferiority complex." But, Mom continues, "The one thing I will always say is every one of us had a sense of humor, and still do. And I think that's what got us through so much. We were never competitive or jealous. We were always so without that anything good that happened to one or the other, we were always happy for that one. I didn't realize [until later] there is a lot of competition and a lot of little jealousies among families."

The Depression hit South Dakota at the same time Harry White left the family. It was particularly hard because "...they [South Dakota] had...seven years of drought...very few crops...everybody was having a hard time." Mom said in those years many Iowans and Dakotans migrated West to Oregon and California. The White family stuck it out in Mitchell. Since everybody was struggling, "...nobody felt they were poorer than anybody else." Gramma White got work with the WPA. It was left to the kids to keep the house clean. By then oldest sister Grayce was working at the dime store helping to support the family. "I adored her," Mom said. "She was nine years older than me...she was so good

to us. And I'd a done anything for her. I think she just felt sorry for us."
The house chores fell to Mom and Jean, and they fought over who was
supposed to do what jobs. "We stuck up for each other...it was just when
we were alone and she tried to boss me around and...I rebelled then. She
tried to beat me up and I'd run and hide and tried to get out of what I
was supposed to do."

In junior high and high school Mom played basketball, field hockey,
volleyball, and swam. And "...baseball in the summer...we were divided
by ages...and we used to play little outlying towns." By the time she
was a senior she was president of Mitchell High's GAA—Girls Athletic
Association. "I loved anything that had to do with outdoor sports. And I
had been a girl scout—camping out and stuff like that."

Her favorite subjects were English and music. "I had an excellent
English teacher. Sentence structure, grammar, literature. Except I
realized later we got very little in classic literature. I loved music. Sang
in the choir. Some training in identifying classical music. I wished we
would have had more. At the time we thought 'oh boring', it didn't sound
good."

In the late thirties the girls wore saddle shoes, bobby socks, plaid
skirts and sweaters. They wore their hair in a pageboy. "Pageboy is when
[the hair] turns under. If you could afford it you could have a permanent,
and you just brush it back. You didn't set it up in curlers," Mom said. I
have a black and white photo of Mom in high school, taken outdoors,
perhaps on an athletic field. She's dressed and looking exactly like she
described, with her brunette pageboy and dark eyes and long slender
figure, smiling broadly, resembling like a twin my sister Ann at that age.

By high school there were three of them left at home: Mom, younger
brother Jim, and Gramma White. Oldest brother Bob left the day he
graduated from high school and little was ever heard from him. He had
a sixteen-year baseball career in the minor leagues. Grayce married and
moved to Bismarck, North Dakota to live with her new husband Bert
Olsen. Jean was in Oregon.

Mom did her studies, played sports, went to dances at the Corn
Palace, and worked part time. Roosevelt's New Deal afforded Gramma
White work on the WPA. "She got a job for $15 a week. That was good.

　　　　　　　　　　　　　　　　DREAM FAMILY ♦ A MEMOIR

And the reason she got that is because she had her education, and she was made supervisor of one of the sewing rooms. The sewing rooms made clothing for the poor people, dresses for women, and shirts and pants for the men working on the CCC. They made baby clothes. It was her job to keep track of every yard of material, every inch of thread that came into that sewing room. How much was produced and everything. She worked six days a week for $15. You had to be destitute to get on it. If one of us got a job and were earning money, that was deducted from [mother's pay]. I did usher at the [Roxy] theater and ran the popcorn machine...one summer...and kind of cheated and didn't declare it. I got 25¢ an hour. But Mother was always leery...she didn't want to cheat, so she didn't encourage it. But I wanted to work so I could have extra money...[because Mother] just didn't have much to give us for spending money for fun."

This "cheating" can be rationalized—the Depression, the single parent household, the dismal pay. But for Gramma White and Mom these small acts of desperation were never forgotten. It was wrong in their eyes, a shame. The lesson was to work and make the money honestly. Shake poverty. Don't let it happen again. No one is going to do it for you. These people from Dakota were hardy and independent people yearning for a better way of life. By hook or crook they were going to make it.

Mom left for Eugene after a short visit with her sister Grayce in Bismarck, North Dakota, before summer's end after graduating from high school.

14

I WAS A star by my ninth-grade year at Wilson Junior High, a legend in my own mind. I was the Student Body Vice President, played on the soccer, volleyball, basketball, and baseball teams, planned dances and presided over student government meetings, played judge in a mock court room battle, talked to underclassmen about their futures, played first chair cornet in the school band, and won the outstanding overall student award. I had the world by the tail. Or so it seemed.

Wilson was so decrepit that we claimed it was built by the ancient Greeks or some lost tribe of bricklayers. Before it was Wilson Junior High it was Eugene High where Dad and Auntie Nelda and Uncle Dan had graduated in the 1930's, and cousins Doris, Evelyn, and Paul in the late 1940's and early 1950s. Three stories tall and constructed almost entirely of bricks, its first story was half buried in the ground from the weight of the other two. Rows and rows of tall double hung windows wrapped around each level, and though the school looked from the outside to be heavy enough to sink the world, it was, because of these myriad windows that let in natural light in each classroom, airy and light from the inside. Except for the basement, or first floor, which was designed after a medieval dungeon.

Wilson was the first place I saw "hoods" up close, one guy in particular had a long drooping face, slicked back hair, wore a black leather jacket, drove a car to class, and, it was rumored, was on his third try at graduating. There were fights every week, usually after school in one of the nearby alleys off Lincoln Street, which ran along the west side of the school. News of upcoming fights reverberated throughout the school like a clarion bell, informing us who, where, when, and why. Within minutes after the final bell everybody would be gathered in a large circle in the alley watching two brutes go at it in the middle, sometimes it got ugly with bloody noses and lips, a black eye, but usually the fights ended as fast as they started, someone would land a good first punch and that was that, or a teacher would show and break it up.

My brother had warned me about Mr. Brooks, my seventh-grade social studies teacher. Like all other seventh graders, I was new to the school and going to different classes each hour and having personal lockers to store things in was pretty heady stuff. But if I was seeing junior high through rose colored glasses those first weeks, then it was Mr. Brooks who quickly changed that.

"He's a hogsbreath," Bill said. "And watch out for his 'perforated persuader'".

"What's that?"

"You'll find out."

He was tall and barrel-chested, styled his black hair in a crew cut, grew a thin black moustache, and wore black rimmed glasses. He walked with a swagger. In his off time he was a Pinkerton cop, and once John Hall and I and some other buddies saw him New Years Eve patrolling the Heileg Theater before the midnight showing of Around the World in Eighty Days. Decked out in dress blues, wearing a leather holster with a revolver tucked inside, he acted gruff like we'd better behave or he'd shoot us. We indulged him, made him feel the power he had over us, then, as he sauntered out of sight, we rolled our eyes and said "What a dickhead."

Brooks introduced us to grading on a "curve". After each test he'd write down everybody's score on the blackboard, the best at the top and worst at the bottom. No matter how good the class did as a whole, he'd divide the grades according to preset portions: 10% A's and F's, 20% B's and D's, and 40% C's. Even if everyone scored 80% or better, he'd apply his "curve".

"Too easy of a test," he'd say.

We'd squirm in our seats when he'd chalk in the borders between the scores, delineating the grades.

"Should it be 92% or 93% for an 'A'?" he'd say, roughing in a line between the two, then erasing it. He'd go through this process with each letter grade, going back and forth between scores, changing his mind a dozen times it seemed, talking out loud for all of us to hear. When he finished the class was a nervous wreck; it was like watching a basketball game with three overtimes.

"He's a secret Nazi," someone said. "Remember when you brought that flag to school with the giant swastika on it, Keefe?" Ray Jackson, a family friend who captured a German flag while fighting in the Battle of the Bulge, loaned it to me to show the class while we were studying World War II. A large red flag with a black swastika in the middle, it was impressive enough for Mr. Brooks to hang it in the hallway.

"Wally Stoneburg saw Brooks walk up to it and click his heels."

"No shit?"

"No shit."

One day Mr. Brooks caught me talking to someone when I should have been reading.

"Keefe, come with me."

As I headed for the door I saw him pull something out of his desk drawer and hold it along his leg so I couldn't see it. I followed him down the hallway into a little room, almost a closet I remember, where he closed the door behind us.

"You don't know when to shut up, do you Keefe?"

"No sir, I guess not."

"When I want it quiet in class, I mean it."

"Yes sir."

"Do you know what this is?"

Mr. Brooks pulled out and revealed to me what he'd been hiding behind his leg: a two foot long and a half inch thick piece of solid oak. On one end was a narrow handle with carved finger grips, on the other a wide flat area drilled full of beveled holes.

"I think I do," I gulped.

"Good," Mr. Brooks said. "For your information, this is called a 'Perforated Persuader'. These holes leave nasty welts."

I nodded.

"If I catch you talking again, you'll be wearing this on your backside. Understand?"

"Yes sir."

"Good. Now get back to class."

From then on I kept my mouth shut.

I loved playing sports and looked forward to playing on organized teams in junior high, but the teams at Wilson were pathetic year in and year out. As perennial losers, the other junior highs—Roosevelt, Spencer's Butte, Jefferson, Cal Young—always counted on us for a win in any sport. But in the Fall of my ninth-grade year, after losing our first soccer game against Jefferson, we went on a winning spree that brought us first place. I was the top scorer, never failing to make a goal in each game, and at the end of the season our school newspaper, *The Wilsonian*, under the broad heading "Wilson Claims Soccer Crown", proclaimed:

Keefe Paves Way to City Championship

The Wilson Knights, after losing their first game to the Jefferson Jays, came back and won the remaining five and came out ahead of defending soccer champions Cal Young Pioneers (the Knights were 5-1, while the Pioneers were 4-1-1) to take the unofficial city championship.

 DREAM FAMILY ♦ A MEMOIR

The Knights may have set some school records, but it is not known for sure. The questionables are the total amount of points for the team (24) and the total amount of points by one player (Jerry Keefe, 14). At any rate, Wilson won and that's all that really counts.

Catching wind of the article, Uncle Buryl began calling me "Paves—the—way" at Thanksgiving and Christmas dinners. Why we won all those games I don't know, we neither played much soccer during the off season to get a jump on the other schools, nor did we have a store of great athletes. I attribute my goals to the fluke of being left footed, thus fooling our opponents who thought I was going to make that last kick with the other foot. But ever since that soccer season I've been fascinated by teams who win when they shouldn't. How does it happen? How can a team faced with incredible odds beat a superior opponent? And it happens all the time—they're called "upsets," "miracles"—and when I see them on T.V. or live, and it could be soccer or basketball or ski jumping for that matter, I get a knot in my throat and my eyes tear up.

There was one personal incident, however, that marred that near perfect soccer season and led to a dark period in my life. It began during our winning streak in a game against Roosevelt at Washington Park. One of Roosevelt's players kicked the ball out of bounds, and since I was nearby, I saw exactly where it rolled out. But the referee Mr. Jackson—our 9th grade Science teacher—wrongly placed the ball in favor of Roosevelt for our team's inbound play.

"It should be right there!" I yelled to Mr. Jackson, pointing to the precise spot on the sidelines where the ball rolled out of bounds.

"No, it's right here," he said, placing the ball a yard or so further downfield, making it an advantage for Roosevelt.

I couldn't believe Mr. Jackson could be so blind. Hadn't he been standing next to me watching the ball roll out of bounds too?

I continued protesting after our inbounds play, making a pest of myself over the next few minutes. We went on to win the game, but afterwards someone told me he overheard Mr. Jackson saying that "Keefe's a baby". It stung. Had I acted badly? In the heat of battle should

I have kept my mouth shut and played on? Did the placement of the ball make that much difference? As one of my favorite teachers I liked Mr. Jackson for his sense of humor and his uncanny ability to make science interesting. But the truth of the matter was he didn't place the ball where it went out of bounds!

The more I rolled it over in my mind the worse I felt. I was a student body officer and soccer player, fans were watching from both sides of the field, and there I was acting...what?...like a jerk?

What I knew was coming but couldn't face was this: the next day, at third period science, I'd have to walk into Mr. Jackson's class and act as if nothing had happened. I found this impossible to imagine. I simply couldn't do it. If my actions were wrong, then I should go up to Mr. Jackson and admit it. But I didn't have the guts. Furthermore, I wasn't convinced I was a "baby". Maybe my actions were wrong, but I knew I was right about where the ball rolled out. That night, tossing and turning in my bed, and sweating as if from a mysterious fever, I devised a plan.

My second period class was gym. The boy's locker room was located in the bowels of the school below the gym, and the gym itself, with an elevated stage on the south side, doubled as an auditorium for plays, concerts, and assemblies. Stairs from the boy's locker room wound up past the entrance to stage left. After gym class we'd file past there and out through the door to the gym, whereupon we'd continue to our next class.

That next day I held back after gym class after everyone else had showered and filed upstairs through the gym. I then climbed the stairs and rather than going through the door to the gym I turned right onto the stage. Dark and enclosed, I found myself among thick green curtains and long ropes hanging from the high ceiling, all seeming to dissolve into a shadowy nothingness. Nearby was an electrical box with a row of red levers and switches. Immediately to the right was what appeared to be a closet with a flat top, sticking out from the wall and easy to climb on. No one could possibly see me there. I lay down and began counting the minutes, waiting for the next period buzzer to ring. Maybe by tomorrow, I thought, everything would blow over.

Time moved like molasses. I got restless. I jumped down from the closet and was about to slip behind one of the curtains when Mr. Owens, the vice principal, appeared out of nowhere, as surprised seeing me as I was seeing him.

"What are you doing here?"

We were well acquainted with each other through student council and other activities. He wrinkled his face.

"Well, I...I..." I couldn't lie, or more accurately, I couldn't think fast enough to make something plausible up. In a moment my defenses broke and I blurted the truth:"...it's about the game yesterday..." Over the next few minutes I told Mr. Owens the whole story.

Somberly we walked to the school office. I saw my whole world crashing down: I'd get kicked off the soccer team, impeached from office, disgraced and humiliated in the eyes of my peers and family.

The story was told again to the principal Mr. William Williams in his office. Next to Mr. Owens, a tall plodding man destined to be a career vice-principal, Mr. Williams was a young up-and-comer, smart, savvy, immaculately dressed and groomed. Some hushed discussion took place between Mr. Williams and Mr. Owens. Then I was excused to my next class. A couple of periods later it was lunch and I told John Hall I was getting kicked out of office. Later that afternoon I was called back to the office. I remember Mom being there, along with Mr. Williams and Mr. Owens, but she doesn't recall it. An agreement had been struck, a wink among the old boys club, except this was the old parents club. All would be brushed under the carpet if I'd apologize to Mr. Jackson during his free period the next day.

"Yes sir."

The following day Mr. Jackson was alone in his classroom, sitting at his desk next to one of the big windows, when I walked in. He stood when he saw me.

"I'm here about yesterday," I said, voice trembling. "The game I mean. I'm sorry. I was really a jerk."

"I know." Mr. Jackson smiled.

"I don't know what got into me."

"It was a tough game," he said.

"Yea, I thought we were going to lose."

"You know Keefe, sometimes in the heat of battle things happen. A bad call, a flubbed shot, a teammate screws up. Little things build up and the next thing you know you pop a cork and the ref kicks your butt out of the game. What good are you to the team then?"

"Well, not much."

"Not much at all, really. Think about it. You let the team down, not just yourself."

"Yeah, I guess."

"Look, Keefe. It takes a lot of courage to come here and tell me man to man you acted like a jerk. Not every kid would admit it. You did. Now shake it off and go win the next game. You guys are playing pretty well."

"Thanks Mr. Jackson."

He held out his hand and I shook it. When I left the room I felt a great weight lifting from my shoulders.

"What about you getting kicked out of office?" John Hall asked later.

"It's nothing. Forget it."

* * *

Before entering Wilson a classmate of mine at Adams Elementary played his clarinet for our sixth grade class. It reminded me of the boy who played the ukulele in third grade: he impressed everyone, including myself, and reignited my desire to play music. Early each morning before school he went to band practice at Wilson Junior High, and would anyone else be interested in joining him? I was, but the guitar wasn't one of the instruments; this band comprised flutes, tubas, French horns, bassoons. So which instrument to play? Dad played the French horn as a boy but said it was a difficult instrument to learn. Granpa had an old trumpet in the attic covered with dents and scratches, in need of valve oil and polish, but for me, a beginner, it was perfectly adequate. I soon began playing it, getting up early each morning to make the beginning band practices at Wilson, then catching the special school bus back to Adams to start the regular school day.

I played trumpet my sixth grade year and through junior high and one year of high school. It was in my ninth grade year at Wilson when

I was first chair first cornet that Uncle Dan, once an excellent cornetist himself, loaned me his King cornet (similar to the trumpet, same fingering). A rare and expensive instrument, it had a golden tone and a sterling silver bell, the best of its kind, and I certainly didn't deserve to play it. In those days you had to "earn" your instrument by achieving a degree of proficiency, but for some kind reason Uncle Dan saw fit to let me use his King.

To move up in our section we had "challenges." If the second chair cornet thought he was better than the first chair cornet, he could challenge him for his chair. An exercise was chosen by the director, and on the following Friday the two would go into the adjacent practice room behind the partially closed door and play the exercise for the entire band to hear, sometimes two or three times. Band members would vote on who played the exercise the best, with the winner either retaining his/her chair or moving up. I remember these challenges like upcoming games of soccer or basketball where you'd practice week long for an opponent, drilling over and over to achieve perfection, getting butterflies before tipoff, then diving in unblinking, hoping and praying for good bounces.

Ninth grade year Dan Larsen and I went head-to-head for first chair cornet. He was President and I was Vice President of the student body. So to me there was something more to this competition than music.

Our directors were men of great patience since they were dealing with beginner musicians playing loud blaring instruments. I remember two of them, though their names escape me, for both had a distinct way of slapping his baton against the music podium when he was mad. Our second-year director, who resembled Hitler with his shortened moustache and upright posture, was able to somehow slap the backside of the podium with such a snap that it sounded like someone being horse whipped. It got so quiet you could hear the ants scurrying beneath the old wood floors. Our first year director, a stooped old man with thinning hair, couldn't muster up the full fledge slap like our second-year director, his was a meek tap-tap-tap, and consequently much of that first year was wasted in the chaos of band members playing whatever they wanted to play while he absent mindedly tapped away. Having been in the business for years he should have known better (he helped conduct Granpa's

Eugene Community Orchestra). I remember him looking pathetic at the podium, his thin stringy hair askew, weakly tapping his baton while all came crashing down in chromatic clink and clang.

I would have been a better Student Body President than Dan Larsen. He won it on popularity because his brother was a popular president two years before. A nice guy, a gifted athlete, Dan was many things but he was not a leader, didn't speak well in crowds, embarrassed easily. So I subconsciously got back at this personal injustice through music, competing against Dan for first cornet to prove that in at least one thing I was tops.

By sophomore year of high school I was spending less and less time practicing; school politics and sports were taking over my extra time, and I began listening to The Beatles and Dylan. But there was one event that broke the camel's back regarding the cornet. That first term in high school I found myself dressed in a purple and white marching band uniform, complete with braids, epaulets, and military dress hat, marching in front of my friends at a home football game.

Afterwards one of them said "You look like a girl!" Bill gave me grief about it too: "Real manly, eh?"

I knew I was done with it, and for the rest of the year I went through the motions of playing and attending band classes knowing it was my swan song.

But it was those years of playing cornet in school bands, particularly at Wilson, that framed my overall appreciation for music. After playing dozens of pieces from Sousa to Stravinsky, I developed an ear for music and was able to discern the different parts and arrangements and tell what instrument was playing what part, even to anticipate transitions to the next movement. I didn't have a natural ear for music—perfect pitch or memory—yet I learned enough by sheer repetition that later it became easier and easier to learn new pieces. Dad was offered a music scholarship to the University of Oregon to play the French horn, Mom once said, but declined it, choosing instead to join the Navy. He never played again, nor did he ever show much interest in music when I was growing up. Granpa, on the other hand, couldn't live a day without music, whether it was playing it or listening to it or reading about it. Bill and Ann liked Elvis too, and it was Bill who turned me on to Dylan and the Beatles.

Even today it is difficult for me to concentrate on anything if there is music playing, especially when there are lyrics, when my ear is drawn by the melody and words like the earth is to the sun. I have no control over it, so if I have something important to do I go to a quiet place. Later I combined what I learned playing the cornet with the excitement of what followed Elvis: the music of the 60's. I returned to the guitar and began playing pop and folk music. Friends took up guitar too and we formed bands hoping to be the next Beatles or Rolling Stones. These days some of these same friends get together a few times each year and play the same songs we played 50 years ago. The wives sigh and go off to the movies.

* * *

I started getting acne at Wilson that by ninth grade year had turned into a full fledge plague that would last another decade, through high school, college, even through my stint in the army. My battle with it, which took many forms and resulted in tears far more times than I want to admit, left permanent scars. Eventually the nickname "craterface" was bandied about, but I never accepted it. Brother Bill, who could have devestated me with a variety of other nicknames too, must have been warned by Mom and Dad to lay off knowing how sensitive I was. (My nose, on the other hand, which was long and hooked like Granpa's, was open season for Bill. In the beginning he used many names, anything he could think of, but the one he finally settled on was "Beak," which was instantly picked up by John Hall and other friends and to this day I'm still occasionally called it.)

I spent a lot of time in front of mirrors assessing the ever increasing fire on my face, wondering how long it would last, wondering if everyone was as repulsed by it as I was, wondering "why me?" of all people, and secretly wishing I'd wake up the next morning cleared skinned via some great biblical miracle in my sleep.

Rather than make me less vain—after all, what was the use of trying to appear good looking?—the acne began an obsession with my appearance that continued long after it was gone. I became Michelangelo with Clearasil, a skin colored lotion made to mask the acne, dabbing and layering it with a cool steady and practiced hand. On bad days I caked it on. But far from relieving the acne, which it also purported to do, by end of the day upon washing my face the fire reappeared once again, reminding me that masks are temporary and what lies beneath is the real thing. As mentioned before, I tried a sunlamp, dangling it over my bed to burn the acne off, a flamethrower rooting out the enemy, and in desperation I'd lie under the lamp too long and emerge red faced except for around the eyes. In high school Mom took me to a dermatologist who said I could get rid of my acne if I'd cut my balls off. She wasn't amused but I secretly laughed.

I cut down on candy because the folklore at the time claimed candy caused acne. I used Sucryl, a liquid sugar substitute, on cereal and fruit. I avoided ice cream and pizza and cokes—all the things teenagers craved. Later I found out that I was producing certain oils more prodigiously than other people did and that someday my body chemistry would change and my acne would go away. Pizza only aggravated the problem. But this was small consolation for someone who wanted the problem over with now.

In spite of my craggy looking face, I had a girlfriend in the ninth grade: M. K., clear skinned, her brunette hair worn in a "bob", "stacked," (friends said she wore falsies); she had gone with an older guy the year before and jilted him, was thus rumored "experienced," and was stuck on me for what reasons I was oblivious. She'd call me on the phone which embarrassed me but tickled Mom and Dad for they'd never heard of a girl calling a boy.

Of course I took advantage of the situation. Having "made out" with Vickie Thorkelson for the first time the previous summer, I had a vague idea how to "get a piece," and the peer pressure was such that everyone was getting a piece but me, so it seemed.

One Sunday afternoon after a rendezvous with M. K. at Washington Park, Fred Beckley, brother Bill's friend who lived across the street from the park, let us into his basement while his mom was gone. On a dilapidated couch M. K. and I laid together and in time she let me undo her bra.

When I arrived home later that day it was dusk and Sunday dinner was soon served and not only were Gramma and Granpa at the table but also cousin Jimmy from Northwest Christian College across town. He was older than I was by five or six years and studying for the ministry. Gracious and humorous, he was one of my favorite cousins. He asked me how things were going, what I was up to.

"Oh, just the usual," I answered, "studying hard and playing sports." At the same instant M. K. flashed across my mind laying beside me on Fred Beckley's basement couch, my hand up her sweater.

"Got any girlfriends yet?"

"Oh no, not really," I gulped. "No time for that stuff, you know." A ton of guilt grabbed me then and pinned me down in the presence of Jim the Good, representative of The Lord, his eyes holding mine; I was fibbing while thinking how hard it was undoing M. K.'s bra. I knew I was going to Hell.

* * *

My best friend was John Hall, and though we didn't know it at the time, we would become lifelong friends. In 1995, thirty-five years after we met, we drove to Pasadena, California to watch our beloved Oregon Ducks play in the Rose Bowl (the last time they played there was 1958). The trip entailed eighteen hours of driving each way, and in those long hours we remembered many things, among them watching the Ducks play football on Hayward field when we were in grade school and junior high, paying 50¢ admission to watch from the end-zone with the "Knothole Gang" before the team moved to the new Autzen stadium in 1967.

On our trip we discussed our first encounter which John doesn't recall but for me remains as vivid as yesterday. In sixth grade I attended Adams Elementary and John attended Francis Willard Elementary. That year a monthly dance was held at Washington Park for sixth graders in the neighborhood, and those who came were from one or the other grade school. We did the Twist and the Hop, played shuffleboard and drank cream sodas, the music coming over a loudspeaker from a 45 RPM record player inside the rec. office.

We were shy to ask girls to dance—especially to slow tunes—so we brought attention to ourselves via the shuffleboard and bravado talk in front of the girls. In this atmosphere a rivalry between Adams and Francis Willard began, and soon emerged a gang from Francis Willard called the Rebels whose members turned up at the dances wearing baggy olive drab sweatshirts emblazoned with mustard colored "Rebel" across the front and back, pegged Levi's tight around the ankles, and hair styled a la Elvis. John Wise was their leader, John Hall one of his foot soldiers. Before long Dave Hodges and I were face to face with them at one of the dances.

"Your school's shit," John Wise said, locking into Dave's eyes while jawing a wad of gum.

"So's yours," Hodges said, staring back.

"Whacha going to do about it?"

"Wouldn't have to be much."

The trash talk continued while John Hall and I were eyeball to eyeball sizing each other up, albeit with a trace of fear in our eyes. We were not of the same temperament as Wise and Hodges. John's black rimmed glasses hung below his curly close-cropped hair, his lanky body topped by broad shoulders. He had huge hands that he cupped while he worked the saliva in his mouth. His eyes darted about for an opening, as did mine, and I suspected that neither of us wanted to punch it out over who went to the best school, a pretty stupid cause in any case. But invisible forces had put us face to face, as if we'd been dropped into a children's army, and though we couldn't articulate it at the time, pride and honor were at stake—in this audience we couldn't back out without losing face.

"I won't have any of that going on here," a voice rang out as she pushed us apart.

It was Marge Beal, the Park's Recreation Supervisor, a stocky matter-of-fact red head who Bill and I knew from previous summers at the Park. She had seen what was brewing from across the dance floor. "Go dance," she said.

After long menacing looks at each other we ambled off. "Later," John Wise said to Dave Hodges, meaning things weren't over.

Certain a rumble was in the making, I called Bill from the rec. office phone: "There's a bunch of guys called the Rebels from Francis Willard and they wanna fight after the dance."

With his learner's permit in hand Bill welcomed any chance to drive.

"I'll be there," he said. Playing God to a bunch of measly sixth graders was too good for him to pass up.

A palpable specter rose above the crowd when we filed out the door following the last dance. It seemed darker than it really was. John Wise and Dave Hodges were exchanging insults like heated alley cats. I didn't want to fight, but the momentum of the thing swept me up and there was no backing out.

At the same moment Bill pulled up in our '58 aqua green Plymouth and parked in full view under the streetlamp across the street, revving the engine once or twice in the process. Heads turned. He switched the engine off. Dad relaxed in the passenger seat. Bill emerged, a picture of insouciance, all eyes on him, now swaggering across the street to the crowd and eyeing the scene with a King's imperious demeanor. At age fifteen Bill was a head taller than the rest of us and big enough to take us all on single handedly.

"Who's that?" one of the Rebels asked.

"Keefe's brother."

"I'm outa here."

"Me too!"

In a moment they were gone, disappearing into the Park's darkness like the true cowards I later claimed they were. "Punks," I muttered to Bill, "Panty wastes of the first degree!" And among them John Hall. The specter above us dissipated in a blink.

In the Plymouth watching this scene unfold must have amused Dad, bringing back memories, for as the youngest of three brothers something similar had to have happened to him. He was taught by Granpa, and he in turn taught it to us, that brothers stick up for each other no matter what. This is what I banked on when I called Bill earlier in desperation.

Though he does recall the Washington Park dances that sixth-grade year and the Rebels and the Wise and Hodges rivalry, John doesn't remember this first meeting. He recalls meeting the following year in the seventh grade and gravitating to each other over the course of our junior high years when, by ninth grade year, our last at Wilson, we were both playing on the school's basketball team, chasing the same girls, attending the same parties, gambling together, and playing sandlot games at Washington Park on the weekends. With our backs leaning against the cyclone fence on the lower field at the Park, after a game of "down the line" baseball or football, we'd tell each other jokes, insult each other, drop a few "shits" and "damn" into our conversation. He was smart, athletic. I liked him because he laughed until he cried.

The house John lived in on College Hill was a cut above ours, a two story with a daylight basement and formal entry, large living and dining room off either side. John had his own bedroom upstairs, his older sister, whom I seldom saw, had one too, but by the time John reached high school she was off to college and rarely home. John's dad owned the Sleep-Aire mattress company franchise downtown, appearing on local T.V. commercials squeezing pieces of foam rubber and exclaiming "Foamy John Hall here...getta load of this baby..." It was John who said his dad drank a six pack of beer before going on the air live. John's mother did the books in the store, and in the summer John worked there doing odd jobs. I'd stop in and say 'Hi" when I was downtown and John was there. In the back was a veranda where John's mother worked at a desk and from where she could see everything happening below, where Foamy John worked the showroom floor.

Every summer John and his dad flew to San Francisco to see the Giants play. For a week they watched a home stand, staying in a hotel each night in that big city, eating out at restaurants, taking cabs. Flying to San Francisco and watching big league baseball was not so much a vacation to me as a dream—so foreign was it to our vacations and our way of thinking that I never gave it a second thought asking Dad about it. I envied John for it and was curious about all the details when he returned each summer.

John and I continued attending the same schools and buddying around until John's junior year at the University of Oregon, when he dropped out and went to Vietnam. He was a lost soul without a clue about what he wanted to do. In Army Transportation he made it through

　　　　　　　　　　　　　　　DREAM FAMILY ◆ A MEMOIR

his stint without incident and returned home to finish his degree in broadcasting using the G.I. Bill. In those years we never lost touch with each other, writing letters when both of us were in the army and connecting again when we both returned to Eugene. These days we go to Duck football games together, he's got the goods on everyone on the team, knows the history of the opposing teams, remembers heroic plays from years ago. "You could have caught that pass at Washington Park, John" I say when a Duck player drops an easy pass. "Yea, right," he says. It's all pandemonium with John when the Ducks make a touchdown and win, and we hug each other.

* * *

I remember with clarity my final day at Wilson Junior high. In the same gym that I had hid in earlier in the year, there was a year-end assembly where awards were presented for sports, scholarship, and citizenship. I thought I might win something, like the most valuable soccer player, but who really knew?—maybe I wouldn't be forgiven for skipping Mr. Jackson's class after all. As the awards were being given out to my friends I began to realize I was coming up empty handed, passed over, nothing coming my way though I had been on the honor roll, been a good Vice President, played first chair first cornet, scored more points than anyone else on the soccer and basketball teams, had been a model citizen since the Jackson affair. Finally, near the end of the ceremony they threw me a bone—I was named the most improved baseball player, a joke because in truth I was a lousy baseball player and played for lack of something else better to do in the Spring. I was feeling shortchanged when the final award—the American Legion Award for the outstanding overall male student—was announced by the Principal. It was sure to be Dan Larson, Mr. Clean Cut Model Student, our student body President, top athlete, trumpeter, honor roll, pleasant personality. He'd kept his nose clean. He didn't make waves. Who else could it possibly be? Mr. William Williams, the man who made me apologize to Mr. Jackson earlier in the year, announced the winner. I was dumbfounded when I walked up to the stage. Mr. Williams handed me the plaque and I muttered some incomprehensible thanks into the microphone to the students and teachers, hundreds of them, who were clapping and whooping it up in the audience. I was euphoric.

Afterwards a group of us walked to Seymour's Restaurant downtown for rootbeer floats, me laden with leftover notebooks and my cornet and case, my shirt wet with perspiration from the warm Spring day. It was a festive time among us, and I reveled in the attention, in the congratulations, being at the center of things. I couldn't wait to tell Mom and Dad. It made sense why I didn't win those other awards—the powers to be had to spread the wealth around! I couldn't win everything! I was full of myself. I felt fortunate, yes, but also, in a way, absolved. Did Jackson and Williams think I'd become more of a man because of the soccer incident? Maybe. I felt a mighty burden lift from my shoulders and I felt weightless in time, suspended in mid-air. To everything I was involved in there was closure—the studies, the music, the sports, and student government—and in spite of my worst fears, in spite of all the worrying I'd done about everything, everything had turned out fine after all.

Indeed I was a star, but soon enough, with high school around the corner, I found my good fortune short-lived.

15

I THINK OF Mom and Dad before they met that Fall evening in 1941, going about their lives unaware of the momentous event about to occur. Then they meet and though they can hardly put words to it, for it is one of the great mysteries of life, they fall in love. They can never shake or undo what they have begun, the die is cast, their separate dreams at night now overlap each other. They soon marry, have children together, move to a different town. They laugh and cry together. They drift apart, come together, drift apart. Over time they take new husbands and wives, drive different cars, wear new clothes. Nevertheless, and in spite of themselves, their lives are forever intertwined since that first meeting so many years before, like a double helix trailing off into a corner of the universe. These days I see in my mind's eye a tail of that helix, like the memory of an old trumpet or the smell of a favorite sweater, seemingly close at hand, always at a little different angle, always reminding me of Mom and Dad together so many years ago. Is it any irony that as time passes I can see these things with clearer eyes?

* * *

The sun eased down in the west as Betty Russell and her date Larry Scrogs and Dad sat talking on the steps of the boarding house on Pearl Street. Most likely sharing cigarettes among them, the bright porch light silhouetting their profiles, Dad had come to know Betty and Larry from his work with Larry at the local cannery. Betty and Mom shared a tiny room at the boarding house, where men were not allowed inside. A few moments later Mom appeared from around the corner, returning on foot from bowling with other friends that evening. She immediately took notice of the man with wavy red hair, blue eyes, broad shoulders. Introductions were made, conversation ensued, Mom discovering that Dad recently finished a four year stint in the Navy and planned to go to university winter term. He was 22, three years older than Mom. Dad's late model Chevy coupe, painted fire-engine red, which he had bought from his meager Navy savings, was parked on the nearby curb. Betty and Mom agreed to drive to the coast in it with Larry and Dad the following Sunday.

"He was mature, sincere" Mom said. "He'd been around and wasn't like those college boys at the university. I liked the way he carried himself. He had a good physique." They were soon dating.

Two months later the Japanese attacked Pearl Harbor. Dad figured that since he'd been a Chief Gunner's Mate on the USS Quincy, the Navy would soon be knocking on his door to re-enlist. Prior to Pearl Harbor Dad had told the family about the Quincy firing depth charges at German submarines in the Atlantic. To his 10-year-old cousin Doris, it sounded "really scary". In 1956 Dad took Bill and me to the movie "The Battle of the River Plate", about the scuttling of the German pocket battleship Graf Spee outside Montevideo harbor in December 1939. I believe it was the first movie I ever saw in a theater.

The Graf Spee had sunk nine Allied merchant ships and the British had tracked it to the River Plate, between Argentina and Uruguay, where it was damaged but found protection in the nearby neutral port of Montevideo. There, surrounded by overwhelming British warships, the captain scuttled his ship rather than risk the lives of his crew (three days later the captain committed suicide). In the movie I recall wide angled camera shots of open seas, a burning ship. Dad's interest in the movie stemmed from being in the same waters as the Graff Spee in those months when the Quincy was involved in "Neutrality Patrol" activities in the western Atlantic. From his experience and what he'd heard about what lay ahead, he believed the Navy was due for a rough haul in the coming war and was especially apprehensive of the Pacific theater, where the Japanese Navy was flexing its muscle and where the Quincy would surely go next. He'd done his stint in the Navy—four long years beginning after graduating from high school—and was eager to move on, get an education, and now, just as important, he'd found a woman he might be serious about: she was pretty, smart, energetic, down-to-earth.

Believing it a safer bet, Dad pre-empted the Navy by enrolling in the Coast Guard in March 1942, which was delighted to take Dad given his Navy experience. He reported for duty in Seattle; in June he was at "Patrol Chaser" school in Boston. By late summer he and Mom were engaged, and by Fall, a year after they'd met, he was at Alameda Coast Guard Station—Government Island—near San Francisco where he began making runs up and down the west coast and to the Aleutians.

As Dad feared, on August 9, 1942 the USS Quincy, Dad's old navy ship, on patrol in the channel between Florida Island and Savo Island during the invasion of Guadalcanal, took several direct hits from the Japanese fleet and sank, with "all her guns out of action" according to Navy reports. Many of the crewmen were lost overboard, several of them most likely mates Dad had previously shipped with.

On February 3, 1943, less than a year and a half after they met, in a small family ceremony at the Methodist parsonage in Eugene, Mom and Dad married. Dad was on short leave from the Coast Guard, and the next morning they drove to San Francisco where they soon found a small apartment in San Leandro, close to Government Island where Dad's ship was docked. Mom, working as a night operator for the Pacific Telephone Company, got a transfer from Eugene to the Oakland office, then later found work with the Caterpillar Tractor Company. In those first months Dad shipped out every other week, but in May 1944 he received top secret permanent orders to ship out, which meant a lengthy tour and open ended as far as where he was going and when he'd be back. Mom moved back to Eugene, returning to the telephone company, living with her mom for awhile, and with Gramma and Granpa, waiting out the war and getting power of attorney to buy the two-bedroom house on 20th street where we kids were later born.

Due to a deal struck between the U.S. and Russia for Russia declaring war on Japan, Dad didn't return home immediately after V-J Day like most of his shipmates but was ordered to train Russians in ship gunnery on cutters the U.S. was giving them, extending his tour two more months. Finally in late 1945, arriving at his new home in Eugene a year and a half after last seeing Mom, she stood before a man who in her eyes had somehow changed.

"He looked so relieved when he walked through the door," Mom said. "And he was so glad to have something to look forward to. He looked pale and thin." And speaking of the Russians he'd just trained, Dad confided to Mom: "They are the most rugged men I know. I hope we never have to fight [them]."

"Then the realization hit," Mom said. "After the war, where do we go from here? It was a scary time. Your Dad was very undecided about what he wanted to do. He was a little depressed. It broke my heart he wasn't out stomping the streets celebrating."

The new GI Bill made it possible for returning servicemen to afford a college education previously attainable only for the better off. Dad enrolled at the University of Oregon winter term 1946, the campus being a convenient walk from home. With his constant juggling of study, family obligations, and part time work, Dad nonetheless hit his stride at university, but not before struggling with several courses and the heedless younger students ignorant of what he and other GI's had gone through in the war.

In those same years Mom was as busy as Dad, giving birth to Bill, me, and Ann, nursing us, changing diapers, taking us to the doctor, teaching us to walk, night after night fretting over our health. Paradoxically Mom felt, as mentioned earlier, "Those years following the war were the best years ever. Everyone was in the same boat trying to get ahead."

Six years after his discharge, and now with three children, Dad had his degree in architecture.

Mom and Dad appeared to the outside world the perfect couple—affable, good looking, hard working. If there were differences, it was hard to tell. Furthermore, if there were problems you worked them out and stayed together, regardless of how severe they were, for that's how it was done in those days. By nature Mom and Dad kept check on their emotions, there were no smoldering passions or maddening jealousies or ostensible displays of adoration underlining their marriage, at least from what we children could see. In public they rarely kissed or held each other, even each other's hands. They seem to reserve their tender physical moments for us kids, for I remember sitting on laps, riding on shoulders, Dad washing my hair over the kitchen sink, his hands scrubbing my scalp until it was red. We kids got whatever emotional tidings left at the end of the day. As marriages often do when children arrive, Mom and Dad must have instinctively shifted into another gear, buckling in for the long haul, finding themselves in the midst of chaotic and hectic times, Dad establishing himself in a career, Mom keeping us kids from killing each other. Romance and passion, war and long absences, these were replaced by the monumental task of raising a family and getting ahead. It wasn't long before cracks began to appear.

I was age six or seven in Salem when I witnessed Mom and Dad argue for the first time. Like he did every Fall Dad was planning his deer hunting with friends, getting his gear ready, guns prepared, choosing a site, but this year for some reason Mom didn't want him to go. Did she fear him getting shot? Or getting lost in the woods? She was adamant he not go. It began in the living room after dinner and both were pacing back and forth making their points.

"I'm going to go!"

"No you're not!"

"Yes I am."

"Over my dead body."

Dad exploded, his face turning beet red, and taking a step forward he grabbed Mom—was it around the neck?—and held her close, face to face, bearing down on her, filling her view, and telling her he was going no matter what and no one, especially her, was going to tell him otherwise. Now diminished and shriveled, a powerless shrew under Dad's overbearing menace, Mom began sobbing, one heave after another, which I took for a sign of escape, it was no place for me, and without a glance backwards I ran from the room and scurried upstairs. Perhaps it's not a stretch to believe that in their red hot anger they forgot where they were and that a few feet away stood a wide eyed and puzzled kid. But it was the first time for me. I don't recall if Dad went hunting that year, but I suspect he did.

Later when we moved to Eugene from Salem they argued behind closed doors—was this because of what happened before?—and Mom explained them away as "discussions between adults". But we kids caught on and knew better. They took place in Mom and Dad's bedroom, their importance underscored by the announcement beforehand we were not to disturb them under any circumstance. Once they began, it seemed our ears were stuck on the bedroom door listening to their voices rise and fall in low murmurs until we suddenly heard the recognizable "no!" or "why not!" like a punch in the dark. Then quiet, as if they thought we were listening on the other side, and we would strain to hear more, seemingly pressing against the door but probably sitting on a nearby couch. For me it was high suspense—like waiting for the outcome of an Eisenhower/Khruschev summit meeting—wondering what the fuss was about, wondering if one of us kids was in big trouble, wondering if the world was coming to an end. It seemed the meetings went on for hours and the uncertainty almost cruel. "What's the problem!" I screamed in my head. Then finally Mom and Dad would emerge from the bedroom looking exhausted but relieved, as if a rock had been removed from a shoe, and I'd feel the yoke of anxiety lift from my shoulders, especially when Mom would say, "everything's o.k.", which she always said afterwards.

And what did they argue about? It was the usual stuff, for one, money, which Dad didn't have a head for and Mom did. Dad gave you his last dollar if you needed it, thinking nothing of it, Mom worried about it constantly, on daily watch for sales, paying monthly bills, buying groceries, budgeting Christmas, birthdays, vacations, school. Given her hard scrabble upbringing in South Dakota, it's no wonder she wanted more than just getting by, yearning for a piece of the good life promised in post war America: the beautiful house with the white picket fence, membership in the country club, college educated kids, a new car in the driveway. There's irony in this, because most of all, and no doubt by a long measure over everything else, she wanted something you couldn't touch or smell or hear, something that remained elusive and unreachable for her family back home in South Dakota: respect. Mom longed for that seal of approval, acceptance, esteem, that admiration she saw others have from their friends and family. Mom's most horrid dread was ending up like her father—impoverished and destitute, a source of shame and a blot on her name, on her past. She could barely utter his name without a hiss. So when things were tight and clients owed Dad money, it was Mom who cajoled him to make collection calls after the dinner dishes were cleared away, shaming him to dial each and every number, Dad detesting it each step of the way, each word of request as if he were a beggar. In these tight months we joked about eating hotdogs and oatmeal for dinner to make ends meet.

They fought over how to raise kids in general and in particular what to do about Bill, who from the beginning fought with Mom over the tiniest things. Both had low flashpoints and were capable of exploding into a vitriol usually reserved for jilted lovers. Flabbergasted by Bill's daily insubordination, Mom resorted to the "Wait 'till your Dad gets home from work" threat—"He'll straighten you out!" But when Dad got home and heard Mom's complaints, his reply usually went something like "He's just a boy growing up. Give him some rope." As the youngest of three boys himself Dad knew how boys were and knew what was important enough to make a fuss about. When Dad's reply didn't sit well with Mom, she'd throw up her hands and say "O.K, if you won't support me, then you raise the boys, I'll raise Ann," which never panned out because, after all, we were an interactive family living under the same roof eating the same food. So the fights continued and over time Mom and Bill grew to hate each other, her discipline becoming less and less effective with Bill, and Dad being the enforcer, well, he had little stomach for it since he'd seen his own dad manhandle his brothers and the adverse affect it had on their relationships later in life. He didn't want that with Bill. Mom's biggest weapon in her arsenal of discipline was shame—no surprise— since it was so closely tied to her upbringing, and she fell to using it on her children as easily as using ABC's. A few cutting words of shame was to immediately fall from grace, from favor, to feel guilt, humiliation. To right oneself from this was a great act of will. Were you up for it? Dad, less complex with these emotions, and perhaps influenced by his career in the armed services, focused more on what should be done, the task at hand, and rarely introduced embarrassment or chagrin into the mix.

They fought over their social life. Dad was a loner and preferred the company of his family, and though he liked his several business acquaintances and clients and often talked about them at dinnertime, there wasn't one of them he made a close friendship with. He had no boyhood friends he palled around with. He liked my friends, was friendly and frank with them, joked with them, and to this day they speak highly of him. He always seemed to be there in the moment, never aloof or irresponsible, never loud or boisterous. But underneath you got the feeling there was more to him, perhaps a force to be reckoned with.

Mom never met a person she didn't like unless they were full of themselves. She hosted monthly bridge matches with her golf cronies where in the days leading up she'd be in a flurry of house cleaning and dessert making. On party night Dad and us kids would go to a movie or visit Gramma and Granpa across the street, staying out of sight until the party broke up later. Mom loved parties, liked to dress up, like to drink, though not excessively, and liked to meet new people. But getting Dad out on the town was like pulling teeth. I think he had his fill of drinking and carousing around in the service, and in truth I don't remember them going out much to dinners or movies or parties, either by themselves or with other people. I can't recall a single babysitter.

Sometimes the cracks became crevices.

   DREAM FAMILY ♦ A MEMOIR

Once when I was in junior high Bill, who was then in high school, approached me in the kitchen one night.

"You're not going," he said.

"What?"

"You're not going, period."

"What do you mean?"

Bill was in his boss mode and thus not agreeable to a long cogent explanation, which would have been helpful, plus it was easy to see he wasn't taking no for an answer. He said this:

"Mom's leaving for North Dakota and thinks she's taking you and Ann with her. But you're not going."

"I don't get it."

"Mom and Dad had a big fight. She's going back to live with Gramma White and Auntie Grayce."

I couldn't fathom Mom leaving, it was a preposterous idea, and I couldn't imagine leaving school and my friends and family, disrupting everything I had come to know in Eugene. Furthermore I'd never been to North Dakota, it was a foreign country to me, and what was there to lure me other than Mom's family whom I hardly knew and didn't know if I would like. We'd moved around enough in my opinion and I was content to stay where I was. And lastly, was Mom really leaving? Or was it a bluff? If I refused to go then maybe she'd stay.

"Well I guess I'm not going," I said.

"Good. That settles that," Bill said.

Mom did go back to North Dakota once or twice in a huff, I don't recall if she went that particular time, but she would stay with Gramma White and Auntie Grayce, and we kids would remain in Eugene, never joining her. I guess sometimes the fabric of their marriage would tear to such a degree as to expose a higher level of fragility heretofore unknown to us kids. We'd be in shock for a few days. Mom would stay a week or two while behind the scenes she and Dad would somehow mend the fence—was it by long-distance phone?—and later Dad would make a small announcement that Mom was returning and all was well again, as if it ever was. I'd come home from school one day and she would be there in the kitchen busying herself as if she'd never left. For a few days there was tenseness in the air, everybody walked on eggshells trying to be nice, but over time things would gradually fold back to the way they were before she left. Nothing really changed.

It was a couple of years later when I was in high school that Mom suddenly rushed me off for a round of golf at a course on the McKenzie River, which was unusual. I wasn't sure why she was so adamant about leaving the house so quickly, or why I was suddenly her golf partner, but as we were going out the back door I saw Dad lying on his stomach in the backyard, his arms covering his head. I'd never seen him in that position before. I couldn't tell if he was crying or simply deep in thought. He didn't look up when we left.

Mom let me drive, I was age 16, had recently got my driver's license, and perhaps this was the hook that got me to go with her. I drove safely enough through Eugene and Springfield, Eugene's sister city opposite the Willamette River, and east of Springfield we headed up the highway that shadows the McKenzie River, a tributary of the Willamette. But soon Mom began complaining about Dad, his lack of money sense, his unwillingness to socialize outside the family, his stubbornness. Was I brought along less for the golf and more to hear her gripes about Dad? And why me? On and on she went, jumping from one topic to another, from one insult to another, while I concentrated keeping my eyes on the road, keeping the car on track. There was plenty to think about. But soon her tirade hit a critical mass and I began to tear up, the road now becoming blurry, and at one point I swerved across the center line then jerked the car back only to hit the gravel shoulder, kicking up dust. An oncoming car veered to give me a wide berth. After a couple of these abrupt swerves Mom had me pull over and from there she took over driving, not trusting me anymore. Today I wonder if these swerves were real or if I manufactured them to stop Mom from ranting on and on about Dad, since I recall she stopped complaining after that.

By the time we kids left home Mom and Dad had grown so far apart that it was as if they had begun walking the Grand Canyon together but ended up at opposite corners, unable to hear each other's voices let alone the beating of each other's hearts. What precipitated their divorce was Dad's alleged affair with a young apprentice working in his office.

                              DREAM FAMILY ♦ A MEMOIR

Through the years Dad often used architecture students from the U. of O. to help on big jobs, and I knew this woman, since years earlier we shared a study hall when I was a sophomore and she was a senior at South. The marriage unraveled quickly. At the time I was in Korea with the U.S. Army, Bill was living in California, Ann in Eugene. Ann, closest to events, remembers it as a dark period of relentless anguish and grief, and to this day is unable to shake the pain and bitterness of it.

When I returned home from the Army less than a year after the divorce, Dad was living alone in an apartment, the apprentice had left town, and Mom was on a rebound marriage and living in a mobile home park. The Monroe house had been sold.

In his earlier letter to me in Korea Dad explained very little about what happened, so during one of the first nights I was home we sat together in his apartment and talked. Yes, he admitted, he was smitten by the apprentice and the attention he received from her, but he claimed nothing improper happened. "But your mom went off the deep end about it," he said. She stalked Dad, pestered him, made outlandish claims about what was going on. I suspect Mom felt her worse nightmare of her father was now happening to her. "I cringed coming home at night to face her daily cross-examination. Finally I couldn't take it anymore and left."

After the divorce Mom found a new man and was married shortly before I returned from Korea.

In the same conversation that night Dad told me how Mom, in a fit of vindictiveness, told him she was having a sexual relationship with this man she was about to marry. As he explained this episode to me, of Mom being with another man in such a way, his voice cracked and he could barely get the words out. Then he brought his hands up to his face and began sobbing. I'd never seen him show such strong emotions for Mom. What did he feel? Was it that he felt he was Mom's one and only true love, that he was the alpha and omega in spite of the divorce and Mom's pending marriage? Oh sure, Mom might be close to someone later on, in a pro-forma sort of way, but never like she was with Dad. But it was his conceit. Now, realizing he wasn't her true love anymore, that he wasn't the center of her universe in any stretch of the imagination, and that there was someone else at the center of her life, he knew then he had lost something he thought he would always have, and had taken for granted.

A few days after this conversation I discovered Mom had secretly checked herself into Sacred Heart Hospital; she had kept quiet about a surgery she needed. Not sure what to do, I told Dad, who automatically picked up the phone and called the hospital. He wanted to know which room she was in and what kind of surgery she had had.

"What is your relation?" the receptionist asked.

"I'm her... ex-husband."

"Sorry, but you have to be family to get that information."

"But I was married to her for thirty years!"

"Sorry sir, but I can't..."

"That's a bunch of baloney!"

"I'm sorry sir... but..."

Dad slammed the phone down. A few moments later I followed up and found out her room number.

The surgery was a secret from her new husband too, who worked for the railroad and was out of town for a couple of days. Why Mom did this is still a mystery to me. So when Dad and I showed up in her room at the hospital later that day we were Mom's first visitors. She was sleeping, sedated from the operation. We found out she had a breast cancer removed. She must have sensed us standing there next to her bed, for she slowly opened her eyes and, though at first they had no focus, they soon followed a path to us. "Oh," she let out when she recognized us. Had we startled her? She certainly didn't expect us. I don't remember what happened next, but a few moments later I remember Mom rolling over on her side and covering her face with her hands and crying uncontrollably into them.

Mom was married barely a year to her second husband when she divorced him and, a few years later, married Lee Jeans, a childhood friend of Dad and his brothers. Lee, a retired navy man who worked for the state, often skippered Uncle Dan's charter boats in the summer when Uncle Dan needed help. With this marriage, Mom found herself in the fold of the Keefe family again, albeit in a fringe way. Her marriage to Lee, which lasted some twenty years into Mom's late 70's, had its own problems, and turned out more a marriage of convenience and security than of love. Once on a trip to Mexico with Uncle Dan and Auntie Arline, Mom was talking about Dad with Lee in earshot. She went on and on about how difficult Dad was to be married to, similar to what she had done with me on that trip up the McKenzie River years before. She had had a Martini or two and was pulling no punches. Finally Uncle Dan cut her off by shouting "You're still in love with the man!" Intended as a joke, an icy silence followed.

When Dad unexpectedly passed away in 1984, a private family viewing took place the night before his funeral. Mom went with Lee. It might have been awkward given that Mom was not officially family and Dad had been married to second wife Virginia for several years, but it didn't keep Mom from going. At the viewing Mom placed a single carnation in the corner of the casket, then bent over and kissed Dad on the cheek.

She explained to me later: "When we were first married and living in San Francisco, I was so amazed at all the flower ladies there. And your Dad would always buy me carnations from them, bring them home to me. I was just a hick from the sticks. I'd never been in such a big city and seen so many flowers and these ladies selling them. It kind of became our flower."

The next day at the funeral, following the eulogy given by my minister cousin Jim and anecdotes from friends and family about Dad, we had our final viewing before he was laid to rest. Family and friends filed slowly by Dad's open casket, all with teary eyes and lumpy throats, all looking for one last time. Like they were the previous night, Dad's hands were folded neatly in front of him, one over the other, but something was different from the night before. Between them was tucked Mom's carnation. Startled at seeing it there, Mom lingered over the casket, wondering how it got there.

16

FOR AS FAR back as I remember we picked beans, the season lasting from mid July until school started in early September, seven weeks of hard, dirty, exhausting, demeaning work. In fact, as I got older and finished college I ended up doing just about everything you could do to prepare beans for eating: stringing, picking, canning, boxing. But it was the picking I remember most, and I picked with Bill.

In the early sixties dozens of beanfields on the outskirts of Eugene—Cantrells, Frosts, Browns, Watson's—many located north off River Road, sent their decrepit yellow school buses out each morning on serpentine routes throughout the city to collect pickers, many of us young teenagers making money for the coming school year. The early morning sun would be poking its shiny head from behind the Cascade Mountain range as we waited on dozens of corners. We were sent—or more likely compelled—by frugal parents to make a few bucks to pay for new school clothes or supplies for the upcoming school year, or to help make ends meet for the family. I suspect too that Mom and Dad sent us to learn important lessons in hard work and responsibility: getting up on time and making the bus, picking the most pounds we could each day, staying out of trouble, working the whole season to get the half cent per pound bonus at the end. There was another lesson we learned too.

Bill and I picked at Frost's bean yard north of Eugene off River Road, halfway to Junction City. Our bus driver lived up the street from us on Monroe Street, a block from Uncle Ed and Aunt Alice's house, where at night he parked his bus and where Bill and I caught it every morning. We'd arrive just as he emerged from his house with his steaming cup of coffee steadied in one hand while his black lunch pail swung from the other. He was a good-natured man up in years—he seemed as old as Granpa—who wore mangled wire rimmed glasses and a frayed and sweat stained baseball cap that looked like he'd slept in it. Over the season Bill and his friends teased and goaded him unmercifully about a variety of things: his driving, his age, his hat, his absentmindedness. But it ran off him like water since he was a gem of a man who liked people in general and appeared to get a kick out of a busload of rowdy teenagers. He was an old crony of Mr. Frost's.

The bus pin-balled through south Eugene, first heading down Monroe Street to 18th, then turning east past Woodrow Wilson Jr. High School where I was attending at the time, following Willamette Street for a block up to 19th where we turned east again, and in a couple blocks passing through the South Eugene High School parking lot, all along stopping—I can still recall the squeak and moan of the brakes—and picking up kids on every other street corner. By the time we hit the parking lot, the bus was noisy and bursting at the seams, and if all the seats were taken and more kids needed to get on, then we laid plywood boards between the seats and squeezed more in. By the time we finished our pick-ups and headed out to the fields the bus was a solid mass of bodies from window to window, front to back, and looking out from the driver's seat was like looking out upon a gang of galley slaves.

     DREAM FAMILY ♦ A MEMOIR

Being on the bus first and watching it fill up had its special rewards. You got the best seat at the window halfway between the driver and the rear wheel. You got to see who made it to work that day and who didn't. You got to see the bus come alive block by block, like viewing a behemoth slowly waking from a night's sleep. I always had my eyes on the girls who climbed aboard, picking out one or two that I wanted to get to know better. There was comfort knowing someone you liked was in the same line of work, but I was torn if they were girls from my own school because they certainly knew by me being there I was from a family that needed the money. It didn't occur to me they probably felt the same about themselves. In truth I felt more comfortable contemplating girls from other schools because I could, in my fantasy, strike up a romance without worry of seeing them in school in a few weeks. In all, it was my first experience at serious people watching and making up stories about them. I kept these romances in my head.

Along this line, what the beanfields exacted in toil was partially paid back in the half-baked education I received about sex: who did it, who didn't, how it was done, how often, what body parts were used, what happened when you were finished, and the best times of the month to do it. I heard for the first time jokes with words like "Fuck" and "Cunt" in them. I heard a variety of words for the penis: dick, cock, prick. This talk addled my fantasies about the girls on the bus, whom I'd scope out while working, finding out which row they were picking in, who their friends were, or if one of my friends knew them. There was also talk about hot rods and horsepower, dual carbs and posi-traction. And plenty talk about sports. We smoked our first cigarettes and watched Jack Walrath's girlfriend unwittingly walk to lunch with a bean stem sticking out the crack of her tight denim shorts. I couldn't have seen this at home watching T.V.

On the other hand, what the beanfields exacted in toil adds credence to the theory that we all go through the Army at some point in our life, though we may not actually get drafted or enlist. We have an experience so demeaning and so dehumanizing, so exhausting and so illogical, that we just as well could have been in the Army or even wished so. My experience with this theory was at the beanfields, and in particular my dealings with the bean bosses.

They would often materialize out of nowhere and be leaning over your shoulder, a cigarette dangling from their lips, a long metaphorical shadow crossing over you as if the Grim Reaper suddenly appeared in your room for a bedside chat. Ostensibly they were there to see how cleanly you picked your row of beans, but they were also there as the eyes and ears of Old Man Frost, The Owner, to make sure order was upheld in His Beanfield.

A beanfield is linear, like a huge green pin striped dress shirt, each row a football field's length with six-foot stakes every ten feet, cable wire running along the top and bottom, with string looped back and forth between them forming five foot high isosoles triangles. Early in June the bean plants sprouted and began curling up around the string like a corkscrew, and by the time we arrived in July they had reached the top cable wire and were altogether bushy from top to bottom. The leaves were rough and sticky on the backside, and I used my fingernails to cut letters and emblems to stick them on my clothes like logos.

The first—or "early"—beans were at the bottom of the plant, and picking them was the hardest part of the season because you had to keep low to the ground to get the scant beans that were there, which meant a lot of bending and contorting without much to show for it. I developed methods to keep from crouching all day: scooting butt first with legs extended, atop my gunny sack; or, using my five-gallon bean bucket as a chair and throwing the beans between my legs. In these early days Bill and I often returned home sore to the bone.

As the season progressed the picking got better, and by August the beans were sprouting higher and higher on the plants and were in such abundance that I could stand there and grab handfuls at a time, even if I was blindfolded, and fill my five gallon bucket in minutes rather than hours.

But down along the long rows the bosses were slinking and prowling about. To our undiscerning teenage eyes they all looked the same: portly women who breathed raspy breaths through their mouths; they squinted their eyes from smoking unfiltered Chesterfields; they had two or three moles on their faces; they had missing teeth. Not really knowing what we meant by it, we nonetheless figured they were too ugly to have husbands so they made love to each other using the beanfield's forklift.

"Oh shit" I thought when I'd see a boss at the far end of the row, head and hands stuck in one of the plants. These witches checked our rows with magnifying glasses, or so it seemed, and if we missed any beans we had to pick the row over again, which was bad news because it took time away from better picking and more money.

"Don't look too close!" I said to myself, a rush of adrenalin flooding my body. As best I could, I acted like nothing unusual was happening, picking happily and, hopefully, cleanly along. She'd get closer and closer, periodically rummaging through a bush along the way, and by the time she was standing over me with a smirk on her face, she'd have a hand full of beans.

"Here", she'd say, dumping the beans in my bucket, each one a personal insult to her. "You're leaving too many."

"Sorry. I'll do better."

"'Better' ain't good enough."

"My Dad smokes Winstons too," noting the pack stuck in her shirt pocket (where were the Chesterfields?).

"Don't try buttering me up."

"Oh no, I was just..."

"You leave this many again and you're fired." Her eyes were slits of steel and her mouth bent at the corners like a horseshoe.

"I didn't mean to..."

"You can start doing better by doing the row over." She nodded her head at the end of the row, pointing a nicotine-stained finger. "And no stripping." "Stripping" was picking not only the beans but also the stems they're growing on, depriving the plant from another round of beans. It was akin to murder and could result in instant firing, a simple case of economics that Old Man Frost taught his bean bosses.

"No problem. I'll clean it up."

"Yes you will."

From the time we started picking in Salem, when I was six or seven, Bill and I were required by Dad to pick a certain number of pounds per day. This rule was relaxed or tightened depending on how good or bad the picking was, but by and large it kept us on track day in day out. There was no loafing around. I remember lying in the grass in the front yard of our High Street house in Salem, tired from picking and still in my dirty clothes, waiting for Dad to drive up in his Plymouth from work.

"How'd you do?" he'd say, getting out of the car.

"Thirty pounds." It wasn't much compared to how much we picked as teenagers, but for then it seemed like a mountain to climb each day.

"Good job."

That's all he'd say and I'd feel like a king.

Expectations were higher when we picked at Frost's later as teenagers in Eugene, my pounds ranging from a hundred to a hundred and fifty per day. Bill's, being older, was higher. We kept daily track of our pounds on notebook paper tacked to our kitchen cabinet. At the beanfield our weigh-ins were recorded on a long sheet by a recorder, and every two weeks we got a check from Old Man Frost and we'd compare our figures with his, but there were rare mistakes. The first time I went bean picking with Mom in Salem we received tickets punched with the weight of our weigh-ins. On payday each Friday we lined up in front of a table outside the owner's farmhouse, which sat on a little knoll, and presented our tickets. Calculations were made and we were paid in cash.

Being nearly three years older and physically stronger, and a no-nonsense picker who was in it for the money, I could never keep up with Bill. He worked his tail off. As hard as I tried, and sometimes I did strive heroically to outpick him, it was a fruitless venture. If I was having a good day, having picked a hundred pounds by lunch, Bill would have two hundred. In his zeal he got caught more than once "stripping" plants, but because he was caught by different bosses who never put two and two together, he was never fired. Amazingly, one day he picked over five hundred pounds, which meant with his bonus, he made fifteen dollars in one day! The most I ever picked was three hundred, or three hundred and fifty pounds. But never five hundred!

I daydreamed for most of my time in the beanfields, often finding myself in a semi-conscious state thinking about what I'd rather be doing, fixating on some girl or wondering about the upcoming school year. It

   DREAM FAMILY ♦ A MEMOIR

was not conducive to high productivity, and not unlike the daydreaming I do today.

We got the weekends off. Sometimes, if the beans weren't good, or the weather was especially bad, we got a weekday off too. These free days seemed like a gift from heaven. And too, for the Lane County Fair in late August, just before school started, Old Man Frost gave us a Wednesday or Thursday off to go to it. That gesture alone proved he wasn't an absolute ogre. Since the fairgrounds were just a couple of blocks from where we lived, we made full use of our holiday, especially Bill, who loved doing everything: riding the Hammer and the Rock-o-planes and the Twister, eating the corndogs and pizza, playing the arcade, listening to the battle of the bands. Whatever money he took was gone by the time we got back. Though I went on a ride or two and loved eating my cherry snow-cone, I held most of my money back. Dad joked that I always returned home with the same amount I went with, although, I pointed out, that was mathematically impossible.

Each beanfield had a reputation, and I'm certain Mom and Dad knew this and checked out Frost's before we started picking there. It was considered a good field. Brown's beanfield, on the other hand, was at the other end of the spectrum, their buses full of ex-cons and juvenile delinquents—we suspected—whose unruliness was well known in the community. If you wanted to have a good time, meet sleezy girls, pick fights rather than beans, not worry about making any money, then Brown's was the place to be. Lots of kids got fired at Brown's, and don't even think of applying at Frost's if you got fired at Brown's.

Like Frost's, Brown's was located off River Road, and we'd pass their buses going to and from the fields in the mornings and evenings.

"Speed up!" we'd scream to our old driver, encouraging him to race Brown's. He never bit, but sometimes on the drive we got close enough to their bus when suddenly a barrage of beans and banana peels and apple cores would fly from the windows of both buses, some landing on target, most slapping against the side of the buses and falling off, all accompanied by extended middle fingers and torrents of four letter words. There was no love lost there.

As the season wore on and the drudgery and monotony set in, the only redeeming hope was that school would start sometime and soon enough we'd quit the slavery and go back to civilization, back to living. Ironically, as we closed in on our season, expectations weren't unlike that of the last days of school when all you could think about was sleeping in and not doing anymore homework. But here our freedom was school—the beginning of it—and there'd only be a few days between our last day at Frost's and the first day of school when we'd begin another slog, sort of speak. It was a bittersweet tradeoff for sure, but it seemed to fall into place as far as how our small world worked then.

And how much money was there at the end? How much with the half cent per pound bonus for staying all season? I remember a hundred dollars or more, and in the early sixties that was a lot of money for a teenager, and of course it was ours to spend, but with strings attached. A few days before the start of school Mom would take Bill and me downtown to Willamette Street to shop at J.C. Penny's and Sears and the Bon Marche. We'd spend most of our money on bright Madras shirts, cotton pants, black low top Converse All-Stars, and my favorite—a new pull-over sweater, usually a V-neck in burgundy. The sweet and unmistakable whiff of new clothes often takes me back to those days before school started, in late summer after beanpicking, when everyone seemed eager to shed their old skin and start anew. At night we had Mom rip out our new pants and peg them with her sewing machine, tapering the legs so that we struggled to get our ankles through the bottoms.

For those of us who worked the beanfields the rewards were plentiful: we earned our own money, met new people, learned about sex and cars, bought new clothes with the money we made. We experienced hard physical labor, paid attention to detail, obeyed orders, and kept our heads down. If we made it through the season in spite of the odds, and whatever shame we felt, it was offset by the feeling we could do just about anything. But far and away any other lesson I learned at the beanfields is that I clearly came to understand what I didn't want to do the rest of my life. I didn't want to pick beans or any similar kind of work. Later, memories of bean picking kept me at my desk in college, and I believe it was the primary lesson Mom and Dad intended us to learn.

     DREAM FAMILY ♦ A MEMOIR

Sometimes when I eat greenbeans now I take special note of them, regarding how long and round they are, whether they are smooth or undulated. I even open them and examine the spacing of the seeds inside and note their pale green coloring. I see how much meat there is to the bean, how fresh it tastes, though I don't particularly like them, in fact hate them, all part of the vegetable fixation. There is no other vegetable I do this with.

17

IN THE BEGINNING there was Bill, Ann, and me, and though we lived together as siblings throughout our childhood, it wasn't long before Bill and I veered off into our own world and Ann was left to hers. It seemed no less a natural law that Bill and I were stuck together playing cowboys and Indians or baseball or going on bike rides each day, instructed by Mom and Dad to play together and for Bill to keep an eye on me so I wouldn't get hurt or stray off. For that, my memories of Bill are more distinct than those of Ann, and I sometimes think she was brought up by a different family. This followed up to our teenage years which by then Bill had had enough of me and would make a fuss to Mom and Dad about having to take me to the state basketball tournament.

"He's a dork! Says the stupidest things! He yells to Freddy (Beckley) at the basketball game 'hey you with the hair on your head.' How dense can you get! All these guys are looking at me wondering who brought the jerk? Why can't he just go with his own friends?"

But then later the same night Bill would let me ride with him and his buddies up and down Willamette Street dragging the gut in the Campbell Soup car, the family's Heinz colored '56 Chev. Whoever called "FO" first got to sit in the front outside seat, the best seat in the house, and we "pressed hams" by squashing our naked butts against the car windows while bystanders looked on in dismay. In those years on Friday and Saturday nights Willamette Street from 8th to 24th was bumper to bumper cars—hopped up Chevy Impalas and Plymouth Barracudas, Ford Model T's, tiny red Volkswagens—honking horns, their passengers hanging out rear windows, racing from one stop light to the next, their engines revving like growling tigers at each juncture then lurching forward as the lights changed from red to green. At the turnaround there was an A&W Root Beer where uniformed girls served hamburgers and shakes on trays attached to the car window. At other turnouts along the way, like the bowling alley parking lot, guys sat on their car hoods in the summer and beckoned girls to stop and talk.

"Hey slick kitty from the big city," Freddy, one of Bill's friends, would yell to a girl in another car, and she would smile back and Freddy would point to a place to pull over with hopes to "hustle" these girls to "make out" or to "cop a feel." Being Jerry the Younger, I could do no more than look on as Bill and Jack Walrath and Freddy Beckley plied their trade, usually to no avail.

One night of cruising I remember sticking my head out the car window and yelling "get a job!" at a bum curled up on the sidewalk, his shaking hands clasped around a brown paper sack, a bottle inside. I saw his broken life as no more than an opportunity for ridicule to get Bill's approval, and it worked, for he and his buddies laughed and laughed thinking I was pretty clever for a fourteen year old. I thought so too because it seemed a big deal being age fourteen and riding in a car with a bunch of older guys. My own friends were eager to know all about it.

     DREAM FAMILY ♦ A MEMOIR

Since Dad taught Bill and me to stick up for each other, it was in our case a duty that fell squarely on Bill's shoulders since I was of no size or shape to defend him against any of his older and larger enemies. One evening I'd given lip to some bigger guys down at Jefferson pool and they followed me home, calling my bluff that I had a big brother who would deal with them when we got there. I was maybe age thirteen. Bill caught wind of my predicament and ran to meet me and my trailers on the corner of 19th and Monroe, a block from home. Breaking to a stop he demanded of me "which one?"

"That one," I said, pointing to the guy who'd given me the most grief, wielding in those two words and the pointing finger the power and might of a warring Pope.

There was a thud. In an instant the guy's head snapped back and he tumbled to the ground, his nose bursting with blood. Dazed, he didn't know what hit him. He tried to get up but stumbled, his legs rubber bands, and he began crying. His friends, now scared of what Bill may do to them, quickly pulled him up and dragged him away. One of them tore off his T-shirt and put it to the bleeding nose hoping to stem the flood. They then quickly disappeared into the night and I never saw them again at Jefferson pool.

I played this Big Brother card more than once in my childhood, but only under provocation, only in defense, pushing back on someone who could have snuffed me out in a heartbeat save for the knowledge there'd be hell to pay later with Bill if they hurt me. So they'd take my insults with a testy reluctance, heartily vowing to get even someday. Bill was like having a Smith and Wesson in my pocket.

He was a good looking kid. When he was a young child he had light curly hair (and a widows peak) that over time it was thought—hoped for by some—would change to Dad's curly red hair, but in fact turned a darker brown and lost much of its curl by the time Bill was a teenager. He had an open face with thick eyebrows, alert brown eyes, skin which freckled in the summer, an athletic build, a quick grin. He was likable but hot headed. He and Mom fought from the first days and it appeared on the surface to be the grandest of ironies since they had the same temperament. Watching them was like watching a *Reader's Digest* version of the Hundred Years War, and for me, at the outset, it made Bill someone worth scrutiny. I kept a close eye on him.

And for good reason. His childhood was much more adventurous than mine—chock full of fishing, hunting, games, fights, girls. It carried through later on as an adult when he built houses, blazed trails for the state, hunted big game in Alaska, coached sports, married three times, flattened a guy for stealing a can of peanuts from his store. His ideas were concise while mine were nebulous, his decisions quick while mine were endlessly fretted over. When he was clearly wrong about something it never ended the battle for him while I was certain the world was crashing to an inglorious end.

It was only a matter of time when the price for his insubordination would come due. The first time I remember, Bill was age nine or ten and Dad had warned him that if he was late for dinner again he'd get a licking. A few days later he was late again. He either didn't believe Dad or forgot about time. We were a tongue-tied family sitting around the dinner table that night, nary a word spoken, Dad steamed about Bill, and afterwards Dad marched him upstairs to our bedroom. Bill told me later what happened:

"Give me your belt," Dad said.

"You're kidding,"

"No I'm not," Dad replied.

Trembling, Bill slipped his belt off.

"Give it to me."

Bill, his hands shaking, gave Dad the belt.

"Now drop your pants."

"No, please!"

"Now."

Slowly Bill slid his pants down.

"Skivies too," Dad said.

"No!" Bill cried.

"Drop 'em."

I was downstairs in the living room, ears perked. Bill had gotten out of trouble before, suddenly there were extenuating circumstances, but this time there was no going back, it was going to be different. The question was how bad was it going to be?

I quickly ran to the nearby bookshelf and grabbed our family Bible, with its orange peel black cover, upon hearing Bill's first pathetic scream, the crash of noise filling the house like a flood of dam water. I sat down and haphazardly opened to a page and began reading it, or at least pretending to read it, since I was age seven or eight and couldn't possiblly have understood most of the words in the King James Bible. But for some reason it seemed the appropriate thing to do as the succeeding yelps echoed down the stairs, one after the other, and I bore down more intensely and in earnest "read" the Bible, believing perhaps that by this act alone I could absolve everyone and make the problem go away. Well, I was certainly willing to try.

But Bill was different than I was, so resilient and irrepressible that by the next day after getting in big trouble, like being late for dinner, he'd act as if nothing had happened. He'd be real chummy and chatty with Mom and Dad and they would act in kind. How could he do that? Didn't he remember what happened—the licking, the yelps, the harsh words? How could he live with himself or with Mom and Dad under those circumstances? Because I was different it appeared that Bill's recoveries were a miracle—maybe my Bible reading helped!—or some kind of sleight of hand, since my troubles with Mom and Dad, which were far fewer than Bill's, lasted days and included endless hours of solitary brooding and sulking, often giving Mom and Dad the silent treatment at dinner because I believed I was either wronged by them and my silence spoke loudly for my righteousness (returning Mom and Dad's punishment in spades), or that I was so clearly guilty for what I did that I was too ashamed and humiliated to move on with my life. Finally, after Mom and Dad repeating once more that brooding and sulking wasn't healthy for me, I'd lighten up and get back to normal.

* * *

Ann couldn't have been more different from Bill. Apart from being a girl, her temperament and personality were distinctive enough from Bill's that it was hard to imagine they came from the same parents. Her first memories from our High street house in Salem at age five and six include hearing our 45 RPM of "Hound Dog" with the line "you ain't never caught a rabbit so you ain't no friend of mine" so many times that when a neighbor's rabbit escaped from its cage, she ran outside thinking that if she caught it she'd be a friend of Elvis's. In Salem she started the first grade at McKinley Grade school, the only time the three of us children went to the same school, and she remembers the principle Mrs. Rea as "a battleaxe...hardnosed," and that Bill had trouble with her. There was "morning milk" for four cents and one cent bubble gum. She remembers the Spring Maypole dance when she grabbed the tail of one of the long brightly colored streamers attached atop the Maypole and danced and weaved among the other kids until the tall pole was wrapped like a gigantic multicolored candy cane. She attended Brownies, read Dick and Jane books, collected Barbie Dolls, and thought that by wearing PF Flyers she could fly. Every night when Dad got up to go to the bathroom he woke Ann too because she was a bed-wetter. With distaste she recalls wetting her pants at neighbor Johnny Dallas' house and scooting home on her butt and leaving a tell-tale track on the sidewalk.

She had thick dark brown hair and smooth skin, distinct eyebrows like Bill's, a slender but not skinny build with erect posture, and lively eyes. From early on her front teeth protruded and had gaps, but braces during her teens made them perfect. Her hands, like Dad's, were nimble and creative and capable of doing minute work—she drew and painted and was closest to Dad in artistic talent. She played with her dolls and dressed in tutus and danced around her bedroom with friends. In time we teased her about her long line of boyfriends, which began in grade school, and Dad later feigned concern she'd bring a Russian home next time. She did mediocre in school, getting B's and C's, and in hopes of getting her interested in high school politics I put her on a committee I chaired—my first and only nepotism—but it wasn't her cup of tea. All she ever wanted from life, Ann once told me, was to be a stay-at-home wife with a couple of kids and a husband who went to work each day.

Bill and I resented her because she had her own bedroom; because she didn't have to pick beans; because Mom made her bed every day; because we couldn't lay a hand on her; because she got braces and we didn't (in truth we didn't need them like Ann did). To us she lived a life of privilege.

But unbeknownst to Bill's and my undiscerning and prejudiced eyes, she lived in a world best described as a tyranny, living under Mom's oppressive thumb while we boys, given more rope, grabbed most of the attention. "It was considered the coolest thing to hunt and fish and play basketball [in our family]... and if you didn't you weren't cool," Ann says.

To make matters worse, she didn't get along with Mom. "We always had a friction between us," she said. "I never felt it with Dad. It was either her way or the highway. Though Mom was nurturing, a provider, the older I got I didn't respect that. Later I rebelled a lot. Dad at the same time was saying 'let her be free to experience life so she learns on her own.'"

She went to Dad with school problems in math and science. "Dad had the ultimate knowledge of everything. I didn't go to Mom. He put on the impression he was the boss. I talked face to face with him. We played checkers together sometimes. There was a respect there."

But it was Dad who gave Ann her first spanking in Salem. "He put me over his knees and he whacked me and I wet my pants all over him. I was five. He looked me straight in the face and told me 'that's the soft one. The next one's going to be hard.' He told me later it was all he could do to keep a straight face."

Beginning in her teens Ann's menstrual cycles took on a fierceness bordering insanity, with sudden mood swings that left the rest of us not only angry but flabbergasted, and whatever gap existed between her and Bill and I was only widened by these monthly attacks.

"[When] I got those hormones...yuk!...it was ugly," Ann said.

It led to her most famous, in my memory, run-in with Dad, which followed a screaming match between Mom and Ann with Ann bolting to our only bathroom at Monroe Street and locking the door. Over the next half hour the shouting continued, Ann refusing to unlock the door even though some of us had to use the toilet! More words passed, harsher now, but Ann still refused unlocking the door. In the meantime Dad was in a slow burn sitting in his living room chair, you could see the color rising in his face as he got more and more fidgety under the screams and yells, and it seemed only a matter of time before he blew his stack. Finally, having heard enough, he jumped from his chair and flew to the bathroom. "Open the door," he yelled at Ann, "or I'll break it down!"

Ann froze, too scared to speak or move.

"Open up!"

There was silence.

"Open up!"

More silence.

With a quick turn of the shoulder Dad rammed the bathroom door with a violent blow, splintering it in several places and breaking through, where he found Ann cowering and panicky. As he carried her through the now fractured door, she wet her pants in his arms. Not long afterwards we built a half bath upstairs.

It appears a contradiction, but in spite of the wide gap between us I got along better with Ann than with Bill. We had more things in common than we would care to admit to at the time. Like me she was sensitive and took things to heart. Like me a wrong look or word could send her into a tailspin. Our family wasn't always tender of heart, and a boy's life is by nature a rough and tumble affair with its movement and action, deed and combat; it leaves little time to contemplate or sort things out. With Ann I could see that life was more than shooting baskets and playing cards, that beneath was a hidden world of feelings and emotions that didn't fit into set rules regardless of how much you tried to order them. I have often looked for the Holy Grail in philosophy with that exact mix of sensitivity and sophistication that makes for a better understanding of life. But to no avail. Ann was indefinable, conflicted, multi-faceted, and like a heroine in a Russian novel she somehow made it through childhood with two older brothers bent on her anonymity. A life philosophy is only as good as the degree of acceptance and buoyancy it contains. Ann gave me a view of a girl's life. She was as human as you can get. I came to love her as much as I loved Bill, though I never wanted to kill her.

Bill, I both worshipped the ground he walked on and secretly desired to run him through with a rapier. It was ambivalence on a grand scale, another turbulent Russian novel, but from Bill I realized the fruitlessness of my moods, that letting things roll off my back and moving on is sometimes the best route. He got me out from behind my thoughts and books and into a life of action. With Bill I knew something was bound to happen. One moment I was sneaking out in the middle of the night to meet girls while in the next moment I was jumping off train bridges in my underwear. He told a good story too. These days his trophies are not so much the heads of elk, bear and moose that hang from his museum-like walls in his house, but the intriguing and fascinating stories behind them, some of which I've been in.

18

I HAVE A black and white photo of Dad standing in front of the scrawny and abandoned train depot. Across the tracks but out of the photo is a grain elevator. There's a trace of a grin on his face, but not too much, since he didn't like photos of himself. His right hand is tucked into the rear pocket of his slacks, his cardigan sweater buttoned in front, his other hand slightly grasping his pant leg. If the photo was colored you'd see his faded and thinning red hair, the light blue eyes, the fair Irish skin. He is six feet tall.

Above the entry to the depot is a large wooden sign painted white with a black boarder and the bold letters "Hurd" written across it. The depot is no more than a wood framed rectangle with a triangle roof, four shuttered windows on each side, a smaller window on the entry door, and painted pale brown. I take the photograph to prove that Dad was born somewhere. It is 1966, I am seventeen, Dad forty-seven.

I have another photograph of Dad at age 3 or 4 when he was living in Rolla, N.D. It is in sepia, looking as if it had been dipped in gravy upon development, and Dad is wearing a dark sailor suit with striped cuffs on a wide sleeve, a broad V—shaped collar covering part of his shoulder, also striped, and a large silky bow tie. It is hard to tell if he's wearing shorts or a skirt, but unmistakingly he's wearing leggings, the same shade as his sailor suit. On his feet are black laced up boots; they appear scuffed on the toes, the only part of his clothing that looks worn. The small rectangular wood table he's sitting on is dark finished with fluting near the crown of the legs and inlay on top. His short stubby legs dangle over the side of the table and cross at the ankles. His left hand, which in its lightness contrasts with the dark cuff, is curled under and balances on his left thigh. His other hand, more open, rests near the right corner of the table. Dad's narrow smile barely reveals his two front teeth. His face is open and slightly chubby, and even in sepia you can tell he has red hair, piled on top and pooched out above the ears. His soft eyes are looking off at something pleasant in the background, maybe Gramma Keefe, making him appear happy in the picture.

The photograph is mounted on a brown textured linerboard frame with folders on the front. There is a "Jorgensen" signature with a long thin flourish off the last "n", imprinted on the frame under the photo, with "Cando, No. Dak." below it. Cando is a small town about twenty miles southeast of Rolla. Whether a representative from Jorgensen took the picture while in Rolla on a sales trip, or Gramma and Granpa took Dad to Cando for the photo session is not known. What is known is that the photograph was taken sometime before 1925.

He was born April 11, 1919, in Hurd, North Dakota, a small town on the Soo railroad line twenty miles northeast of Minot. As Gramma mentioned in her interview, Dad was the boy she was "...going to put a dress on...and call him my girl." It was the following summer when their crops failed on the farm they sharecropped, that Gramma and Granpa pulled up stakes and moved to Rolla, North Dakota, near the U.S./ Canadian border where Gramma's mother, my great-grandmother Ollie

Belle Scott McDaniel, ran a restaurant. Gramma worked the restaurant while Granpa did odd jobs.

Dad soon ran afoul of the harsh Dakota winters with his severe bouts of pneumonia, as Gramma earlier said, that they had to get him out of North Dakota and into a milder climate. Gramma said a special bond grew between her and Dad during these bouts of pneumonia, and rather than being the boy who should have been a girl, Dad turned out being the boy who needed all the love and care Granpa and Gramma and the doctors could muster to keep him alive. Having lived in Oregon after he ran away from home fifteen years earlier, Granpa remembered its temperate winters and warm summers. In 1925 the family, with three young boys, moved to Eugene.

* * *

It was from Eugene in 1966 that Dad, Mom, Ann, and I drove to Bismarck to visit Gramma White and Aunt Grayce and Uncle Bert, Mom's side of the family. Dad and Mom agreed he'd take a day out of the vacation to drive up to his birthplace, having not been there since he'd left over forty years before. There were rumors Hurd no longer existed, and over the years it became a family joke that Dad wasn't born anywhere. He was determined to find it and I was delighted to accompany him.

We drove north from Bismarck on highway 83, passing through Washburn, Big Ben, Lake Sacagawea, and Minot. There were few bends in the highway, the land flat, farms and ranches stretching from horizon to horizon. Over and over we saw couched in the middle of a thousand acres of wheat or corn a white wooden house and a barn with a shiny cupola on top, a small green yard in between with a clothesline and a row of pine trees for shade, a tractor or two stirring up dust, an old Chevy truck up on blocks, a gravel road leading up to the front lawn. And there were flax and sunflower and barley and rye fields too, one after another, and we were near the geographical center of North America—Rugby, North Dakota—where the land's value is based on what it grows rather than where it's located. If you looked both ways you could see the earth's curve, or so it appeared.

North of Minot we started looking for Hurd in earnest. It was not on the map, as Dad knew, though he had a sense of where to look from talking with Gramma and Granpa, who reported it being not far from the tiny town of Landsford. Using Landsford as a marker, we crisscrossed the countryside on old gravel roads, turning here and there, doubling back, finding more farms and vast wheat fields, but despite these initial efforts we could not find Hurd. It seemed the more we looked the more we were lost.

We next found ourselves driving parallel to a railroad. Dad was looking left and right, trying, I could see, to get a bead on where he was. Was he looking for something vaguely familiar, something he recognized from his childhood? We came around a clump of trees. It was then we saw the depot with the sign on it.

After I took the photograph of Dad in front of the depot, a strange thing happened. We looked at each other thinking the same thing, a sort of instantaneous impulse, but the idea behind it was odd because it was out of character for us. We had come all the way from Oregon to North Dakota, driven north from Bismarck to crisscross the countryside searching for Hurd, come so far to prove Dad was born somewhere, that why should we come away empty handed? Nobody would know, nobody in this far away place would ever miss it. And what a prize it would be back home in Oregon as material proof of Dad's very existence!

Like a couple of outlaws we threw ourselves at the sign above the entry door, me jumping on Dad's shoulders and pulling and tugging on the sign. But it was too secure, too well nailed to the exterior. From the glove compartment we got pliers and screwdrivers and pried around the edges, but still no give, then from the trunk came tire irons and wrenches. For twenty minutes we took turns tugging and pulling and prying at the sign, careful not to damage it, coming at it from every conceivable angle using these tools plus our bare hands, which by now were scratched and bruised, but the sign wouldn't budge. As hard as we tried, as hard as we put our shoulders into it, without proper tools we couldn't get the sign down. I want to believe our fingers bled from it.

As much as it would have been a coup bringing the sign home for Gramma and Granpa to see, we had to settle for second best. Inside the depot we discovered a dilapidated potbellied stove as black as a well hole. It could have been there since creation. On its front door dangled a wire pull, oblong and coiled and made of thick gaged cable. It was easy to slip off. We threw it in the glove compartment of our Thunderbird along with the screwdriver and pliers, and with that Dad turned the engine on and with a final wave at the depot we left Hurd. A week later back in Eugene, Gramma attached the wire pull to the handle of her dining room light fixture where it stayed for the rest of her years. For me, the wire pull was not only proof of our discovery of Hurd, and Dad's birthplace, but also a symbol of one of the precious times we spent together as father and son. Dad never returned to Hurd, but I would.

* * *

It was apparent early in his childhood that Dad was good with his hands, and later with ease tied knots for his Navy training and even later wove macramé patterns when they were popular in the 60's and 70's. I have two of the toys he played with as a kid, one a tin windup racing car of 1920's vintage, about a foot or so long, that once had black rubber tires stretched around its oversized wheels. The second toy is a grey and red metal elephant mounted on a platform with tiny wheels at each end. The elephant is about a foot long and eight or nine inches high, the very model of a circus elephant in those days. They must have been top of the line toys when Dad was a boy, and I imagine he got them on a special occasion like Christmas or a birthday. I picture in my mind's eye Dad playing with them back in Rolla, or Eugene, slowly turning them around in his tiny fingers, running them along the wood floor of the house, spinning the wheels again and again, winding up the race car for yet another imagined race, preparing the elephant for a parade or circus.

It was natural therefore that Dad enjoyed playing cards given his agile hands, and in our family a certain status went along with playing a good hand of cards. He taught us that at High Street. When we lived on Monroe Street nearly every Sunday after dinner Mom and Dad played bridge with Granpa and Gramma. Dad was cool; when playing cards he kept most of his thinking behind his eyes. I watched these games, loved the way everyone handled the cards, watching their fingers and hands and wrists make the cards come alive first by slicing the deck in half and then with the thumbs bending each half deck back and letting fly, the cards instantaneously buzzing and whizzing and flapping perfectly into each other like two converging columns of a marching band at the speed of light. Then with the hands forming an "O" a magical reverse shuffle occurred, the cards arching high the opposite way, causing them to fall all at once into place in a near perfect pile set for dealing.

I watched closely how dealing was a subtle affair with timing the cornerstone as the left thumb readied the card just before the right thumb and forefinger picked it up and tossed it. I noticed how with the proper flick of the wrist the card spun in the air seemingly airborne before it landed and smoothly slid across the table like a feather from heaven, coming to rest with the other cards, neither a flutter nor a traceable track as evidence. Dad, with his magical hands, was the best at this.

He had an idiosyncrasy once he picked up his dealt cards before looking at them when he'd arrange them face down and slowly slide the top card to the bottom using his thumbs, doing this several times as if in some kind of rapture. Then he'd bring his cards up close to his face and squeeze them out one by one, making a compact fan making you believe that this ritual would somehow make him a winner regardless of what cards he got. The expression on his face gave no news about what he really had.

During high school John Hall and Keith Derry and Ed Walker and I and sometimes Bill would get together for penny ante poker on a Friday or Saturday night in our rec. room in the old garage on Monroe Street, and Dad would sit in for an hour or so until he wiped us out then throw all the pennies back in the pot and with a wry smile leave. We'd beg him to stay because we wanted another go at him, another shot, but mostly we wanted him to stay because just watching him play was worth losing our shirts to him. But he seldom did.

✳ ✳ ✳

When I returned to North Dakota in the summer of 1994 for the first time since Dad and I visited nearly thirty years before, I tried to find Hurd again, this time with the help of my wife Connie and thirteen-year-old daughter Katy. I warned them beforehand the odyssey might be fruitless and boring and there was no guarantee we'd find Hurd. We were in Bismarck on the last leg of a swing through the Midwest for a wedding and reunion with Mom's side of the family, including a celebration of Aunt Grayce and Uncle Bert's sixtieth wedding anniversary. Like I did before with Dad, we took a day off to find Hurd.

Earlier that Spring before our trip I had talked to my great uncle Ed—Granpa's younger brother—about where Hurd was. He was the only one left who knew where it was since by then Dad and other relatives who came from North Dakota had passed away. He was turning 90 and had lived outside Hurd when he was a child.

"Hurd's one mile north and eight miles east of Lansford, on the Soo railroad line," he said.

Luckily, the official North Dakota state map I obtained included all the railroads lines, including the Soo, but I didn't see a road indicating where Hurd might be based on Uncle Ed's directions. Where was the road Dad and I took?

Once again I was on a journey headed north out of Bismarck on highway 83, past Washburn, Big Ben, Sacagawea, and Minot. Things had not changed in thirty years for it appeared the very farms Dad and I had passed before were still there, granted with a few more coats of paint on the barns and houses, a modern tractor out back, and a new generation working the land, but still the same.

Just as the map indicated, the Soo line crossed highway 83 about 20 miles north of Minot. We took a gravel road—#228—near the rail crossing and headed east. We drove down it for a couple of miles, but the further we went the more the railroad trailed off to the north. I sensed we were on the wrong road when Katy spotted a truck across the way going west on a road paralleling the railroad. It was easy to see because the land was so flat, and at the next intersection we turned north and connected to this road, which indeed followed alongside the railroad. We then came upon three houses that rang a bell from my trip with dad.

After we left the depot in 1966, I remember Dad going up to a house and talking with an older lady about the Keefes in Hurd. She remembered Gramma and Granpa.

* * *

We kept driving along the gravel road hoping to find the train depot or the elevator that I remembered from before, but I saw nothing familiar. We crossed back over the tracks and headed further east for a while, but by then I knew we had gone too far. The road was well graveled and there wasn't any traffic to speak of, so I let Katy drive, having learned some basic driving skills on her cousin's farm outside Bismarck the day before with my Mom as instructor.

We decided to go back to the houses we had passed along the way hoping that someone would know about Hurd. Outside the first house was a man barbecuing hamburgers.

"Hi," I said as I approached.

"Hi," he replied.

He was about my age and was wearing a straw cowboy hat unraveling at the edges, a simple blue work shirt with smudges on the front, threadbare blue jeans and black scuffed cowboy boots. He had perfect white teeth like two rows of Chicklets gum and his face was leathery and tanned and appeared thick as a steak. His eyes were lively and heavy lidded, and he looked at me directly though I felt no threat since he seemed to have an easy and honest manner about him.

"Is there something I can help you with?"

"Yes. My dad was born in a town called Hurd back in 1919, which I think used to be around here. Would you know anything about it?"

He smiled slightly and paused, then turned his head and looked east down the road. "You bet." He raised his index finger. "It's right down there, near the end of that row of trees, about a quarter of a mile."

I turned towards where he was pointing. "Right there?"

"Right at the end of that tree line. There's a sign on a post there that our family put up during a reunion a few years back. There's a turn-in there and you'll see it."

"I missed it. I was here about thirty years ago with my dad and I was looking for a depot and a grain elevator."

"Well, the grain elevator burned down about eight years ago, and the depot was moved to Blaine, about three miles north of Lansford. It's the township hall there now."

"No wonder I couldn't find it. I was looking for something that wasn't there."

"Well the sign's right down there, like I said, and if you want, down at the end of the road turn north and go for about a mile and you'll see a monument to my grandfather Joseph Cunningham, who was the first to homestead this area in 1901. You'll see it, just off the left of the road."

"O.K.! I sure appreciate the information. By the way I'm Jerry Keefe from Oregon."

"Glenn Cunningham. Please to meet you." We shook hands. "Keefe...I don't remember that name."

"Well, it's been a long time since my family lived here."

I got back in the car and directed Katy to where Glenn had pointed to the sign. Inching the car down the road she was careful in keeping it centered on her side of the gravel road and watching her speed, and near the end of the tree line she pulled into the turnoff for the railroad. We got out of the car and glanced around to find nothing different from when we passed by before. Then in mid distance something caught my eye, and upon careful examination, we saw nestled under one of the cottonwood trees, where there were several leaves and branches covering part of it, a metal plate about a foot long and 6 inches wide with the name "Hurd" painted on it. It was nailed to a round post about shoulder height. Excited, I fetched the camera from the car and took several pictures of us leaning on the sign and pointing at it while remembering the black and white photo of Dad. Next, we wandered over by the railroad and peered across a huge wheat field where black and orange monarchs fluttered about and bluebirds and small insects flew at odd angles and a mild breeze created waves in the wheat and above us puffy cumulus clouds dotted the otherwise clear blue sky. It was comfortably warm. As I looked out over the expanse of fields and further to the horizon, which seemed in another dimension, I knew I had done the right thing coming up here. Something special was happening but I couldn't put my finger on it. Even Katy and Connie remarked how peaceful and serene it was. We lingered for several moments then returned to the car, a purple Ford Escort rental, and Katy insisted on driving again. She was having fun on these back roads, the same ones Dad let me drive on.

She drove us to the Cunningham monument nearby, a headstone-sized memorial easily noticeable on the roadside, and as I was getting out of the car a pickup truck came speedily around the corner kicking up dust and pulled behind us and parked. Amidst the settling dust out jumped Glenn Cunningham.

He approached and said: "Say, I thought if you wanted to know a little more about the history of these parts, I got a couple of names I can give you and maybe you can look them up."

"Great," I said. Connie handed me a notepad and pencil through the window and Glen began talking, giving me the names of Lloyd Worth and C.L O'Keefe (no relation), both old timers from Lansford who might know something about Hurd and the early settlers. We might find them at the Lansford restaurant. He went on to tell about his grandfather, the monument's namesake.

"He was the first homesteader, came out to North Dakota from Iowa after getting liquored up at a Christmas party. He slept overnight on his pile of wood for his homestead shack, and when he woke up the next morning there was four inches of snow over everything. Then across the way he noticed some smoke, and thinking he was the only one around, was surprised to find a man by the name of Mike Kitzeman living in a cave. They became fast friends and Kitzeman helped grandfather build his homestead shack. This was January 1901."

"Quite an introduction to North Dakota," I said.

"It was tough. Grandfather had to go back to Iowa for a period of work. While he was gone a neighbor stole his shack and dragged it half a mile up the road. When grandfather returned he stole it back. Our family still has the original homestead title signed by Teddy Roosevelt."

Glenn suggested I go up to Bottineau, the county seat, where I might find a plat of old Hurd at the courthouse. He said Hurd had a couple of banks, some churches, a school, a general store, a blacksmith.

　　　　　DREAM FAMILY ♦ A MEMOIR

"Glenn," I asked, "what happened to Hurd?"

"Well, the trains used to stop every eight miles to take on water for their steam engines. That's why the towns were spaced eight miles apart back then. But when the new engines came along they didn't have to stop so often. So most of the towns along the way like Hurd got bypassed. Over time they just disappeared."

We talked for fifteen minutes or more with Connie taking her own notes to back mine up. Again I thanked Glenn. It was apparent how proud he was of his family and its history. He and his brother owned about 3,600 acres including the land that was once Hurd and the land we had just looked across, growing wheat, barley, and soybeans.

Katy drove out to the main highway where I took over and drove to Lansford a few miles west of highway 83. The Lansford restaurant is in a single storied building that also houses the local library, meeting hall, bar, beauty salon, and motel. I asked around but none of the old timers Glenn mentioned were there so we ate and hi-tailed it to Bottineau, about forty five miles away, hoping to get there before the courthouse closed.

We arrived around four o'clock. The courthouse and library are housed in a modern brick structure two blocks off Main Street. Inside I introduced myself to Karen Bergman, a plump congenial woman who ran the Register of Deeds office.

"I'm looking for a plat of a town called Hurd that was around in 1919, but is gone now," I said. "It was near Lansford on the Soo railroad line."

"Well let me see," she said, tapping her forefinger on her lips.

I watched Karen examine a nearby shelf of books until she finally bent down and with both hands pulled out a gigantic cloth bound tome with a black "1910" printed on its spine. She started leafing through the large pages, each one a town plat covered in a plastic sheath and arranged in alphabetical order. I was hovering over her shoulder when she came to the "H's" and suddenly Hurd appeared. Karen was as surprised to see it as I was. The plat was full of various shaped rectangles and lines and numbers and words indicating the depot and elevators, the school, the Congregational Church, the Post Office, the Bank, the plat numbers on the town lots, the street names: First through Fourth going east and west, Rose, Violet, Main, Geranium, and Daisy going north and south. I didn't recall anyone in the family talking at length about these specifics of Hurd, so it was news to me. As I gazed at the plat Hurd began taking a shape and form that until then had never occurred to me. It was no longer just an odd name or a family joke but rather a town where people loaded hay and learned geography and prayed in church and posted letters and were born and died. It was once a town where lived a baby boy who many years later and far from Hurd became my father.

On the long drive back to Bismarck that evening we were nearly ran over by a pickup crossing the freeway. The sun was low in the west and the driver claimed he didn't see us. We were at top speed when I swerved off the freeway to miss him, avoiding by inches a light pole. Several other drivers who saw the incident pulled over to see if we were o.k. The driver of the pickup was an old farmer mortified by what he'd done. I was able to drive the car out of the ditch, albeit with a few clumps of grass and turf hanging from the chassis.

Sometimes when I think of Dad now, looking back over his life when I was a child and even as a young adult before he passed on, I remember in him a certain melancholy and loneliness, a sadness and sorrow, like electrons circling his big heart and generous soul. They didn't define him but rather were pushed to the periphery and apparent only if I looked close enough. If the war brought on an inescapable fatalism or a shadowy destiny from some event or an accumulation of experience, I'll never know. Or maybe because he was so ill as a child, so close to death with pneumonia in those years in North Dakota, that from then on he always felt his time in the world was borrowed on a sheet of ice, that in an instant he could be gone with little more than a slip and that the war only added to this premonition. It is odd how things ultimately ended for him, dying on a golf course, the last place he'd want to be.

The monument to Joseph Cunningham was the same Joseph Cunningham in Granpa's memoirs who said Granpa's father worked him too hard.

19

MOM AND HER sister Jean were the only family members on her side living in Oregon while I was growing up. The other Whites, including Gramma White and Mom's oldest sister and her two brothers, lived in faraway places like Bismarck, North Dakota, Miami, Florida, and Germany. But for Gramma White, who would stay with us for a week or two each summer when we lived in Salem, I seldom saw those other Whites and in fact Mom's oldest brother Bob, who is in the Florida Bowling Hall of Fame, I didn't meet until I was age forty. It wasn't until I was a teenager when Uncle Jim, Mom's younger brother, retired from the army and moved to Eugene that we began to see more and more of Mom's kin, which by then there were nine of us cousins around the same age which meant there was a lot of horsing around when we got together.

The Keefes, on the other hand, seemed to be everywhere. When we moved back to Eugene in 1959 it was hard for Mom to get equal time. If we went to Auntie Jean's for Thanksgiving, then we spent Christmas with Gramma and Granpa. If we went to Auntie Jean's for Easter, then we spent Memorial Day with Dad's brother Uncle Dan. If we went to Auntie Jean's for July 4th, then we spent Labor Day with Dad's other brother Uncle Bob. And so on. When we moved across the street from Gramma and Granpa on Monroe Street we were literally surrounded by Keefes and any chance of equal time from the Whites was lost forever.

As I mentioned before, in addition to Gramma and Granpa across the street, around the corner on 19th street lived Granpa's younger brother Mike and his wife Maurine and daughter Mary Jane. Great Uncle Mike was the middle of the three brothers and married Gramma's sister Josephine in 1923 and between them had daughters Doris and Evelyn and son Howard Paul. They were arguably the smartest Keefes born in that generation. When Jopsephine was pregnant with Evelyn in 1931 a fortune teller told her she would die before Evelyn was born. Shortly afterwards she and Great Uncle Mike became "born again" Christians— Great Uncle Mike was raised Roman Catholic and had been an altar boy—and from photos of Josephine you can see how her hair changed from a stylistic bob to a simple pinned bun; they stopped playing cards and going to dances; their 1936 auto was painted in Bible verses. In 1933 the family came to Oregon from North Dakota at Granpa and Gramma's urging where in Eugene there were revival meetings in tents and a group called the Plymouth Brethren that soon started a Sunday school. In 1945 Josephine suddenly died from complications following surgery and two years later Great Uncle Mike married Maurine Turner. Daughter Mary Jane was born the following year, the same year I was born. Great Uncle Mike began working for EWEB in the 1940's and continued there until he retired in the late 60's. Like Granpa, he was a meter reader for a time, then a cashier, then worked in the warehouse. I spent many hours in his company when we lived on Monroe Street. He was slight of build with a small stoop, had translucent skin and deep liquid eyes, delicate hands, and I seldom saw him dressed in anything but coat and tie. He was the kindest and gentlest man I'd ever met, remarkably soft-spoken in spite of his high-pitched voice, and he always wanted to know how I was doing. I candy coated everything I told him because I admired him and didn't want to offend or disappoint him, bragging about my good grades or sports prowess while at the same time wondering what a condom was. Though he sprinkled his conversation with verses from the Bible, he never tried to convert me or transform my views, at least overtly, to his faith. Maybe he figured under Granpa's spell I was a lost cause. That he was Granpa's and Great Uncle Ed's brother seemed a hoax to me, the only clue being that he looked like them.

Three blocks up Monroe Street lived Granpa's youngest brother Ed and his wife Alice. In those days Great Uncle Ed ran the local bus company with a partner, and when I stayed at Granpa and Gramma's for a week when we lived in Salem Uncle Ed would stop by the house early in the morning driving a big green city bus and pick me up. He was shorter and stockier than his brothers, rounder in face but having the same lively Keefe eyes, and the knuckles on his huge hands would protrude and turn white when he clinched them and punch me in the shoulders as a form of greeting when I was a teenager, which I always faked hurt me, saying "No more Uncle Ed, no more!", but in fact it did hurt and under my breath I'd say "shit!". His son Leon told me he had worked in a traveling circus and boxed in his younger days before marrying Aunt Alice. Gramma would be with me on the curb as the bus approached and the brakes squealed, and I could see through the glass Uncle Ed pulling the silver handle and the front doors opening with one half turning in while the other half turning out. No one else was on the bus. Gramma gave me a little nudge up the first step and with a wide grin and a mischievous look in his eyes Great Uncle Ed greeted me as a special customer. I looked around. Far beyond anything before it was the largest vehicle I'd ever been in, with endless rows of seats split by a long narrow aisle, windows front to back spilling in handfuls of sunlight from every angle, horizontal and vertical and curved aluminum railing helping riders get on and off the bus and get seated, high ceiling that kept even the tallest person from having to stoop while finding a seat. From the side seat up front I watched as Great Uncle Ed revved the engine and began commandeering the bus around Eugene through intersections and up hills, navigating Willamette Street with its shoulder-to-shoulder stores and stop lights, over bridges and around tight street corners, along tree lined neighborhoods with fancy homes, forever watching out for pedestrians and oncoming cars while every couple of blocks stopping to take on passengers. I watched as they slipped their coins through the slot of the fare box next to Great Uncle Ed's seat, recalling the hard clink of the coins as they hit the bottom. Near the end of the route when there were few people on the bus Great Uncle Ed sat me on his lap and had me grasp the black oval steering wheel that was nearly horizontal to the floorboard and was as wide as I could stretch my arms. He guided my hands as I turned the wheel to pick up passengers, to navigate the next corner, to back the bus into a parking spot, he working the long transmission stick extending from the floor below my dangling feet, shifting from first to second and higher gears, pushing the bus forwards or backwards and sometimes grinding the gears in a metallic and clanging ring. From the driver's vantage point I could look over cars and people walking along the sidewalks and believe I was flying high above them. I could hear the pitch of the engine as it would slide into an alto or growl into a bass. I saw puffs of gray blue exhaust out the back window.

The rhythms and sounds of the bus—from its engine, breaks, doors—infatuated me to such a degree that it seemed a virtual symphony to my ears! Upon returning to Gramma and Granpa's later in the day I replicated them while powering toy boats, cars, and airplanes that Gramma gave me as toys. By day's end my lips burned like fire and my voice hoarse from overuse.

It was rumored that Great Uncle Ed and his partner split the profits at the end of the day and Uncle Ed would hurry home and bury his share in Folger coffee cans in his backyard. Each year he bought a new Chrysler with a trick horn that he'd toot at us every night on his way home from work. People in the neighborhood called him "The Horny Man". He showed me how he could change the channels on his car radio by simply waving his hand in front of it. He told me my motion wasn't right, or my mouth was too drawn, when I tried it, only to find out later he was secretly pushing a button on the floorboard with his foot.

Across town lived Ed and Alice's sons Leon and Kenny, and

daughters-in-law Corky and Marilyn. Leon was a school principal, Corky worked in retail; Kenny was a butcher, Marilyn a secretary. Dad's oldest brother Bob and wife Nelda and children Jimmy and Roberta lived in Roseburg, Oregon, an hour south of Eugene, where Uncle Bob was a State Policeman. His position in the police afforded a car full of us Keefes to pass through the otherwise cordoned off Roseburg when a truck of fertilizer blew up part of the downtown area in 1959. Uncle Dan, Dad's next oldest brother, and wife Arline and children Carolyn, Susan, and Linda lived in Winchester Bay, on the coast, where Uncle Dan taught high school math and ran charter boats during the summer break. For a week or two each summer we'd camp nearby while Dad helped Uncle Dan "swivel neck", or help out, on his boats. These Keefes were hard working, sociable, durable, opinionated.

Gramma and Granpa's house was the meeting place when relatives were in the neighborhood, and I could tell who was visiting from the make of the car in the driveway: Auntie Alice drove a green '54 Chevrolet coupe that had a fan mounted on the dashboard to keep her cool during the summer; Uncle Dan drove a brown Olds Rocket 88 that was heavily chromed and sleek with fins; Uncle Bob drove a purple Plymouth Barracuda that seemed contradictory to the police cars he drove on the job. When we'd see one of these cars parked it might be Dad and I who'd go over to see what was up, never knowing what we were walking into when we passed through the front door.

"Kennedy's too damn young to be President," Granpa would be saying, as Dad and I entered. "And he's Catholic to boot."

"You're going to vote for Nixon then?" It was Uncle Dan baiting Granpa. "Eisenhower's done a good job."

"Jesus Christ, Danny, you can't be serious! Look at the economy. Look at crime. And the commies caught Powers red handed spying on 'em. Eisenhower lied through his teeth."

"Now Robert, watch what you say," Gramma would interject, eying me.

"Godammit Forrest, I know what I'm saying!"

"Granpa secretly likes Nixon," I'd throw in like a hand grenade, knowing that Granpa was a staunch Democrat.

"Tricky Dick," Granpa would begin, a smile slowly creasing his face. "Now there's a piece of work for ya. Phony as a two dollar bill and nothin' but Eisenhower's go-fer. Ike hates his guts."

"So why you votin' for him?" Dad would tease.

"I'm not votin' for Nixon, godammit! Never voted Republican, never will.

"Sure Pop."

* * *

By the time I was born in 1948, and into the early 1950's, the Keefes were seeing their first wave of college graduates, including Dad and uncle Dan, who had been in the war and used the G.I. Bill to pay for tuition and books, and Dad's younger cousins Doris, Evelyn, Paul, and Leon, who like Dad went to the University of Oregon across town. It was a source of pride for the Keefe family to have members at university, for until then the sum total education of the three brothers—Granpa, Mike, and Ed—and sister Florence, was sketchy at best. Granpa went as far as eighth grade. This new college educated generation gave credence to the notion that the Keefes were indeed smart after all, as some in the family secretly suspected but couldn't readily prove if diplomas or material wealth was any indication. The university was the Keefes' meal-ticket to the middle class. They became architects, businessmen, educators.

The family possessed obscure claims to fame. Uncle Bob appeared in police uniform on the front page of state newspapers in 1959 when that truck blew up in downtown Roseburg killing several people. Gramma's cousin Emma and her husband Lester were featured in Life magazine when their son Jerry had disappeared in Trujillo's Dominican Republic after unwittingly flying a dissident Dominican there (Oregon congressman Charles Porter flew there to investigate but never found Jerry, who some say had been fed to the sharks). Granpa was on first name basis with U.S. Senator Wayne Morse, or so he claimed.

It was this milieu that I found myself in after moving back to Eugene from Salem at age 10. There was no mistaking my place in this tribe as we quickly became entwined in Gramma and Granpa's lives once again.

There was no knocking on each other's doors to enter. From their living room window they waved to Bill and me and Ann each morning as we walked to school. From their porch Gramma set off firecrackers each Fourth of July. Mom too fell under the spell of the Keefes. "There was something there" she once said, something she couldn't explain that wasn't in her family. Mom had lived with Gramma and Granpa when Dad went off to war, forming a strong attachment to Gramma. "I learned so much from her then," Mom told me later. While searching through an old box in my basement, I came upon a letter Mom had sent to Gramma postmarked January 4, 1953, from Olympia, Washington, where we had moved after Dad graduated from architecture school. I was four years old at the time. Though the letter was to "Dear Folks", it was directed to Gramma:

Dear Folks:

I have started this letter several times…Wish we were just a little closer—miss you every day.

Poor old Bill—he went strong on his (new) bike until the day before New Year's. He broke out all over with chicken pox. I don't know what he had in Eugene, but he definitely has chicken pox now. Was really covered but is healing now—feels like himself again. Three of the other little boys are down with them here in the neighborhood, so they probably got them at school. Hope Jerry and Ann get them soon and have it over with. If they don't…I'll be surprised.

Ann seldom crawls now. So cute to see her walking all the time. She knows she is doing something smart and does she show off. She feeds herself real well now. Seems kinda funny not having "one in arms" around here. Jerry really wanted to go with you (back to Eugene). Sure laughed at him when I got him ready for his nap. He said we couldn't sleep in Gramma and Granpa's bed because they would come back.

We enjoyed having you here so much (for Christmas) and thanks for everything. Seems like everytime I turn around I see something that reminds me you have been here. Have mended something everyday on the (sewing) machine. Going to get my

ticking next week and do the pillows—also going to make Ann
a jumper. We have had popcorn everyday. In fact we are out of
corn now.

    My Love, Gayle

    P.S. Bill says he is going to spend his summer vacation with
you. Said he ought to have his spinning outfit by then and you
could go fishing "with him" every day.

When we moved back to Eugene Gramma fell ill several times because of her weak heart and Mom would take care of her and make doctor appointments and shoo people away when Gramma needed rest, and cook for both her and Granpa as well as for us. She spent hours at Gramma's bedside. It was unfortunate years later when they had a falling out over Mom and Dad's divorce, Mom trying to get Gramma to side with her. Gramma couldn't—wouldn't—think of turning against her own kind, especially her favorite son, since "wrong" had no place in the Keefe vocabulary if it meant going against the family—the Keefe blood was too thick. After the divorce Gramma and Mom kept their distance from each other, each recognizing the emotional baggage between them, each knowing that regardless of the facts, regardless of the particulars, neither would change their minds about their own righteousness or the wrongness of the other's. In many respects they were alike. I want to believe that although Gramma was a cool customer and rarely sentimental, if she had the opportunity to bare her soul to a higher being without anyone knowing about it, then she would have professed a special love for Mom, a special place in her heart, for in all her time spent caring for Gramma, Mom certainly earned it.

After Mom and Dad's divorce, and Dad's and Gramma's passing a decade later, Mom gravitated back to the Keefe family. After a short rebound marriage following her divorce from Dad, Mom married Lee Jeans, a boyhood friend of Uncle Dan's and Dad's, who had skippered Uncle Dan's charter boats in the summertime. She was again invited to Keefe reunions and to some in the family she was never considered anything but a Keefe.

＊ ＊ ＊

In contrast, the Whites were handsome, happy-go-lucky, amiable. Except for Gramma White they were a less formidable force of nature and there was less tension among them, at least at eye level. Get-to-gathers with them were wild affairs in comparison and anything might happen among us kids. When Uncle Jim and his family moved to Eugene in the early 60's, there was suddenly a handful of White cousins living in the same town: Auntie Jean's and Uncle Buryl's kids Patty, Denny, and Peggy; Uncle Jim's and Aunt Mary's kids Janice, Lisa, and Jay; and we three.The boys among the cousins would often peel off after a Thanksgiving or Christmas dinner and head upstairs to Bill's and my bedroom where we would tie Jay up and torture him. He was the youngest of our White cousins (Denny was between Bill and me in age) with fair skin, short light hair, a toothy grin, scrawny-looking to us older teenagers, who would have thrown a protective familial blanket over him were it not for his motor mouth which seemed to have no "off" switch and got him in considerable trouble with us, much to our joy and pleasure. Jay would start it by saying something stupid to Bill, for example, like "Hey punk, get outta my way," as we scrambled up the stairs.

"Excuse me, did somebody fart?" Bill would say.

"Yeah, you."

"Step into my office to discuss it."

Next thing Jay was parallel to the floor having been grabbed and wrestled down by Bill, who now held his arms while Denny and I each latched onto a leg. Frantically squirming and wriggling trying to escape, it was a fruitless exercise for Jay in the face of overwhelming force—we'd lug him up the rest of the stairs and into our bedroom and close the door behind us. In the next moment we'd shove him onto my desk chair and tie his feet to the chair legs and cinch his hands behind the back of the chair, telling him if he screamed for help we'd cut his balls off. The interrogation began after that:

"What's your name, shit-for-brains?"

"Jay White."

"You lie!" we'd bellow in unison. "Tell us your *real* name!"

"Jay White."

"You're one dumb piece of hog's breath, aren't you? You think we don't know? Think we're stupid? We know who you *really* are."

"Who am I?"

"One dumb piece of hog's breath!" We'd laugh.

Then Bill would pull out his loaded squirt gun and twirl it around his trigger finger.

"Stop, stop, please!" Jay would shriek, eyes now wide.

"O.K., we'll stop, if you tell us your *real* name."

"It's Jay White, like I said," and then after a slight pause he would add "...punks."

Bill would let him have it four or five times in the face, point blank, and Jay now looked like he'd been face up in a rain storm.

"Like that shit-for- brains?"

"Did something happen?" Jay would smirk a moment later, water dripping down his face.

Again Bill would nail Jay with several rapid shots to the face with the squirt gun, then point the barrel downward and for good measure give him two or three more shots to the crotch of his pants so it looked like he'd wet them. Jay would wail.

From the stairwell we heard Dad holler up: "Hey, what's going on up there?"

"He's coming up the stairs!" Denny would whisper, an anxious look crossing his face. He was as rambunctious as Bill and me, he had an open face and expressive eyes, front teeth that protruded slightly, an athletic body.

"Untie him, fast," Bill would say, "and don't say a word Jay, or you're dead meat".

In a hurry I'd untie Jay and throw the rope under my bed just as Dad was coming through the bedroom door.

"Sounds like you guys are dropping bowling balls up here. What's going on?"

"Oh, just fooling around," Bill would say.

"Is that right Jay?"

"Ah...yeah...no problem Uncle Jim."

"What happened there?" Dad would point to Jay's pants.

"I, ah, splashed water on them when I was washing my hands...in the bathroom."

"Really?" Dad wasn't buying it, stretching out 'really' as if it were a four syllable word. "O.K., listen guys. I don't want any more racket from up here, right? The living room's right below and we can't even hear us talk. Got it?"

"We'll keep it down," we would echo together.

By the time Dad was at the bottom of the stairs we had Jay tied up again and asking once more what his real name was.

Another time we hung him up-side-down in our peach tree and peppered him with tennis balls. We stuffed him in our deep freeze and threatened to throw the key away (Aunt Mary, usually tolerant of our shenanigans with Jay, was upset at this one). As it turned out Jay grew up topping out at six foot two and weighing over two hundred pounds, playing football in high school and college. By then, Bill, Denny, and I agreed, he was a real nice guy and always knew his name, knew it in fact because we made a man of him. Even later as Bill, Denny, and I were graying at the temples we began abusing Jay again by denying we abused him at all as a kid, telling others that we were nurturing cousins, nice and proper. Or if there was abuse we couldn't recall who did it. We smile at our revisionist history in spite of knowing exactly what happened. This drives Jay mad these days, who still fumbles finding the "off" switch to his mouth.

Mom and Auntie Jean looked so much alike with their slender figures and brunette hair and dark eyes that they were often mistaken for each other around town. They traded giving permanents to each other, turning our kitchen into a chemistry lab with bottles of pungent wave solution and black combs, spiky curlers and hairpins, all splayed across the kitchen table like pick-up sticks. They gossiped too, and I remember walking in one time to get something from the refrigerator when Auntie Jean ended a funny story by calling herself a "boob". I was fourteen and "boob" was a strong word for me. We both turned crimson.

She was kind and thoughtful and through the years she'd seen how I loved dinner rolls, how I would eat three or four at Thanksgiving or Christmas, so she always pulled some off to the side for me. For my 21st birthday she made me the Mother Of All Dinner Rolls using an angel food cake mold and topping it with icing and candles, which pointed to her imaginative side that included writing exquisite poetry. She did this with other nieces and nephews too.

Along with staying at Gramma and Granpa's, Mom and Dad used to have me stay at Auntie Jean's in Eugene for a week and I'd play baseball, ride bikes, and swim with Cousin Denny. They lived in a small bungalow on Jefferson Street where Denny and I slept in an open unfinished room upstairs where the ceiling was the tilted roofline. One night in the middle of the summer it was hotter than a furnace and after we were put to bed Denny and I slipped out of our skivvies and t-shirts and using the beds like trampolines began jumping up and down hoping to cool off. Then Denny grabbed a flashlight and beamed it at me, first shining it in my eyes then at my belly button. It wasn't easy to do since we were bouncing up and down at different speeds, so when the light eventually veered to my flopping penis we burst out in peals of laughter. He threw the flashlight to me. But for the beam of light it was pitch black in the room. In turn I shined the light on him, doing the same by capturing his eyes and belly button and penis. By now we were delirious, laughing and howling and jumping higher and higher trying to touch the ceiling.

Suddenly the overhead light switched on and up the stairs bounded someone in a rush. Because there wasn't time to dress, I slipped into bed naked, pulling the cover up to my chin.

"What are you boys doing up here?"

It was Auntie Jean coming around the banister.

"Just talking," Denny said.

"Doesn't sound like it." Auntie Jean strolled towards me, a look of concern in her eyes. I pulled the covers further up. "Aren't you hot Jerry?"

"Oh no, Auntie Jean, I'm fine."

"Well let me help you there." She leaned over to pull the bed cover down. I held my ground, my hands now a vice grip on the covers.

"Really Auntie Jean, I'm fine."

"But you'll roast in there. It's so hot up here."

"No, really."

Nevertheless, Auntie Jean grabbed the cover.

"Auntie Jean?"

"Yes, Jerry."

"I'm o.k." Four hands now clutched at the bed cover.

"This will be cooler." She tugged at the covers.

"Auntie Jean?"

"Yes, Jerry. Is something the matter?"

"I don't have anything on."

For the remainder of that week I refused to take my clothes off. When Auntie Jean and Uncle Buryl tried getting me to take a bath, I vehemently refused. They worried I'd return to Salem smelling like a clothes hamper, and then what would Mom think? They begged, bribed, and coaxed until I finally relented the final night, when by then I was a walking dirt clod. I dictated the ground rules for the bath: no one would be in the bathroom when I took the bath; I would take my clothes off in the bathroom; I would wash myself; I would dry myself and put on clean clothes; no one was to peek through the keyhole.

This story about me refusing to take a bath was a favorite of Auntie Jean's and Uncle Buryl's and they kidded me about it later because they liked me and never took the story too far, never mentioning the part about Denny and I jumping naked on the beds, never making me out to be anymore than the innocent rascal I was. I'd chuckle and shake my head at my immaturity. Later Uncle Buryl began calling me "Paves the way" because of the sports story in the Wilsonian about our City Soccer Championship."

"Hey 'Paves the Way!'" he'd say when we arrived for dinner, or "Pass the butter 'Paves the Way.'"

When uncle Buryl unexpectedly died when I was in my twenties, Auntie Jean called me to her bedroom the next day in the midst of a house full of well wishers, and containing herself as best she could, she described to me how uncle Buryl had passed the previous night and that she was doing fine, just fine. She hid her grief for my benefit, but behind her eyes I caught a glimpse of fear, perhaps of the future. She was in her 50's and had many years ahead of her. But at that moment it was more important for her to soothe me than it was for me to soothe her. I felt special by her personal touch in the middle of her grieving, and like Gramma she was like a second mom to me and was my favorite aunt.

* * *

It is not easy gathering my arms around the Keefes and Whites. Though both families were from the Dakotas and had homesteaders in their histories, they were like two continents narrowly linked by the rocky isthmus of my Mom and Dad's marriage. If Mom and Dad had taken other spouses I doubt the families would have ever met, each whirling about in their own worlds between vast oceans living distinct and separate lives.

The Keefe sway is still strong these days but there is irony in why it is different and changed. Once Dad and his generation began graduating from university this close knit clannish family came to place education in the middle of the tribe's tradition and heritage. A college education became an expectation. Lo and behold, the children got more learned, worldly, became less provincial. The homespun got slowly spun out of them. Soon they were dispersing into a wider world where they were eager to understand its workings and make their mark. In the meantime, the old guard, now older and dwindling and wondering where everybody went, found themselves left behind on Monroe street.

I too would leave Eugene for the wider world, first to the Army and South Korea, then to live permanently in Portland. Sometimes I return to Eugene and want to turn back the clock and hear Dad's voice again, see Gramma's smile, smell Auntie Jean's dinner rolls. The world is timeless when you're young. Nothing seems to change. When you're older you see how time moves in spurts and starts from one moment to the next, from one age to the next, relentless and ruthless, a conqueror without guns.

The isthmus between the Keefes and Whites is broader now. In the succeeding years I have gotten to know the Whites more than I ever did as a child, in part due to Mom's brothers and sisters becoming closer themselves. In the 80's and 90's reunions and weddings brought some of them together for the first time in decades, perhaps realizing time was getting short for some of them. Mom's oldest brother Bob, who had been incommunicado for half a century, came into the fold. E-mails passed among us. Mom kept me posted.

20

IT WOULD BE 10 o'clock on a crisp Sunday morning when I'd start phoning and by 10:30 AM everyone had been called. In the privacy of our homes we'd begin our preparations.

The conditions were perfect. Earlier in the morning I had stepped outside my home on Monroe Street and felt the lawn: it was soggy to the touch as I bent down and pressed my hand against it, I heard the *squish squish squish* as I walked on it. Good, I thought, the squishier the better. The turf would be the same at Washington Park, three blocks east where we'd gather. A week's worth of Oregon rain always did the trick.

Preparations would be similar among those I'd called this morning. From my closet and basement and garage I gathered old throwaway clothes that one by one I pulled over my body, layering them for two reasons: first, it would be wet and cold outside—being late Fall—and I knew this layering would stand against the chattering teeth and goose bumps that would otherwise test my capacity for wishing I was doing something else. Water and cold would not seek its own level and then stop, but rather seek to chill my warm flesh from all angles, I knew this from experience, so I grabbed what I could from around the house while keeping in mind I needed mobility too.

The second reason had to do with the relationship between pain and muscles tensed by cold weather. Receiving a violent smack when it's cold outside is a physical experience not to be confused with a poke in the rib or a stubbed toe on a warm day. Limbs like icicles would be snapped off, blood squirted in quarts, bones cracked in two, and it felt by day's end that the accumulated pain suffered among us was equal to all the pain suffered in all the battles of all the wars ever fought in the history of mankind. Thus I was looking for protection, a shield against the inevitable onslaught, so more layers meant more recoil absorption and less cringe factor. I put on as many frayed and ragged jeans as possible, and tattered sweatshirts, holey socks, unraveling stocking caps, fingerless gloves; the shoes I wore were throwaways that sometimes from the powerful suction of the mud I'd run right out of, leaving them trapped and half buried in the muck. Fashion didn't matter, the uniform purely utilitarian. I was a mobile but ramshackle Egyptian mummy when I'd leave the house.

I wouldn't blame Mom for rolling her eyes. She knew I would return in some degree of squalor and foulness, but to what degree—encased in a shell of mud, unrecognizable, a zombie of filth and grime and nastiness oozing through the back door—only time would tell. I would tell her not to worry, telling her lies such as:

"There's no real tackling, Mom, just two below", meaning the play stops when the tackler touches the runner with his two hands below the runner's waist. No grabbing and throwing down.

Or: "It isn't that muddy, and I'll clean everything up. Promise. Not a speck of dirt anywhere, promise."

I told Mom these lies because a "no" from her meant a "no" from Dad which meant a "no" to going to Washington Park which meant a "no" to the meaning of life. And why would anyone in their right mind say "no" to that? Mom had an extra sense for smelling a rat, so I would start early and wear her down, assuring her the game was no more than a powder-puff amusement. When she would say "yes" my heart jumped with joy.

Washington Park takes up two city blocks bordered by 19th and 21st streets on the north and south, and Lawrence and Washington streets on the east and west. From 19th street to 21st street there is a gradual incline leading up to College Hill, so the early architects split the park into three tiers: on the lower tier, the largest, are two baseball diamonds that can convert to a soccer/football field; on the middle tier is a full length asphalt basketball court, a recreation hall, a kid's playground and wading pool, and an open grass field for general purpose; on the upper tier is another open area for baseball or football, and two fenced-in tennis courts encircled with lights. We played football on the lower tier, but through the years there wasn't an inch of Washington Park we didn't use, whether it was for sports, flirting with girls, fights, or just hanging around. It was our second home.

In those days everyone had their favorite football players whom they were anxious to imitate: Johnny Unitas, Y.A. Tittle, Jim Brown, Norm Van Brocklin, Big Daddy Libscomb. Not only did we like their play but we also like how their names rolled off our tongues, liked their nicknames. And we idolized teams like the Baltimore Colts, L.A. Rams, Green Bay Packers, and San Francisco Forty-Niners. This game at Washington Park was no less than an All-Star game of these living legends played by these mythic teams and watched by millions of people.

The regulars would be there: John Hall, Dan Jones, Wayne Dickson, Dan Larson, Brad Parish, Keith and Jim Derry. Maybe brother Bill and his friend Fred Beckley too. All of us lived within blocks of Washington Park. We were blessed and fortunate that Sunday, though none of us went to church, set apart from those who didn't show up and who later got razzed at school about being "panty wastes" and momma's boys, and who had to settle on listening to endless stories about the great game they missed as if what they missed was no less than history in the making. While walking to Washington Park I was excitable and my mind would imagine, even exaggerate, some of the heroic plays from previous games—John Hall's diving catch where he gains an extra five yards from the momentum of sliding head first through a pool of water (in normal football the ball is put down where the player first hits the ground, but in our game we added the slide); Dan Jones' header over a pile of defenders for a touchdown, his face landing with a slap in the mud followed by his torso crumbling about him, Dan emerging smiling and looking like Al Jolson in blackface; Wayne Dickson dragging the whole opposing team on his back for ten yards for a touchdown, looking like a beast of burden in a social studies film.

Two captains would pick the sides with the best players getting picked first and the worst last. But in these games it didn't really matter who got picked first or last because the normal laws of nature didn't apply. For example, if a fleet of foot player cut too hard one way or another his feet would often slip from underneath them from lack of traction. Or if a player tried running too fast he would turn into a human treadmill in the mud, going nowhere fast, even losing his shoe. It was hard to get a head of steam, so the best player was not the fastest or the slyest but rather the player who was built lowest to the ground and carried some weight. A wrestler for example. Wayne Dickson was that sort—short, stocky, strong as an ox. The best way to stop him was to rope him and shoot him.

Within a few plays after kickoff we would be initiated to the conditions, each of us taking our first hits and feeling the cold and the pain, each of us getting our first splotches of mud on our mummified-looking uniforms. And after a few trips up and down the field when the turf got churned up, the game would roll into a full fledged mud bowl and running speed would be at 1—2 mph., a perfectly sluggish pace in my opinion. There would be puddles too, big and small, like sandtraps in golf, to be avoided or, for those more tactical minded players, used to an advantage. From afar we looked like a chain gang mired in molasses.

I'd take a short pass from Bill and immediately get nailed by Fred Beckley, the cockiest person in the world and rich by his dad's lumber mill, who would mutter "eat shit" while I pulled myself from the mud. Heading back to the huddle my head would be ringing and convinced the two of them had planned it that way.

   DREAM FAMILY ♦ A MEMOIR

"Nice catch" Bill would whisper in the huddle, a smirk on his face. I admired Bill in a big brother way, but not always.

"Thanks asshole."

As we moved our team downfield we would remember from last year's games the strategies and tactics that worked: keep the passes short because the wet and muddied football was like a penguin fresh out of water, hard to grab let alone catch, plus our fingers were wet and cold. We fumbled a lot so we did a lot of end sweeps and reverses to keep the ball away from defenders for as long as possible. We kept handoffs and laterals to a minimum. A stranger looking from afar would think the ball had financial significance since everyone was trying to get it, but then the stranger would be baffled when play stopped and the ball would lay quietly on the wet field undisturbed and serene, oblivious to the plans being made in the next few seconds.

We would break huddle for another play. We were near the goal line now and our play was designed for a score. In retrospect it was the outstanding play of the day and it went something like this: Bill received the hike from Keith Derry. John Hall, who was playing left side tight end, stepped back from the scrimmage line and received a quick lateral from Bill. He followed Bill while Bill ran interference. Keith and I pulled out from our linemen's positions and gathered on either side of Bill forming a "Flying Wedge" in front of John. I could see it was coming together like a gunfight at the O.K. Corral. We each picked a defender to take out. Accompanied by groans and grunts we began knocking down defenders left and right, pow, pow, pow. All was going according to plan until suddenly someone somehow slipped through the human wall and hit John head first in the solar plexus. The football popped out of John's arms, and John, turning jellyfish, slumped to the mud in a heap, his eyes rolling up. Someone yelled "fumble!"

The airborne football reached its apex and then turned end over end, and like everyone else I was looking the wrong way—down at the ground—rather than in the air for it, so when it hit me on the head I thought someone had poked me. The ball bounced up again and Fred Beckley, who it turned out had sneaked through to make the hit on John, snapped the ball out of the air and began running to his goal line at the opposite end. Our team, except for John, who was now gasping for air like a beached salmon, wheeled around and, seeing who had the ball, began chasing Fred. He had stolen an imminent touchdown from us and was destined to pay dearly.

"You're dead meat, Beckley," someone roared over heavy breathing and the sound of sloshing tennis shoes trudging machine-like through the mud. The gap was closing between Fred, a slow runner anyway, and his pursuers. Mud kicked up from our heels. I knew what was going through Fred's mind because the same thing had happened to me in previous games: it's a bad dream where you're being chased by sick but speedy monsters with open wounds, one of which is gaining on you while your shoes fill with wet sand. Fred heard our footsteps, our taunts.

"Give it up, Beckley, you're dogshit!" someone else screamed. Keith and I were the first to catch up to Fred. I jumped on his back while Keith dove and wrapped his arms around Fred's legs. As he began to tumble he stuck his arm out to cushion the fall, only to lose control of the football cradled in his other arm, it popping out and now rolling in slow motion in the mud, still in play. I jumped off and scrambled over and grabbed it. For the second time this play the ball was in our team's possession, but now our goal was fifty yards away!

I began trotting slowly, assessing the defense in front of me and yelling to my teammates for help. With Fred and Keith behind me, that left three blockers to take out four defenders before making the touchdown. But could I count on John Hall, who sill appeared a jellyfish, at the five-yard line? The math wasn't good. I would have to employ some fancy footwork to make it all the way.

Jim Derry, Keith's younger brother, was the first to take a swipe at me, taking the bait of a perfectly timed head fake and flying past me in a whir. Bill saw that I was heading for the right corner of the field, so he trapped Brad Parrish there, bowling him over and pinning him; he out-weighed Brad by twenty pounds.

Dan Jones had his hands full with Wayne Dickson, the beast of burden, who was making a beeline at me determined to spoil the play and turn the tide once again. But Dan's quick and constant bumps deterred Wayne's pursuit enough to give me a seam to slip through.

Slogging through mud as fast as I could was not easy work, like running with weights on your feet, but at that moment I felt I was skipping along the surface with the grace of a figure skater. I was "in the zone". I was now crossing the fifteen-yard line and closing in, anxious to make the goal, but there was one defender left between me and the goal line that could destroy my ambition: Dan Larsen, the fleetest among us, destined to become a track star in high school. There wasn't a chance in hell I would get by him, he was too quick and agile, and had an angle on me, due to pounce at the ten-yard line. But I had an idea, ignoble as it was.

I turned from the right corner of the field to the center, running almost parallel to the goal line. A moment before I had seen John Hall showing signs of life, as if miraculously returning from the dead, rolling over and shaking his head, raising himself on his hands and knees. It was then I saw the opportunity. He was between Larsen and me, and Larsen in a flash must have seen everything, seen what I was seeing, and thought "Oh my God! This can't be!" The mound of flesh and bones comprising John Hall, no more than a bump in the road and easily jumped had metamorphosed into a human hurdle the size of a St. Bernard. It was too late for Larsen to change direction, he tried to put the skids on but couldn't, and in that split second of hesitation and extra effort to leap high over John to catch me, there was enough time to change everything because the mathematics of the angles and the physics were inexorable. Seeing Larsen approaching, John's eyes went from narrow and glassy to grand and luminous. "No, no! Not again!" he must have thought, clutching his chest. I ducked as Larsen leaped over John and whirred by me in a blur, his hands outstretched to get a piece of me but missing altogether. With a thud he hit the muddy ground empty-handed, now powerless to stop me. I trotted the few more yards. John had inadvertently taken out Larsen without laying a hand on him! It was beautiful! It was divine! It was holy! It was the end zone!

At least that is what I remember.

By game's end there was no telling who was who from a distance. Caked in mud from head to toe—mud behind my ears and in my hair, chunks on my eyelids and in my pants—I even tasted it in my mouth. I smelled like mud too, that turfy fertilizer odor when the sod has been overturned too much.

Neighbors stared at us from living room windows when Bill and I staggered home. Were their frightened children clinging to their legs watching too? Did they think we were returning from a nasty round of the Crusades?

When we turned up at the house Mom would take one look at us and roll her eyes, then point at the garden hose and clothesline in the backyard. She had been on the lookout for us to make sure we didn't sneak into the back door before cleaning off. Using the nozzle at full pressure, Bill and I would douse each other in the back yard while chunks of mud flew here and there from our shoes and pants and sweatshirts, each of us getting final pro-forma squirts in before Mom cried "That's enough!"

We would peel off our water-soaked clothes and hang them on the nearby clothesline, it sagging from the weight, and scamper into the house in our skivvies, a mad dash because we were wet and freezing and knowing we had one more chore.

In the shower, water the color of the Ganges would stream off my body into the drain, doing cleanup work for whatever the hose didn't get. Repeated scrubbings turned the water clear, which at first was cold and shocking against skin, but then becoming warm and the balm and liniment for the sunny new face of the skin. From a chunk of coal I became a diamond.

My muscles would heave a sigh of relief once out of the shower. I dried and dressed in warm clothes and slippers. Later lying on the couch in the living room I dozed, the Giants were playing the Rams, and from the kitchen oven wafted the aroma of roast beef. I would soon hear Gramma and Granpa's footsteps on the front porch.

21

WHEN IT WAS hot in the middle of summer Bill and I used to sleep outside in our sleeping bags and once, when we were certain Mom and Dad were asleep, we snuck out and met girls. Mom and Dad's open bedroom window was nearby so we kept quiet as we slipped from our bags and tip-toed to the gravel alley leading to 20th street. It was after midnight and Bill and I took special care while stealthily bounding from tree to tree and hedge to hedge, keeping a keen eye out for other people plus oncoming headlights, fearing that any pair of them might be those of a police car. Our destination was Jefferson Junior High school several blocks away. We slipped down 20th across Friendly Street, then by "Tyler Poked Taylor" streets, as we used to call those presidential streets, then up to 22nd, passing Adams Elementary school on the way.

I'd met Vickie Thorkelson at the Jefferson Street pool—not to be confused or associated with Jefferson Junior High—near where Auntie Jean and Uncle Buryl lived. I used to hang out there between the end of school and the beginning of bean picking season in Mid-July, high season for the pool when kids from several schools, including Wilson Junior high, where I was soon to be a ninth grader, and Jefferson Junior high, where some of my friends from Adams Elementary went, swam there. Admission was twenty-five cents, I paid at the front desk just inside the entry of the small rectangular brick building, the attendant issuing me a wire meshed basket for putting my street clothes in. In the men's section to the right of the front desk I changed into my swimsuit, attached the basket's pin (with the basket's number on it) to my trunks, then returned the full basket to the front desk through a hole in the wall. I remember the dressing room floors perennially wet and slippery from the showers and water dripping from swimmers coming and going. Lifeguards kept an eagle eye that I took a shower before entering the pool area and diving into the water.

We planned to rendezvous in the tall grassy area just beyond center field of Jefferson's baseball diamond. Vickie and Bill's girlfriend Janet were coming from a few blocks north, we were triangulating, and as we converged on our destination I could feel my heart pound like a sledgehammer. Amply nervous and excited, I may have wondered in the quiet of that warm summer night if the cops, for example, could hear my heartbeat and home in on it? Such were my thoughts at the time.

And would the girls really be there just as we planned?

It was an Olympic sized pool with high and low diving boards at the deeper north end. A high wooden paneled wall surrounded that end of the pool, then about halfway down the west side the wall gave way to a shoulder high cyclone fence, which continued around the shallow end of the pool ending at the brick building. Black numbers ranging from three to ten were painted on the rim of the pool indicating depth in feet, and, in my own mind, a quantitative danger level related to drowning—ten feet meaning there were ten times more chances of drowning than in the three feet area. To swim in the deeper end meant you could swim the width of the pool, and lifeguards would challenge you if they thought you couldn't do it.

During the hottest days of June and July, when the sun's heat turned parts of the nearby black asphalt soft and gooey, the pool turned into a sea of flailing shiny bodies resembling a school of migrating fish. You had to come early to find a place to lay your towel on the pool's concrete border. Prime focus was the deep end where the diving boards were and where the older boys—i.e. Bill, Dan Jones, Fred Beckly, Jack Walrath—did great athletic feats off the boards to the amazement of the younger onlookers. It was there I gravitated to learn their exotic dives: the "baroni" (front flip with a half twist); "can-opener"; (an angled feet first jump with one leg tucked under resulting in a high splash); "suicide" (a calculated belly flop with a quick jack-knife at the end that prevented the inimitable sting and ache of a normal belly flop). Diving off the high dive was the most frightening thing I'd done in my life up to then and it was a dose of both peer pressure and sheer excitement that made me do it. Bill pushed and dared me.

"C'mon pussy, scared?" he'd say.

I'd try whatever dive in vogue in spite of being petrified to the bone and knowing better, and my most famous one was a two and a half front flip that took several excruciating belly flops to learn—I couldn't get enough around on the last turn for the head first dive—but once done perfectly I never attempted it again. A year later I would watch Bill do a "baroni" off the superstructure of the Armitage Park Bridge, which loomed a hundred feet above the McKenzie River, his dive finishing with a mere murmur of a spash on the river's surface, the act befitting an aerialist.

But it was not just for the sheer excitement or dare that we did these dives, but for the girls sunning themselves nearby and watching us like hawks though they tried to hide it. Diving was our way of distinguishing ourselves from the hoi polloi, from the swirling masses below us, and it seemed to work, for Vickie Thorkelson took notice of me and over a period of days we got to know each other.

"She's hot for you," Bill said.

She was my age and went to Jefferson Jr. High. She appeared to me exotic, though I wouldn't have known the term relative to girls then. She had black shiny hair, olive skin, arching eyebrows, penetrating and lively eyes, a slender figure, nearly my height. It was rumored she had a "rep", which meant she went *all the way*, which meant I'd bluff my vague understanding of the term to save face, but in truth I didn't know what it *really* meant, my knowledge purely by word of mouth, all adding to the intrigue about her.

But I wondered: "Why is she hot for me? Because I'm Wilson's Vice President next year? Because I can do a 'baroni' off the high dive?" It was bittersweet because I was happy she was hot for me but what was I supposed to do with this volatile information? I was troubled and excited.

"We're meeting her and Janet tonight at Jefferson," Bill added.

"What? Tonight? When tonight?"

"Midnight."

"Damn," I thought. "What are we going to do?"

"You'll figure it out."

At age fourteen my body was changing before my eyes—not only was I growing like a weed but there were physical feelings I couldn't explain. I found myself drawn in by girls and getting "crushes" and infatuations and wondering what it would be like alone with them. Life magazine featured movie stars in slinky dresses that I would blush at first viewing. I masked this with bravado and wit, learning big words, but I was just as often moody and self-conscious around girls. I felt unprepared and untrained for what was coming that night, caught up in a whirlwind of excitement and taboo. I blindly went along for the ride, my fingers crossed, hanging onto a thin thread of guiltlessness, and hoping to emerge undamaged in the end.

What was I to figure out? What was at stake? And what would happen?

Being a couple years older than me, Bill had an aggressive agenda. He had "made-out" with girls, talked of "getting a piece". I liked Vickie, but did she really like me? Did she know what she wanted—in other words, was she "experienced"? Why was she willing to sneak out of her house— to get more "experience?" "What kind of girl would do that?" I wondered. Boys can sneak out but girls who do have "reps".

I rationalized that I was going with my big brother, my possibly asinine big brother if we got caught, who I hoped knew the ropes enough not to get caught. On my own I wouldn't have done it, wouldn't have had the boldness or courage or audacity to do it.

We were ducking between houses and bushes in the final blocks. We saw headlights and crouched behind a laurel hedge and kept silent as the car inched by, an old Desoto, not a police car. We breathed easier and forged ahead.

They were there when we arrived but hadn't been waiting too long. Up to then Bill and I wondered if they would really show—the uncertainty of their getting away, the possibility they couldn't or wouldn't sneak out, losing nerve in the end. But there they were in front of us as real as the night and the kaleidoscope of stars above us. There wasn't much time. It was midnight in the middle of summer. In tall grass beyond center field there was no turning back now.

A few weeks earlier Mom sat me down at the dining room table and told me the facts of life. I don't remember what prompted it. Maybe she felt it was time, sensing my anxieties. The whole episode disgusted and shamed me so much—was it in Mom's presentation, the photos?—that afterwards, in a state of shock and distress, I reeled outside into our backyard. It was a sunny day. I looked upwards into the bright clear sky and vowed then and there to devote my life to Jesus and God and all His infinite Wisdom. Never would I do that revolting thing Mom had just told me about. All that wasted time wondering about what I saw in the bushes at High Street! I'd remain chaste.

The emotional and physical roller coaster I was riding then, at age fourteen, was acute enough that my pledge to Jesus and God and chastity lasted maybe a day or less, but certainly no more than a day. I couldn't control my strong feelings for certain girls. These crushes took on gigantic proportions. If I was rebuffed or snubbed in some way, I sulked for days, awash in enough pity and sorrow to fill a swimming pool. Before Vickie there was Holly Cohen, also from Jefferson, who I fell hard for, but who dumped me for her old boyfriend, a "hood", which I failed to understand and for that I laid motionless in bed for an entire afternoon, my throat knotted up as if mourning a family death, wondering how life could be so cruel and heartless, particularly for me. What had I done to deserve such a fate?

This turmoil was not good for me, I knew that, but I had little control over it. All I could do was forge ahead.

"You made it o.k.?" Bill whispered to Vickie and Janet.

"We couldn't tell if the headlights were cop cars." Janet said.

"Same here," Bill replied.

Bill and Janet spoke a few more words, quietly, while Vickie and I stood awkwardly facing each other. Then we split up in pairs and I was suddenly alone with Vickie—suddenly alone with a girl I had dreamed about. Alone in the tall grass at midnight just beyond center field. My self- consciousness soared geometrically—my heart was now a series of nuclear explosions in a mineshaft, and out of the blue I was aware of having a neck. Every moving part in my body felt like it had recently been attached. What was I to do with my arms, my ears? The sound of energy buzzed in my head like a swarm of bees.

We laid down in the grass. My experience kissing up to then, less kissing aunts and grammas, was nil.

"You like me?" Vickie whispered.

"Sure. Do you like me?"

"Why do you think I'm here?"

"Right."

I leaned over to kiss her. Where was the saliva supposed to go? It was miraculous that she didn't drown, or didn't seem to mind.

I remember the night sky being as dark as a well hole, but I could see the Big Dipper glowing as bright as embers in a campfire, and thousands of other stars too. The grass around us was like a castle wall; I couldn't see anything at ground level. We were truly alone.

"You have another girlfriend at Wilson?" Vickie pulled back from a long kiss, breathless, needing air.

"No. Nothing. What about you?"

"Not really."

"What do you mean 'not really'?"

"Not really is what I mean."

Then she leaned in and we kissed again.

We whispered more things. Were we whispering to each other or whispering to dreams of this moment? Then we didn't whisper, only laid there in silence. I kept an ear and eye out for Bill and Janet, who were a few yards away, invisible in the grass, hardly making a peep.

Since neither of us had any idea what to do beyond a certain point, we kissed some more. I certainly wasn't going to do "it" like my Mom described.

"Hey, hotshot, its time to go." whispered Bill over the grass, moments later. I think Vickie and I were secretly relieved from all the kissing. What more was there to do?

Bill didn't want to push our luck the first time sneaking out. "Let's do this tomorrow night," he said.

"O.K. about tomorrow night?" Vickie asked.

"Sure," I replied.

We kissed one last time and then we both disappeared into the darkness, but not before waving to each other.

The next morning at breakfast Dad acted as if he knew exactly what we'd been up to the night before.

"You guys better not be getting in any trouble with the police," he said.

I gulped.

"Tonight you'll be sleeping inside."

Another gulp.

Later Bill and I phoned Vickie and Janet to warn them, but no luck. We looked for them at the swimming pool. We asked friends about them. We phoned again and again, but to no avail, they were incommunicado. We went to bed that night worried that if they showed up at Jefferson later they wouldn't find us and they would be pissed.

At around one o'clock in the morning Bill and I were awakened by rocks hitting against our second story screen window. Bill looked out to see Vickie and Janet standing below on the narrow side lawn, in front of Mom and Dad's bedroom.

"Come down," they whispered loudly.

"Go away," Bill hissed through the screen. "We can't come out. We tried to call you."

How did they know where we lived and which bedroom window was ours? Could Vickie and Janet see right through our house and into our bedroom?

"Why can't you come out?" Janet whispered.

"We just can't," Bill said. "We're in trouble."

They stood there stubborn about not leaving without us, arms folded in front.

"Come on!"

"No!"

"Fine," Janet said, and after some murmuring between them they turned and disappeared into the night.

From their open window, screened like ours, Mom and Dad must have heard everything—how could they not have? I imagined them lying there, ears perked and hearing the hushed dialog, both grinning, and knowing we weren't going anywhere. We never slept outside again that summer.

I saw Vickie Thorkelson once more a couple months later in the early Fall after a soccer match between our schools. The match had been played at Jefferson on a field next to where Vickie and I met that fateful night. At one point the game had been stopped because I had been kicked in the head and the refs had checked me out for blurred vision, but I was alright. I was getting on the team bus. Suddenly Vickie appeared out of nowhere, buffeted by a couple of friends. I was vaguely aware she was there and had watched the game—had I been looking for her and spotted her earlier? She wanted to talk to me. I was stepping up to the bus. She looked upset. Was she concerned about me getting kicked in the head? Or did it have to do with what happened in the grass beyond center field?

"C'mon Keefe," Mr. Bradetitch, our coach, yelled. "Keep it moving."

"Why didn't you call me?" Vickie quickly asked.

"I thought you were mad at me, about that night."

"You could have at least called."

"We got in trouble, and then bean picking started."

I was being pushed onto the bus. I let on that I had to move on, couldn't talk, the bus was leaving. But in fact I was a coward, frightened out of my wits from Vickie's sudden appearance. In those intervening weeks I had thought a lot about her and what we did that summer night, rolling it over and over in my mind for hours on end, or so it seemed. I was afraid of what would happen to us if we picked up from where we left off. What would it lead to? (To Mom's "it"?) I was afraid of how it would interfere with school and sports and all the other stuff boys hide behind when they can't identify or face up to their feelings. I made a choice.

"Who was that?" a teammate asked.

"Ah, nobody."

It was the last time I ever saw the first girl I ever kissed.

I didn't go to Jefferson pool much after that. Maybe not at all. By then I was entering high school, and working more in the summer, and all those kids at the pool seemed so young and immature to me. I had done all the diving I wanted.

22

"I LEFT HOME," Granpa wrote in his memoirs.

Over the years when I lived across the street from him, Granpa told me bits and pieces the story of him running away from home at age 17, but never in its entirety or in such detail as he wrote in his memoir. The narrative is so powerful and so compelling that I felt transported back to his house on Monroe Street, listening to him once again. Furthermore, I thought the writing in this part of his memoir, though rough in parts, was at the core sufficient and honest enough to stand on its own, and except for some minor editing I could not tell the story any better than he did.

* * *

"On March 7, 1910 I found myself running away again. Father had threatened to beat me with a black snake whip the next time I got in trouble, and I knew it was soon time I received such a beating. For what I do not know.

Mother and I had talked it over and she thought it was best for me to get away. Father was drinking heavily and did not know just what he was about. He would take his feelings out on me whether I deserved it or not. I knew I was doomed.

Mother put my little bundle of clothes and a lunch in my hands and bid me goodbye. I felt so sad as I kissed my little brothers Mike and Ed as they lay in their bed upstairs.

I hurt mother far beyond my understanding at the time. I felt that I was entering the vast field of eternity as I walked through the barn gate into the pasture and started north across the pasture. I seemed to remember every step I took that long first night.

There was a new moon, but the stars were bright enough that [I could see the] shadows of buildings at some distance. I was also able to follow trails and not walk into fences or fall into holes that might be in my path.

I cried most of the night.

I plodded along through water and slush that covered most of the ground. Spring was just beginning and all the snow had not melted. In a very short time my feet were soaked and I became cold whenever I stopped to rest.

I was afraid that I would not get far enough away and Father would catch me in the morning. I walked about fifteen miles that night. In the morning I rested for a couple of hours in a hay stack. I felt better when I woke up except for the crying spells.

I pushed on towards the Canadian border. I felt that if I could get there Father would have a hard time finding me. It was just kid reasoning and not very sound. But that was the way I planned.

About noon the second day I came to the railroad that connected Antler N.D. with the main line of the Great Northern at Rugby N.D. Somehow I turned west toward Antler, which was only two miles from the border. I arrived in town around 3 p.m.

To my surprise there were farmers looking for farm hands. I was fortunate to have a kind gentleman from the Canadian side contact me and offer thirty dollars per month to clean grain and prepare for the spring seeding. His name was Robert Nunn...about 60 years old...[with] a very nice wife...two daughters about 11 and 13 and a son named Sutton. [Sutton] was just married and lived two miles north of the home place.

Mr. Nunn came from England and was English to the core. They had their daily portion of black tea which was new to me. Also, it was confusing the way they pronounced their words with English inflections.

I helped Mr. Nunn for about three weeks when he asked me to work for his son. Sutton was very lazy so all the Spring work fell on me. Most of the time he spent entertaining his new wife, who was a very nice lady who cooked well and cared for me nicely. In truth they were all kind to me except that Sutton was short of money.

Nonetheless I worked steadily during April, May, and June for Sutton. The one thing I got was a case for my violin. I ordered it from Montgomery Ward and had it shipped directly to Mother.

Sutton arranged for me to charge at the store in Antler, so when the Fourth of July arrived I bought a new suit and charged it. He had given me about fifteen dollars to spend. I thought I was well off, but I also knew the weather was hot and dry and it was evident that there would be little grain. The wheat was turning brown in spots and I could expect no more money from Sutton.

That same day I met Jack—I do not remember his [last] name—but he was tall, slim, and dark complexioned and had been working out for some time. He seemed to know his way around...and we decided to get out of that country. We bought tickets to Minot, [N.D]. for the fifth of July. When we arrived we found that the Great Northern needed carpenters at Galatea, Montana.

Together we bought a saw, hammer, and a square, and this was our ticket to Montana. They sent us on our way, and it was then that I knew I was getting away from Father for sure.

Galatea was like the early towns in Dakota with unfinished buildings covered with dust and dirt. The menfolk carried their guns either in a gun belt or in their hip pockets. One would hear shooting most anytime day or night. As soon as someone got too much liquor in themselves they would start a fight. It could be either fist or gun, it made little difference because all were floaters and bums. We worked at Galatea for two weeks until all that was left to do was the finish work, so we were discharged.

We were able to get a ride in the cab of a freight engine to Shelby [Montana?]. We were both thrilled from it except the jumping off that sent us rolling along the track for several feet. But the engineer said we must jump because he did not wish to be caught carrying bums—it would have cost him his job.

From there we caught a freight train. We were kicked off a couple of times more but we got right on again until we reached Higate, Montana, where we knew we were kicked off for sure. It so happenned that Higate is the summit of the Rocky Mountains.

That was very interesting for Jack and me because neither of us had seen mountains before and here we were right on top of our highest range. The trees were just beyond belief: tall stately pines with their beautiful green branches that hid most of the mountain sides. A charming creek ran along side the railroad, sparkling and babbling. The night before we were in that hot, dry, flat country that had great cracks in the ground from the baking since the Spring and where hardly a blade of grass was to be seen. Now we were transported into a heavenly place where nature had only been disturbed some years before by the building of the road. Nothing beyond was that different from hundreds of years before. There was wildlife everywhere—bears, deer, birds, etc. Because of that men did not tarry long.

It was a nine mile walk to Essex, Montana, and we enjoyed every minute of it. We would throw stones at the creek below the road, but the stones seem to hit close to our feet. We did not realize the distances were out of perspective for boys raised on the prarie.

We noticed that the railroad company had employed Japanese to fill most of the jobs on the road-bed work. We even saw that the switch engine was operated by Japs. They were the first of that nationality we had ever seen, and we were impressed with the fact that they were in such a strategic location, there being talk of war with Japan at the time. I found out later that their men were placed in like locations all through the Rocky Mountain region. Therefore, it would have been easy

for them to cut the west coast off from the rest of the United States. All
they needed to do was to destroy the road and cut the telegraph in 1910.
And with a few men they could hold the passes until they gained a strong
foothold on the coast. I remember the plan that was later divulged of
the Japanese landing at Greys Harbor in Washington by an American
working for them in 1909. Today [1964] that sounds unreasonable
because we have planes and radio, but then it was not farfetched.

Jack and I hopped a freight at Essex (Montana?) and headed for
Spokane. When we got to Whitefish (Montana?) we got into a car loaded
with steel rails. The car was so heavily loaded that the ride was smooth,
even though the train seemed to go a lot faster than the one out of Essex.
We went through Sandpoint, Idaho and the lumber mills there, and soon
found ourselves in Hilyard, Washington, which was the railroad yards
about five miles east of Spokane.

We were lucky not to be arrested, but there were hundreds of men
riding the freights in 1910, so they could not arrest all of us. Only those
they suspected of crimes other than riding freight trains. The Brakeman
usually collected a dollar or two from us for riding their division, and
after that they would not see us again.

Jack and I took a streetcar into Spokane and started looking for jobs.
We split up while I was looking for a job in a laundry, but there were so
many girls there that I never went back. I found out there was going to be
some threshing done at nearby Tekoa, Washington, so I bought a ticket.

In Tekoa I met a young farmer by the name of Benton Poole and he
hired me to help in shocking grain. I was very husky and could do as
much work as any ordinary man. I could keep the grain shocked from an
eight foot binder. It was hard work, but that was what I was used to. I got
top wages of $2.50 per day, and worked 10-12 hours per day.

The Pooles were very fine folks and treated me nicely. When the grain
was finished they got me a job on Mr. Al Baughman's thresher driving
a bundle team. Benton insisted I take his team, but I was afraid that I
could not handle them on those steep hills in the Pallouse country. But
Benton persisted and that was how it became.

I was really at a loss just how to handle the horses and wagon, but I
soon learned that one must keep the team moving around the hillside

instead of up or down because the horses could not pull the load up or hold it coming down. The problem was keeping the wagon from tipping over on the sidehill. It takes a lot of experience. After a few days I was able to do very well, so I stayed with the machine until Baughman was through that Fall.

It was my first experience with Fall or soft wheat, which went forty bushels per acre. The smut [from the thrasher] was so bad that many times we could not see the machine thirty feet away. [Its]...thick black cloud...would get into my nostrils, and I could not breathe, and by the end of the day I would be saturated from head to foot with the stuff.

I started to do some Fall plowing for another Poole, but I did not like the job. Maybe because I had some money—about $80—was the reason I just quit and...sent my money to a bank in Palouse because [I heard] there was more thrashing in progress there...

[But] I soon found a job fighting fires near Bovile, Idaho. There was a train running from Palouse ...[to Bovile via]...Potlatch in 1910. Potlatch at the time had the largest lumber mill in the world. We could see it from the train. The trash burner was a huge cone with a great screen over the top that belched a cloud of smoke that could be seen for many miles. It was an impressive sight indeed.

At Bovile, Ida. I had to walk several miles north to the lumber camp where I was to work. It was a typical lumber camp except that there were several tents to sleep in because the crew was larger than usual due to the recent fire. I was hired to put out the fires that were still burning in the tree trunks and stumps. Everywhere you could see fires smoldering. The air was filled with smoke, and at times it was difficult to breathe. Our eyes would stream tears and the odor was pungent. [The Great Fire of August 1910, also known as the Big Burn or Big Blowup, raged across some three million acres of forests in northeastern Washington, northern Idaho, and western Montana, later prompting new legislation in forest management.]

There was no let up morning, noon, or night. We were saturated with smoke; the water, food, and everything was smoked. To aggravate all this the weather was hot and tinder box dry. We could not see the sun but the heat was there. Most of the men there were Greeks who spoke little

English. They were very quarrelsome people. It seemed that they would just as soon kill me as look at me. I was afraid of them. I worked with a young Greek, and we seemed to get along fine. He spoke a few words of English and I helped him out with others.

In two weeks I had had enough of firefighting and Greeks, so I quit and walked back to Bovile. From there I took the train to St. Maries, Idaho. There was fire everywhere along the railroad. Small blazes in stumps and snags, and fallen tree trunks with smoke. There was a heavy cloud over all. It was such a vast desolation that it sickened me to contemplate.

I took a steamer downriver to Coeur D'Alene, ID for the most beautiful trip that I have ever experienced. I would judge the boat was about fifty feet long with about a twenty-foot beam. Wood was used as fuel, so there was a nice stream of smoke pouring from the stack. The engine that drove the large stern paddle wheel would puff along gently while we floated down the beautiful St. Joe River. The water was crystal clear with a slight bluish cast. I could see the pebbles on the bottom with trout swimming around the boat in a leisurely manner. The smoke had vanished so that the reflections of trees were inverted on the smooth-as-glass water. The fires missed this area so that it was nature at its finest. This river trip I shall cherish, along with the crossing of Lake Coeur D'Alene into which the river emptied, as long as I live. It was the most lovely scene I ever looked upon. The wind had come up as we reached the lake and there were whitecaps all across it about 18 inches high. The stiff breeze was just enough to [a]ffect the boat somewhat, but not enough to be dangerous.

The contrast of the rough lake and the gently flowing river made me appreciate the beauty of both more fully. Also, the change from the hot dry harvest fields of the Palouse country and the desolation of the fire around Bovile gave a contrast that I could not ignore. I suppose there are many other sights that were as beautiful, but I did not see them even though I was looking for them. Environment has a way of changing things from time to time so that one cannot fully get the truth. Time, Place, and Circumstances all have a bearing to our thoughts and actions.

I arrived in Coeur D'Alene and took the electric train to Spokane that evening. Somehow my money was about gone. I should have had about a hundred dollars, but I had only five or ten when I landed in town. Blankets, train fare, and just foolish spending took most of it.

For the first few days I looked for work but couldn't find any. By then I had spent all my money and was just about to start begging for something to eat when I saw a sign in the Western Union Telegraph office window saying "Boy Wanted". I asked for the job and I think the manager felt sorry for me because he said I could begin immediately [as a messenger]. I did not know the city but I said I would try if they would excuse my mistakes. There were plenty.

I was the messenger to Senator Poindexer, who was running for U.S. Senate, so that places the time as Nov. 10-11 in 1910. I was able to hold the job very well. I obtained a map and soon learned the city because Spokane is a fine plat arranged in straight lines with streets named in regular forms. Shortly I had a bicycle. We provided all types of services beginning with telegrams...meals to hotel rooms, and guided tours about town. I saw everything from the best and the worst in the city. The slums and the mansions were open to the messenger boy. The Senator and the bawdy women were our friends. It was a very exciting time for me.

About six weeks after I started I finally smashed my bicycle so badly that it could not be repaired. I [wrecked it] by hitting ...rocks in the roads or planks on pavements. I was usually skinned up somewhere on my body from being thrown headfirst off the bicycle from time to time. The only streetlights were in the downtown area. I felt I had to quit because I owed some for the bike and could not pay. I took it back to the man I bought it from and left it.

Now I was in a mess. A couple of fellows let me stay with them a while in their shack on the north side, but I did not like that and was soon in a ten-cent flop house on front street. The next thing I knew I was down to the Police station because I had come to the end of my rope and went there for help. They helped me right because I was broke out with measles. They took me to the isolation hospital where I stayed for two weeks and got cleaned up and a hold on myself somewhat.

After several more jobs including setting pins in a bowling alley and washing dishes, I met Jack Capra, a young man who owned a horse and a delivery wagon. Though he was only 20, he was head of the household because his father had died. It was up to him to support his mother, a 12 year old sister, and two younger children. His uncle, who owned a local saloon, assisted Jack in getting work hauling trunks and other express.

Jack wanted to help me so he had me work with him picking strawberries and lifting heavy loads. We sold the berries by driving along the residential streets and calling out "Berries for sale!" It was lots of fun. He was the nicest person one could imagine. I never saw him angry, never heard him speak a cross word to his family or his horse. He worked hard for his money but was loyal to all his family and friends. I learned to love Italians through him and his folks. Their ties to each other is beyond the belief of people outside their circle. They close ranks at once should anyone of them be endangered, and nothing can make them betray one of their own.

I stayed with Jack until thrashing time came around again [in]... August [1911]. [After] I said goodbye to Jack at the railroad crossing on Division Street...I jumped a passenger train going south to Tekoa, Wa.

I climbed upon the tender of the engine and walked along the top of the coaches until I was on the next to the last coach. I then lay down and held onto the pipes that were along the coach top. It was quite cold and soon my hands were numb, even though the cinders from the engine would burn me occasionally. The next morning the suit I was wearing was full of small burn holes. Years later I can still visualize that train top with the smoke and cinders flying over me as it sped along at 60 mph through the night. It stopped once but no one checked the train top.

When we reached Tekoa the brakeman came on top. I saw I would have to get off. I got to my feet and started forward, and as I approached the brakeman I read the name of the town (Tekoa), and when he asked me where I was going I told him "Right here." He said "That's for sure." I threw my blankets on the depot platform and jumped down after them and vanished into the dark, leaving the brakeman swearing. I found out later if I had jumped off the other side the cops had me [for train hopping].

I had left behind me the most desperate time of my life. I had been hungry several times and without money most all the time I was in Spokane. There were times when I was close to breaking the law and becoming a pursued person. With the work I did I was in contact with the roughest element of the city. It helped little to be on Jack Capra's transfer wagon because we hauled trunks for the fast ladies and theatre groups that came and left. The Italians were always skirting the fringe of the slums, stealing fights, and extortion was a common practice among them. The bums and Wobblies were all about me in that town, so one could easily become one with them when you are down and broke. It was an experience that taught me that there is good in the worst of us as well as bad in the best people.

In Tekoa I went to Al Baughman's place where I worked threshing the year before. I slept upstairs in their bedroom, and it was the first nice place I had been in since I had left North Dakota. Al was a jovial man and too kind to his two daughters Florence and Orphie. They took advantage of his kindness and went with nearly any boy, to their own disgrace. They were good girls but they were wild. I had no experience with girls up to this time, being a bashful boy of 18. But that was soon to change because there were always boys and girls around the Baughman's.

Threshing started at once and I loaded bundles on the wagons in the field at $2.50 per day with board. The cook house was a kitchen mounted on a wagon and hauled from place to place as needed. After a few days I began to spike pitch, which was unloading wagons at the machine. I liked that better because there was always some excitement there. Also, the pay was better at $3.00 per day. But it took a strong man to hold the job since it was a [tough] spot to be in. Everything depended on getting the loads off quickly without stalling the machine with an overload. I was an experienced thrasher by this time and could do anything from running the engine to shoveling grain into the bins. Understanding how machines operate was important, and I knew thrashing machines from beginning to end. Repairing engines and separators by now had become familiar to me. I could lace belts and pour babbit for bearings with some degree of success.

But it was different with girls. I had no contact with them except through my sister Florence, and she was very distant and unfriendly. There was no brotherly and sisterly love between us. In fact we did not like each other much. It seemed she was Dad's pet and mother always tried to make a lady of Florence. The love of my parents seemed to be all given to her, and whether it was true or not I felt it so.

So when I met these girls at Tekoa I was somewhat resentful because of my feelings toward Florence. To my good fortune I suppose.

Here began a series of events that affected my entire future life. The Baughman girls had two girl chums that lived only half a mile from their place. They had a brother who I liked very much. The sisters were Pearl and Elsie Huckreid. It was a common practice to walk to church and to the neighbors in the early 1900's. So the first thing I knew I was escorting Elsie around. The other girls had beaus off and on, but Elsie was too young until she picked me. She was quite homely, having a large square jaw and an angular figure that had little appeal as a young girl. She was fifteen and I was 18. She was, however, very friendly and treated me as an equal, which was new to me. Before long I felt I liked her very much. I think it is called "calf love" that struck me.

In all the time I knew her she never appealed to me sexually. In fact I scolded her one night when she made advances toward me. I just could not see sense in getting too familiar. I never held it against her because it was common in the neighborhood to have affairs with any or all.

The Baughman girls were not the only ones that were loose. Pearl had several lovers. I took them all to church or other places, but I was too bashful to get serious with them. I am proud to say...that I didn't do anything foolish with them even though they sometimes were disapointed to be out with such a prude. Mother taught me to respect women and girls, and even today I hold to that teaching even though I know that some women are not entitled to that respect.

As a group we young people were quite unruly. We had several chicken feeds with stolen chickens. We raided fruit cellers and stole watermelons. We were acting just about normal for a group of teen-agers of that day. We had no automobile, so about all we could do along that line was to rent a livery team and take the girls for a buggy ride.

The last Sunday I spent with the Baughmans was buggy riding. It ended up being an exciting time and a turning point for me. [Me] and a fellow named Earl Gilham each rented a rig from the livery barn in Latah, Wash. In the morning we took the Baughman and Huckreid girls for a days ride to the Indian reservation east of town. On my rig there was a small [jump] seat that was placed between the two persons that sat on the buggy seat, and a third person could set on it though not very comfortably. It was better than setting on the laps of others. Florence and I were on the buggy seat and Elsie was on the jump seat. We were jogging along a narrow road that had been cut out of the hillside, leaving a ditch and a high bank on the right side and a steep drop off to the left. I had cautioned Elsie to be careful of the horse whip she had taken from the whip socket and was swinging around. But she flicked the horse on the right causing him to switch his tail over the driving reins. The team were broncos and were of a wild nature, and when that pony felt the rein under his tail he started to kick. That scared them both, and they started to run away at the top of their speed. As long as I did not pull on the reins the kicking was held at a minimum, but it was almost impossible to guide the team. Of course the girls became scared and started to scream, which only made things worse. I quieted the horses somewhat while watching the first opportunity to catch a moment that the horse would switch his tail a little and release the rein. We traveled about a thousand feet before that happened. As soon as the rein was free I grabbed it and I was able to slow the team down and had them stopped. They were sweating heavily and were lathered up a lot, and to be sure I was about as scared as one could be over the event. Those darned girls laughed and seemed to think it was a lot of fun. I had seen runaways before and saw wagons and machinery smashed into many pieces, so I could imagine just how we would have fared if we had either been forced onto that bank or over the side of the road. With three of us in that buggy—with the top up and one of us on the jump seat—I am sure some...or all of us would have been badly hurt. For a few hundred feet those horses were traveling about 30 mph.

When we got back to the Baughmans so much was said about the runaway that I thought Mr. Baughman would make the girls stay home and tell us fellows to take the team back to town. But good old Al let the girls go again for the afternoon and evening. Gilham got the idea that we should go to Oaksdale, about twelve miles south of Latah.

We certainly had no business to go, but it was something to do. When girls are willing, boys do very foolish things to entertain them.

It was a long trip, and we got the horses into Latah around 1 a.m. Monday. The livery man was fit to be tied. He was so mad because he had heard of the runaway and figured we should have brought the team in early. He really put the price up for their rent. The regular price was $2.50 a day, but he charged us $10.00 each. We paid him half that night and said we would get the rest the next day.

Gilham and I decided after the tongue lashing the livery man gave us that we had had enough. We thought $10.00 was pretty steep. We came up with a plan. Mr. Huckreid was having a sale in a few days and then moving the family [out West]. Gilham was very thick with Pearl, and I felt that Elsie was very nice because she treated me as an equal and seemed to like me a lot. [I found out] we were going to Eugene, Oregon.

Gilham was broke but I had about $90.00. I bought two train tickets for us; Gilham promised to pay me back later, which he never did. At 3 a.m. we boarded the train after slipping by the livery man.

I remember the trip well. The Columbia River was beautiful with its falls and smaller rivers flowing into it. The river was so wide and there were several fish wheels and river boats along the way. In Portland we transfered to the Southern Pacific and then went to Eugene.

I don't remember how we met Mr. Pheleps, but Gilham and I ended up at his place, which was about 10 miles west of town and only two miles from the place the Huckreids had rented.

Gilham was a fast talker and he arranged for us to cut cord-wood for Mr. Pheleps. He furnished us with a tent and I bought saws and other tools as well as cooking gear. Neither of us knew much about wood cutting, but with a little experience we had soon got a few cords of knotty fir in racks so we could measure them. Shortly we were on our feet again as far as money was concerned.

The next act unfolded quickly when Elsie heard that I had paid Gilham's way down [to Eugene]. Elsie was upset at me for bringing

Gilham along because she thought he was a bum and only wished to get all he could from Pearl. It turned out she was right. Next thing I knew he had broke with Pearl and then went to Mr. Pheleps and drew out all the money we had coming and disappeared.

I never saw him again. He left with a debt to me of about $75.00. Elsie would not speak to me and never forgave me for bringing Gilham along. I was sorry for this but did not feel too bad because Elsie's brother Earnest and Pearl still treated me fine. Unfortunately I had no money to face the winter that was coming on.

Thanks to Mr. Pheleps and his good wife Daisy they took me in their home and I worked for my room and board cutting wood, building fences, spraying fruit trees and doing other chores around the house. I did this until I got another job cutting cord wood for Robert Smith, who lived about twenty rods up the hill south of Pheleps. I never forgot the kindness that the Pheleps did for me. Nute was a well-educated man and taught me many ideas that were a great help to me in understanding other people."

Granpa continued to work odd jobs around Eugene from late 1911 until early 1913, when he received a letter from his mother saying she was afraid she would never see him again.

"I was having a good time and enjoying myself for the first time in my life without worry or feeling inferior...I was a free man though quite ignorant having only an eighth-grade education and that a weak one... [The letter] upset me so that I had enough of wandering and bidding my friends that were so wonderful to me good bye, I took the Electric for home, by the way of the Canadian Pacific through the Canadian Rockies...To say that Mother was happy to have me home again is an understatement, after all I was her first baby...[and] she loved me more than any man can imagine, a mother's love is beyond any description... Father was about as distant as a father could be...he started to push and boss me around as if I had not been away for nearly four years...I stayed home for about six weeks and then got a job from Mr. John Olson...

later I worked for Frank Scott doing chores until Spring came. Mrs. Scott his mother was very kind to me and was my good friend in my courtship of her granddaughter Forrest McDaniel, who had then become my girlfriend."

23

I ENTERED SOUTH Eugene High School in the fall of 1964. More a
campus than a single building, it was a mile east of our Monroe Street
house, we called it "South", and was, compared to Wilson Junior high,
expansive and labyrinthine, with a vast front lawn and central flagpole,
spacious parking lots for both teachers and students, a broad sleek two
story modern building bordered on either end by an auditorium and
gymnasium, with athletic fields stretching forever out back. It was truly
a step up in accommodations for us Wilsonites.

Along with students from Wilson, South was fed students from
Roosevelt, Jefferson, and Spencer Butte junior highs, and the pecking
order at South depended on which of these you came from. At the top
was Roosevelt, located not far from South in a neighborhood near the

University of Oregon campus, where the kids were sons and daughters of professors or doctors, or prominent business or community leaders. All the student body presidents came from there. They seemed brainy, haughty, arrogant. Next in the pecking order was Spencer Butte, located at the southern end of town on the lip of a vast suburb of new ranch style and split-level houses built in the 50's and 60's. Of the four junior highs, it was the most up to date, built explicitly for the fast growing middle class population moving to that part of town, and the kids appeared as neat and clean as the manicured lawns and homes that dotted the neighborhood. Lowest in the pecking order was a toss up between Wilson and Jefferson, due in no small part because they didn't feed all their students into South like the other two did. At best half of Wilson's and Jefferson's class went to South, the other half going to North Eugene, or later, Sheldon High off Coburg Road. But if the truth were known and a poll taken, students from Roosevelt and Spencer Butte would pick Wilson as the absolute rock bottom of the barrel rather than Jefferson because of the shear decrepitude of the building—Wilsonites got lots of ribbing about going to school in a dungeon—and because some of the students came from the "tracks" down near 1st street where the trains thundered though in the middle of the night and people drank and cut each other with knives. So when we entered South for the first time we found ourselves, much like the Jeffersonites, adrift in an ocean of unfamiliar faces looking down on us. We stuck pretty close together that first year.

Like I did at Wilson, I followed brother Bill's footsteps into South. Because of the junior high system, Bill and I never went to junior or senior high school at the same time. Sister Ann and I did—she was a seventh grader when I was a ninth grader at Wilson, and a sophomore when I was a senior at South. But with Bill, it was different, and at each juncture he helped prepare me for my new school even though he wouldn't be there. He told me what was cool to wear, what teachers to avoid, which ones were o.k. For South one of the best pieces of advice he gave me was to avoid football.

"Why?"

"It's not like the Park. You really get nailed."

He'd played football his sophomore year and come home from a couple of games looking like he'd been run through with a chainsaw. For a tough guy like my brother, I thought, this was an omen. As much as I loved football and playing sandlot games at Washington Park over the years, I knew that if Bill was over his head with high school football, even with all the protection and padding, then I would be too. I heeded his advice.

Our sophomore class numbered nearly 500. I took World History, English, Advanced Algebra, Band. I worked like the devil. Every night after dinner I marched upstairs to my bedroom and did a couple hours of homework. At nine o'clock I marched back down and ate a bowl of Wheaties topped with the dreaded tasting Sucryl (pure sugar aggravated my acne), a piece of toast, and watched a little TV with Dad, who by then was snoring away in his green stuffed chair, oblivious to the screen. Later I marched back up and read until I fell asleep. Bill was in his first classes at the U. of O. and up to his ears in English Comp., Anthropology, Math 101. By then we had converted the garage into a recreation/bedroom where Bill slept and studied, so the upstairs bedroom was my own, the first time Bill and I had not shared bedrooms since I was born.

In late Fall I tried out for the basketball team. The previous year I had been the top scorer at Wilson and hoped to at least make the JV team, with an eye on varsity.

It was something I wanted to do more than anything else. For years I'd followed the varsity team, idolized players like John Pinkstaff, Bob Officer, Jim Lockhard, John Roche, many of whom went on to play college basketball. John Roach would later coach a state high school championship team. During spring breaks in junior high, John Hall and I lived at MacArthur Court on the U. of O. campus, where the state basketball tournament was played over six days, the tournament featuring morning, afternoon, and evening games with teams from around the state. One of my earliest memories is of "Mac" court—I was sitting in one of the overhanging balconies watching a basketball game with Dad, and maybe with Mom and Bill. Above us hovered another balcony brimming with people who were swaying to the rhythm of the activity below. I remember looking at the vast crowd below us, and at the tiny players on the court running frantically about like ants, up and down, up and down, from one end to the other. Every few moments the crowd erupted in a deafening roar—now on their feet flailing their arms and baring their teeth in paroxysms of religious fervor. I felt excitement. Dad pointed to someone on the court. (Could it have been Dad's cousins Kenny and Leon playing in the state high school basketball tournament?). It was a cavernous and echoing building, bright with a thousand overhanging lights, alive like an animal. It was, like Washington Park when the fans roared at night, a contrast to home and the quiet and small spaces. Oh those scores of people above and below us moving and swaying and shouting all at once. I wanted to return to this place for my high school because I still remembered it as a Mecca from those first years of my life.

For hours I studied the tournament booklet with the team photos and stats and comments, hoping one day my name and photo would be in it. One of our parents would drop us off in the morning and we would watch upwards of seven or eight games in a day. I remember once, between the afternoon and evening games, John and I walking over to Jim Lockhard's parent's restaurant nearby and ordering hamburgers and French fries, my first time in a restaurant—a rare occasion anyway— without my family and ordering for myself. I felt a grown up.

The tournament was especially exciting in 1963, two years before I entered South, when North Eugene, South's bitter rival, and South were ranked one and two in state. The two teams attracted so much attention during the regular season that games between them had to be held at MacCarthur Court because as many as 10,000 townspeople showed up to watch. There were high hopes in our camp that both teams would meet in the state finals and South would prevail and be crowned the state champs, even if "North" was ranked number one and had the tallest team in state. Bill was a junior then and we talked endlessly in those months about which one was the better team: who had the fastest guards, the best rebounders, the sharpest shooters. I wanted the same glory, grandeur, and fame that I saw at those games and at the tournament, wanted to be mentioned in the same breath. Shockingly, South lost in the first round of the tournament that year, one of the

                                    DREAM FAMILY ♦ A MEMOIR

biggest upsets in the history of the tournament but redeemed themselves in the days following by winning the consolation bracket and fourth place. "North", on the other hand, with their hulking giants, went on to win the tournament handily, swatting away their lowly opponents one by one, thus earning not only the town's but the state's bragging rights for the next year.

But it became apparent during try-outs my first year at South that my dream of playing varsity basketball for South was in jeopardy. There were so many good players that in spite of my drive and dedication I wondered if even making varsity by senior year was attainable. I was a big fish in a small pond at Wilson. It was a sobering thought and a setback to my glorious plans. I played for the Sophomore team and scored my share of points, but didn't distinguish myself or show marked improvement over the season—otherwise I would have been moved up to JV—so I knew that if I was going to climb further up the ladder I'd have to improve faster than the other players. Could I do it, was I up to it?

In the Spring I ran for Junior Class V.P. and won. Maybe I did this realizing I might not be distinguishing myself on the basketball court any time soon and needed another way to shine. Doug McCallum, whose father was the doctor who had operated on my left eye so many years before, was elected President (and yes, Doug was from Roosevelt). I had met Doug the previous year at Jefferson Junior High during a seminar for junior high student body officers. He was serious, intelligent, good looking, and I knew his status coming out of Roosevelt as its President was high. My run for class VP was a safer bet than running against him. The victory gave me instant standing, and one quick benefit was dating Lynn Buss, who in the same election was voted Junior Class Secretary. She also made the J.V. rally squad. We hit it off while working on the sophomore class charity drive later in the Spring. She was pretty, intelligent, and friendly, with brunette hair and dark eyes and a wide sincere smile. She'd gone to Roosevelt and lived in a split-level house on a nearby hill. I soon met her father and mother and younger brother, John, who was a year behind us at South. I recall her father was not a professional—I remember him as a plumber or electrician, or something similar—because I was prepared to meet a doctor or lawyer and get the first degree. But he wasn't and found him down to earth and friendly. I was secretly relieved. I was nervous with Lynn since she was from Roosevelt and felt over my head dating her, the peasant boy wooing the King's daughter, so this was my first tip that perhaps the Roosevelt stereotype wasn't altogether true. Lynn's brother and mother seemed to like me too.

We had fun together for awhile, but by the time school let out in June we had stopped dating. The next thing I knew I was chasing Sue Cook, for whom I felt a strong animal attraction. She was one of those balls of energy that everyone had fun being with, she reminded me of Vickie T. in her dark mysterious demeanor, and I wanted in the worst way to be part of her world. Lynn was too much like me, contained and focused, we were very decent and kind to each other and sensitive to each other's feelings, but it was hard work and akin to walking on eggshells. There was no spark like I felt with Sue. That summer I would borrow Bill's silver '56 Chev and swing by Sue's house—she lived in one of those ranch styles in the Spencer Butte area—and invite her for a spin. But it was a losing proposition, I could never connect with her like I did with Lynn, she was always one step ahead of me and on to something else, always had a reason she couldn't get in, and in spite of my gargantuan efforts to woo her she never reciprocated. She was an ephemera; she was an apparition that couldn't be grasped. By later in the summer when I realized it was a hopeless case, I didn't even try to get back with Lynn. She was too smart for that.

I began wondering what other people were doing all the time, especially during those handful of summer days when I wasn't working and there were a lot of empty hours to fill. By then I had stopped bean picking and was making good money umpiring little league baseball in the evenings. But no one was ever home when I called or stopped by. By then I felt too mature to go to the Jefferson Street pool to hang out and swim. That was old hat. And there were other things that used to amuse or interest me that were old hat too, like making model airplanes or playing baseball. I suspected that everybody else was having a splendid time at some secret place that I knew nothing about, doing something new that I would certainly find amusing too if only I had the chance to be there.

Junior year started soon enough. I took math from Dr. Oscar Schaaf, my first teacher with a PhD. The nonstop and rigorous proofs we did under his tutelage were arduous and exacting and I still have a notebook full of them. The same rigor with dreaded Mr. Dedman's English class, with endless in-class sentence diagramming, endless vocabulary and spelling exercises, endless homework assignments, endless papers returned scribbled in red ink. He was a smart dresser and nervous Nellie whose effeminate traits led to rumors about his bachelorhood. In Mr. Hale's Chemistry class I sat next to good friend Keith Derry. Mr. Hale spent much of his time reading science fiction while we fiddled with Petri dishes and Bunsen burners, and he called the two of us Jerry Derry and Keith Keefe, never getting us straight (also: someone had chalked in "Eat the Weenie Hale" on one of the half drawn black window shades, but he never took notice of it over the school year). I took U.S. History from Mr. Goodnough, who also taught Dad at old Eugene High many years before and who occasionally taught at the U. of O. He had an encyclopedic knowledge of U.S. History, especially of important Supreme Court decisions, and made history come alive like Granpa did in his living room. He never looked at notes during his lectures. He had terrible flatulence that made it impossible to breathe for those of us sitting near his podium during lectures. But it was a small price to pay for a ring side seat to history.

Like the previous year, I had my work cut out for me and I continued working like the devil.

That Fall I barely made the J.V. basketball team. I knew from my spare playing time I was hanging on by a thread; perhaps the coaches were hoping I'd have a growth spurt or get stronger over the year, thus making me a hot prospect for varsity my final year. Given an opening I could shoot the eyes out of the basket, but more often than not I was too slow getting there and too weak in muscling for rebounds and getting easy layups. I sat on the bench a lot.

That I wasn't doing better in basketball bothered me immensely, but I had other things going that mitigated my worry. Doug McCallum, a nice guy with good intentions, was more interested in being class president than doing it, so much of the nuts-and-bolts work fell to me and Lynn

Buss. And along with the class V.P duties, I was elected to student council, which I found intriguing for its issues and contentious debates, and overt posturing by some of the students. Granpa gave me a copy of *Roberts Rules of Order* so I could better understand the protocol during these meetings. So as my junior year revved up I once again fell into a routine regarding classes, homework, and extracurricular activities, and the future—except for basketball—looked bright. Furthermore, I had quit band and the trumpet and no more found myself marching in a purple and white band uniform at football games in front of my mocking friends. I began playing the guitar again.

My good feelings, and the school's, were short lived however. One of the girls on the varsity rally squad had become pregnant earlier that Fall, it was a major scandal in the school, and there followed a quick wedding on October 21st. Both JV and varsity rally squads were invited to the wedding, and during the traditional car chase following the wedding the car Lynn Buss was riding in overturned and she was killed. The funeral a few days later was attended by hundreds in the school, and Dad let me drive his powder blue Thunderbird to the church for the service and later to the cemetery for the burial. I remember Doug McCallum, Brad Parrish, and Dennis Phillips rode with me. As I passed by her open casket Lynn looked creepy—waxy, unnatural, a contrived impression made of parts that didn't seem to fit, and certainly not life-like.

I remember afterwards, either that night or a night or two later, when I was alone in our house for some reason, I went into our bathroom and looked into the mirror above the wash basin. I found myself looking hard. Something was different. It was as if I was staring at an absence, a black hole. There was nothing inside the image of me. It appeared—what else could I surmise?—lifeless. Something had left me for the moment, whatever it was that usually animated me and gave me color. I was no more than ether. The thing pressed down on me. I suddenly hated myself and everything in the world. I couldn't fathom how something so horrible and unmerciful could happen to someone like Lynn. There was

                                              DREAM FAMILY ♦ A MEMOIR

absolutely no reason for her being killed. I felt darkness then, almost palpable, maybe coming from the mirror, so I quickly left the bathroom for our more open living room. The face in the mirror, though it was mine, was a face I'd never seen before.

A new substance was added to my soul. What else could I believe? And what was it—a molecule of mud or sleet or fog? A murky specter? Whatever it was had crept in and took up residence in a small space where it remains to this day, periodically reminding me that life runs full tilt right up to the time of death, then stops so abruptly that it cannot be—even defies to be—measured in standard time. I do not know what happened to Lynn.

Soon afterwards the leaves were completely gone and the first frost had arrived in Eugene.

About two years later Lynn's father died of a heart attack. It was sudden and unexpected. So in the wink of an eye there was only John and his mother left. A few years later I ran into John at the U. of O., where he was taking some classes. We chatted a bit, talked about Lynn. He kept up a good front. He talked about some dynamite grass he'd recently bought. I could tell he was lost, but what could I say?

* * *

At the end of my junior year I ran for Student Manager. I don't think I knew then what the Student Manager did, nor do I remember now, but it was an elected position and a post on the student council alongside the President. The candidates had to make a speech before the student body during a Spring pep rally, in the boy's gym. My speech started fine— using Granpa's advice, I started with a joke to lure everybody in—but as I continued on and got to the meat of my presentation, little did I know I was dropping the microphone I was holding lower and lower down my chest until no one could hear me. A murmur began throughout the crowd then grew like wildfire until in short time everybody was talking as loud as I was. By the end of the speech no one was listening to me.

"It would have been a good speech if we coulda heard ya, Keefe," was the general response afterwards.

I ran against Kelly Ray, recently popular from playing a masterful Artful Dodger in a well received Oliver that year. He made sure he was loudly and theatrically heard following my anemic speech, he easily won the election, but then quit the post early the following year in protest of our Student Body President having to resign because of alleged weekend drinking. I never figured out what moral or ethical principal Kelly was trying to invoke in resigning. Since I drink too, I'll resign? He once chided me on an impassioned speech I'd made in student council having to do with sports budgets, claiming I didn't make sense. He was one of the few kids at South who got on my nerves, he was full of himself, and losing to him didn't make it any easier. His eventual resignation gave me some degree of secret satisfaction and just deserts.

* * *

In Fall my senior year I went out for basketball, my last chance to play varsity for South, and my last chance to "letter" for that matter. Possibly I would make the team—I was getting better, especially from practicing in the off-season—but it was a slim chance, depending on how many sophomores and juniors varsity coach Hank Kuchera (called "Kooch") wanted to bring up to varsity. If he was looking for depth, then he'd keep me, but if he was looking to the future, I was out.

I thought I'd puke from the tryouts, no different than in previous years—vigorous and exhausting, with dribbling drills, one-on-one drills, sprints, endless laps around the gym, full court scrimmages. Water breaks couldn't come too soon. I was hanging on, surviving one cut after another, surviving one day to the next, as if in battle hoping to stay alive to fight again. I had high hopes. I was playing well. Even being a bench sitter would be good enough for me. I just wanted to make the team.

Days later in the locker room I read the final cut. I was out. Kooch threw me a bone: "Keep at it Keefe. Go to a small college next year and try out there. Maybe you'll make it."

My heart sank. All that work for nothing, not only at tryouts but in the years of playing and practicing before. My whole basketball career was built on the premise that one day I'd play for South. Play at Mac

                    DREAM FAMILY ♦ A MEMOIR

court. Hear the yells and screams of fans when I scored, blocked a shot, intercepted a pass. Did I half expect it? There were a couple of hot sophomores that Kuch couldn't overlook. He figured that after losing key players from the previous year he had to rebuild and look to the future.

"Thanks Kooch. I'll think about it." But chances were that I was headed for a major college so his suggestion held little consolation.

* * *

So that senior year Christmas vacation was the first in years where I didn't have daily basketball practice. With the free time John Hall and I decided to take up skiing—why not? Mom and Dad let me use the Campbell Soup Car, and in Bend, Oregon, near Mt. Bachelor ski resort, we rendezvoused with John's old friend Chris Mulligan. I don't recall how Chris got there. Chris had grown up with John at Francis Willard grade school in Eugene and attended Wilson one year before moving to McMinnville, Oregon. He had curly blond hair, a wiry build, freckles, an upbeat personality, very likable, charming. His dad worked for the CIA, Chris claimed, and was seldom home.

We rented a room at the White Owl motel, a place known around town for accommodating skiers on a budget, and on the way back from skiing the first day Chris used fake I.D. to buy beer. John and I couldn't believe his moxie and nerve at the tiny store, acting as if he'd done this kind of thing as a matter of course. We also picked up potato chips and a pack of cigars, and in short order a sort of giddiness wound the three of us together once back at the White Owl, where we swooped down on the beer and cigars like our motel's namesake. It didn't take long for things to happen. Having never drunk beer (or any other alcoholic drink for that matter) before, I winced at the carbonated sting and sour taste as it first rolled across my tongue. "How can people like this?" I wondered. But I was keen to discover what all the fuss was about, keen to delve into forbidden territory, keen to forget basketball. It was the first time I'd ever been out of town overnight unsupervised; I was free to do as I pleased, Mom and Dad would never find out, I wasn't going to pass up this opportunity for anything. A rite of passage was laid at my feet.

I lit up a cigar.

The results were predictable, but I couldn't have guessed it then. The neophyte drinker slips and slides along in ignorance and faith. Drinking beer and smoking cigars for the first time, and ingesting hefty handfuls of potato chips in between, (our "dinner" that night) was a recipe for nothing less than disaster. Soon I was green and coughing from inhaling cigar smoke and disoriented and queasy from the ceiling whirling propeller-like above me; I was shortly on my hands and knees horking all over the little bathroom next to our room. Preternatural noises surfaced from murky and hitherto unknown fissures in my body. I thought I was going to die then didn't care if I did. John and Chris were having quite a time of it themselves whooping it up and crashing about the small room, and the proprietor came by a couple of times wondering what the Hell was going on, but Chris, who was a genius at making things appear less than what they really were, convinced him we were suffering from the aches and pains of our first day of skiing, or something akin to that, and that nothing was wrong. Later on, after the beer was gone, we finally settled down and tried playing five card draw, but it was no use. By then the day's flurry of first-time events had caught up with us and soon we were dead to the world.

We were up early the next morning and skied again at Mt. Bachelor, then headed home in the late afternoon. The plan was to drop Chris off at the Santiam Junction, high in the Cascade Mountain Range, where highway 22 continues to McMinnville and highway 20 continues to Eugene, and from there he would thumb a ride home. But we soon found ourselves in a pounding snowstorm that jammed the windshield wipers, which we periodically kick-started by reaching outside and jiggling them. With limited visibility and slippery roads—we had no chains—John and I begged Chris to continue with us and return to Eugene rather than hitching to McMinnville. Who would see him let alone pick him up in this storm? He could freeze to death! But Chris had his own agenda, had his mind made up. Maybe he thought we wouldn't make it to Eugene with our silly wipers. Unable to convince him to go on to Eugene with us, it was with great apprehension and misgiving we dropped him off, he climbing out of the back seat and

    DREAM FAMILY ♦ A MEMOIR

nonchalantly bounding off, and in my mind's eye I can still see Chris through the rear view mirror as we motored off, standing there at the junction getting smaller and fading into the snowstorm, hatless, one hand holding his duffle bag while the other hand thumbed for a ride. He looked as alone in the world as anyone could be. John and I shook our heads.

Later that Spring John and I started getting strange phone calls from Chris. He'd call almost any time day or night, accompanied by Mothers of Invention rock music in the background. Often there were long pauses between his ramblings, and sucking noises, and usually, when all was said and done, he didn't make much sense. Mom wanted to know who was calling long distance, and John and I had long talks about what Chris was up to.

Except for my classes, I was a kid without a mission after Christmas break—no sports, no politics, no nothing. But fortune soon smiled on me when senior class V.P. Marc Lehrman resigned that January because his family was moving out of town. I threw my hat in to replace him, running against Terry Brown, Carol Hunderup, Marsh Johnson, and Rich Cone in a run-off election to fill the position, winning, according to one source, by a landslide. Like the year before, I was paired with Doug McCallum, who had been re-elected class president the previous Spring. Getting elected and holding office again did my heart good, for at the time I was at sea with myself by doing so little at South other than attending classes. Not only was I busy again, but the office gave me some legitimacy, some claim to fame, however minor it was.

There were people at South who stood out, whom I can't forget. When I began as a sophomore, Jon Hoffman was student body president. In my eyes he embodied all that was worthy and virtuous at South. Involved in school politics, the Thespian and Spanish societies, singing in choir, always making the honor roll, by the end of his senior year Jon had nabbed a scholarship to Harvard. He wore a constant smile and appeared as if he knew you intimately upon meeting him. He was roundly liked and I couldn't help but look up to him that first year. As time went on, however, I discovered that Jon Hoffman wasn't the only smart person at South, that in fact there were some really smart people at South who soared intellectually and that comparatively speaking, I was a lightweight. In my own secret way I came to admire and hold in awe such fellow classmates as Jim Ellickson, Liane Kemler, Dennis Lund, Barbara Jo Novitski, Chuck Cunningham. They were brilliant, witty, dazzling; they were getting college credits for classes taken during their junior and senior years; they were National Merit finalists; they would get scholarships to big name universities. It was in this light that I figured the only way I was going to make my mark at South was by working my tail off.

Spring term junior year, while running for Student manager, I also campaigned for Jim Ellickson to upset Mark Lutz for student body president. Lutz had been the vice president our junior year and had the inside track to the presidency. Popular and well liked, he had had lead roles in South's productions of Dark Side of the Moon and Oliver, had the beautiful face, the voice, the charisma, but we had classes together and I felt he didn't meet the Jon Hoffman standard either in character or intellect. For the sake of South he needed overthrowing, and Ellickson, son of a U. of O. professor, tall, cerebral, verbal, I thought fit the bill. We met once at his house, a modern style filled from floor to ceiling with books, to discuss strategy. The lively campaign was capped by a dazzling debate in front of the student body, but in spite of the hard work and in spite of Jim's obvious talents and potential, Mark won handily, his charm in full force, teaching me a quick lesson about the roles "image" and "substance" play in politics. Lutz, though less brainy than Ellickson, had a magnetism, a charisma, people were attracted to him and wanted to be around him; Ellickson, on the other hand, was distant, internalized things, and you felt threatened by his intelligence. A professional politico could have surmised early on he had no chance to win. Unfortunately, Lutz was the one caught drinking later senior year and had to give up his presidency. By then Ellickson had gone off to Norway as a foreign exchange student.

The thespians opened my eyes for good and bad. My love of theater and actors and actresses I attribute in part to the excellent plays I saw at South under the superb guidance of Ed Ragazino, the longtime director. But those kids in my class who immersed themselves in theater at South were by their senior year impossible to be around. If you weren't in the plays then you were a lower life form. Kelly Ray was one of those actors, and I hark back to him not so much that I lost an election to him as that he epitomized the arrogant actor stereotype. Mark Lutz was another one, though not in the same league as Kelly. I remember a year or two later, after graduation, I saw a play Kelly was in at Lane Community College (in Eugene), and afterwards I went backstage to congratulate him on his performance only to have him brush me off. It took me aback. I'd never revealed my dislike for him, and he had had a fine performance. He didn't have a moment to chat with an old classmate.

As a whole the teachers at South were the best I'd ever had. When I think about knowledge and character, I think of Mr. Goodnough, with his encyclopedic knowledge of U.S. History, who called every student "Mr." Or "Miss" like he did when Dad had him thirty years before; Mr. Dedman, wound tighter than a drum, who gave me my only "C" in high school, his hands shaking when he adjusted his black rimmed glasses and his voice trembling when he talked about his dear mother; Mr. Harold Allison, my senior year debate teacher, tough as nails, challenging our arguments at every turn, taught us to mark "SS" in book margins for "speechy sentence" when we found something that would add sparkle to a debate, which I still do.

That senior year debate proposition was a reflection of what was going on in Vietnam, which was becoming more and more on our minds as we read the papers and watched the evening news on TV: Should U.S. foreign aid be used for military purposes? Granpa thought we should either declare war or get out; he backed his idol Senator Wayne Morse in this, who was one of the few who argued vehemently against the Gulf of Tonkin Resolution. We debated other high schools in the district, learning both sides of the proposition because we never knew beforehand which side the judges would choose for us. We quoted Senators and Congressmen, cited statistics, told stories of government corruption. It was contentious and exciting. As for Vietnam, we had no idea what was really going on, the debates were a battle of ideas, not guns; only later, shortly after graduation, when Kreg Viestenz, a classmate and friend since junior high, was killed there did it hit home that Vietnam was more than a battle of words. In the meantime classmates were growing their hair long, wearing bell bottomed pants, singing protest songs.

When Bill bought "Meet the Beatles" and several Dylan albums I was bedazzled by the words and melodies, listening to those albums over and over and writing dreadful songs in the Dylan style using simple chords and stream of consciousness lyrics, thinking I was as clever as Dylan. On the guitar I was remembering chords from when I flipped for Elvis, but this time it was the Beatles and Dylan who stirred me. During Spring break I drove to San Francisco with Bill and a friend. Bill's girlfriend was living in the Bay area at the time and I remember driving through downtown San Francisco and seeing thousands of people hoisting placards and wearing brightly colored outfits and shouting anti-war slogans. It was 1967 and changes were afoot.

In the winter of my senior year I began making applications to college. I wanted to get away. Whether it was a feeling of being hemmed in in Eugene, or wanderlust, or something else, I don't know. As much as I was a Duck fan, I wasn't committed to the U. of O., at least in my own mind. Chapman College in California was the first to offer a scholarship, but it was a partial one, and because it was a private school it would cost Mom and Dad a bundle to send me there. Nonetheless, I thought of how going there would change me, open my eyes, and I would meet new people. I wondered how my family and friends would view me when I got off the plane on my first visit home.

Not long after Chapman offered their scholarship, the U. of O. offered one too, albeit less money-wise, but in the long run less expensive for Mom and Dad because it was a public school. I was on the horns of a dilemma. If I pushed hard enough Mom and Dad would certainly find a way to get the money for Chapman. But did I really want to go there? Did I really want to leave Eugene and my family and friends? Did I want to impose a financial hardship on the family that could be avoided if I just stayed home?

I thought long and hard about it. Indeed I wanted to leave Eugene in some abstract way, but I held back from touring Chapman or signing papers. Eugene was all I knew as a place to live. We'd moved around a lot early in my life and Eugene had become comfortable, sheltered, offering much for a small town. What was Chapman and the greater L.A. area to me? I'd never been there and I could see myself getting overwhelmed and forgotten, simply one in a million. Furthermore, at the U. of O., I could live at home the first year and use the scholarship and my summer earnings to cover most of my expenses. It wouldn't cost the family that much. Bill would be a senior then and could, once again, show me the ropes like he'd done at Wilson and South. Several friends from South were going to the U. of O. too, and if I wanted I could pledge a fraternity and begin meeting people from out of town.

* * *

A funny thing happened the day before graduation. I couldn't attend the graduation rehearsals because I'd just landed a summer job with American Linen sorting dirty laundry and was working. My rehearsal partner Keith Derry told me it was announced at the rehearsal that I and a few other students had overdue library books and unless we returned them or paid for them, we wouldn't get our diplomas the next night. The curious thing was that I remembered returning the particular book to the library—it had been earlier in the year, but I could clearly see in my mind's eye entering the library and dropping the book through one of the slots to the left of the front door. So I didn't have the book, the school did, and I wasn't about to pay for it. I'd call the school's bluff, believing they wouldn't withhold my diploma in good conscience since I'd done well by them.

The next night after crossing the stage and receiving my diploma, I returned to my seat only to open the plastic folder and find a blank sheet inside. It maddened me—they'd called my bluff!—and wondered what it really meant. But ultimately I didn't sweat it. By then I'd been accepted to college and had a scholarship to boot. Someone else's lost library book wasn't going to keep me from moving on. High school was behind me. I soon forgot about it.

* * *

Nearing each class reunion I look at my high school yearbooks. As I turn the pages I recognize the pictures and faces as if I'd just seen them yesterday. When I first got each one at the end of summer after they were published, I spent hours looking them over, seeing who made it on the pages, reading the captions, studying who had done what. The images and words seem imprinted in my mind like a genetic code.

There is Darlene Weber, sophomore year, in the school cafeteria, mugging for the camera, holding up a placard saying "Keefe for Jr. Class Vice President". We went to junior high together. After graduation I heard she'd been a cheerleader for a professional sports team. She's holding up the placard, which covers her from chin to waist, by a stick on the bottom. She's wearing a cowboy hat with a bandanna underneath, a short dark skirt, cowboy boots. A broad grin covers her face.

The club pictures are from a bygone era: The Rifle Association, Future Farmers of America, Future Homemakers of America, peopled by what are now called, by my daughter and her friends, nerds. Where are these clubs now? When did they pass from high school culture? One of the club pictures startles me since I've forgotten about her. A group of girls are gathered near a Christmas tree. The caption reads, "Fingers snap in rhythm as Pat Crowder, center, leads game played at French Club's party". Pat, a couple years ahead of me, was who Dad allegedly had an affair with several years later, which led to Mom and Dad's divorce.

Two photographs of Lynn Buss, junior year, one of her posing in her J.V. rally outfit, kneeling on one knee, arms stretched up and out, at an angle (symbolizing victory?), a smile on her face. Next to the photograph, a quote from her own writings, followed by a couple of paragraphs on how she represented the best at South. It says several others were injured in the crash but doesn't say who they are. The ones I remember are Hilda Bengston and Meg Sticles.

A picture of me, senior year, looking intent, serious, during a student council meeting, hands clasped in front of me, acne showing through the Clearasil, just after Dad had given me one of his bad haircuts.

In the back of each yearbook is an alphabetical listing of each senior and their activities over their three years at South. Under my name is listed class VP, some committees I headed up, basketball, student council, National Honor Society, and Axeman (South's mascot) of the Month. Skimming over the other names I stop at Shelly Lonnquist's, a friend whom I went to junior high with. Our class's Miss South Eugene, she was on the debate team, Quill and Scroll, Spanish club, rally squad, student council. She received a generous scholarship to the U.of O. Not bad for someone from "bottom of the barrel" Wilson. And for Ann Hendrickson—Ann, my fifth-grade sweetheart? Nothing listed. How is that possible? It makes me wonder what happened to her and how people bump into each other and become intimate for awhile and then careen off and never see each other again.

* * *

Sometimes when I'm hiking or simply resting in a forest and looking about, I see something I can't explain. Why is it that a maple or oak tree will have one leaf vigorously waving about while all the others are perfectly still? Could there be a shaft of wind so narrow and confined that it hits only that leaf? How can it be? Or is the leaf at that very moment in an intensely spirited stage of growth, wriggling around in great joy and happiness as its cells swell and multiply by the millions, while its neighbors sleep? Who knows?

South is like this for me, waving about among the stillness, standing out in the crowd. Often I've measured things I've done since then not in terms of my grade schools, or Wilson, or even College, but against a South Eugene standard of excellence. I think: How would this go over in student council? What grade would Dedman give me for that? Would

Dr. Schaff see through this proof? These things I see waving at me in the world remind me, even now, what I'm supposed to do.

* * *

In the end I chose to stick around. Two years later Mom sent Ann, then a senior at South, to the school's office. Yes, they said, they had my diploma. No, they said, they didn't know why they had it. So they gave it to Ann, who passed it on to Mom who passed it on to me. In my sophomore year of college I received my diploma from high school.

EPILOGUE

EACH SPRING MY wife and I plant flowers around our house in Portland, giving it a festive colorful look. I'm up to my elbows in dirt and fertilizer and potting soil like Gramma and Granpa used to be. Friends who come over for dinner on the back porch compliment us on how luscious and vibrant everything looks.

We built a beach house. It has the right mix of design and materials to be both visually striking and strong enough to withstand the salty wind and rain of the Oregon coast. I reviewed floor plans and renderings with the same eyes I looked at Dad's plans and renderings decades ago. The house looks out upon the Pacific Ocean where he used to sail.

When I returned from the Army after college everything was different. Granpa was dead and Gramma lived alone across the street.

Their garden lot had been sold and a new house built on it. Mom and Dad were divorced and Mom had remarried, then found out she had cancer. Both Bill and Ann had left town. Strangers lived in our house on Monroe. This happened overnight, while I was overseas. I was angry and felt immense sorrow and loss. I didn't care about certain things. I'd been on task for so many years and done what I was supposed to do that for a moment I let my guard down and did what I wanted, convincing myself that happiness was more important than duty. But I wasn't happy.

Then, like Dad had done 25 years earlier, I enrolled in school again using the GI Bill. I took music courses and learned what Granpa tried to teach me years before about resolution and chromatic scales and augmented 5th chords. I played jazz guitar and learned to improvise in every key.

Mom went on to have a long third marriage. Bill and Ann eventually moved back to Eugene. I live two hours away and visit often, and over the years have gone to many Duck football games with John Hall. From time to time I drive around the old neighborhood and remember those days from long ago.

     DREAM FAMILY ♦ A MEMOIR

PHOTOGRAPHS

ABOUT THE AUTHOR

Jerry Keefe graduated with a BBA from the University of Oregon and an MBA from Portland State University. He served in the U.S. Army in South Korea in the early 70's. He spent his 25-year business career in manufacturing and sales. He lives in Portland, Oregon with his wife, Connie.

THANKS

Leo MacLeod, David Scott Arnold, Diana Keefe, Danny and Keefe Sullivan, Mike and Susi Leach, Doris Lidtke, Paul Keefe, Mary Jane Coty, Evelyn Hunt, Jim Keefe, John Hall, Leon Keefe, Carolyn Berg.